Gendered Online Abuse Against Women in Public Life

FEMINIST DEVELOPMENTS IN VIOLENCE AND ABUSE

Series Editors: Dr Hannah Bows, Durham University, UK and Professor Nicole Westmarland, Durham University, UK

Feminist Developments in Violence and Abuse provides a feminist forum for academic work that pushes forward existing knowledge around violence and abuse, informing policy and practice, with the overarching objective of contributing towards ending violence and abuse within our society. The series enables academics, practitioners, policymakers and professionals to continually build and explore their understanding of the dynamics, from the micro- to the macro-level, that are driving violence and abuse. The study of abuse and violence has a large scope for co-producing research, and this series is a home for research involving a broad range of stakeholders, particularly those working in grassroots domestic and sexual violence organisations, police, prosecutors, lawyers, campaign groups, housing and victim services. As violence and abuse research reaches across disciplinary boundaries, the series has an interdisciplinary scope with research impact at the heart.

Available Volumes:

Victims' Experiences of the Criminal Justice Response to Domestic Abuse: Beyond Glass Walls
Emma Forbes

Understanding and Responding to Economic Abuse
Nicola Sharp-Jeffs

Rape Myths: Understanding, Assessing, and Preventing
Sofia Persson and Katie Dhingra

Gendered Justice? How Women's Attempts to Cope With, Survive, or Escape Domestic Abuse Can Drive Them into Crime
Jo Roberts

'Rough Sex' and the Criminal Law: Global Perspectives
Hannah Bows and Jonathan Herring

Not Your Usual Suspect: Older Offenders of Violence and Abuse
Hannah Bows

Mind the Gender Gap: A Mobilities Perspective of Sexual Harassment on the London Underground
Siân Lewis

Forthcoming Volume:

Gendered Anxieties: Exploring State and Legal Responses to Violence Against Women and Girls in the UK and the EU
Anna Carline and Sharron FitzGerald

Gendered Online Abuse Against Women in Public Life: More than Just Words

BY

SUSAN WATSON
University of York, UK

emerald
PUBLISHING

United Kingdom – North America – Japan – India – Malaysia – China

Emerald Publishing Limited
Emerald Publishing, Floor 5, Northspring, 21-23 Wellington Street, Leeds LS1 4DL.

First edition 2025

Reprints and permissions service
Contact: www.copyright.com

British Library Cataloguing in Publication Data
A catalog record for this book is available from the British Library

ISBN: 978-1-83549-727-2 (Print)
ISBN: 978-1-83549-724-1 (Online)
ISBN: 978-1-83549-726-5 (Epub)

INVESTOR IN PEOPLE

For Tom, Dylan, Alice and Tabitha – never stop dreaming the impossible.

Contents

List of Figures and Tables

Figures

Tables

About the Author

Dr Susan Watson is Lecturer in Criminal Justice and Social Policy at the School for Business and Society at the University of York, UK, where she leads the university's criminology and criminal justice degrees. Her research is concentrated on technology-facilitated gendered violence in the public sphere. She is currently engaged in an empirical study investigating the reporting mechanisms and policy response of UK universities to the online abuse directed at academics, using Freedom of Information laws to gather data.

She is also a Member of the Executive Committee of the British Society of Criminology, a Member of the Social Policy Association and an Associate Fellow of the Higher Education Academy.

Before embarking upon an academic career, she worked as a political campaigner for the Labour Party between 1992 and 2005. She has also worked on criminal justice research and policy development, including time on the House of Commons Home Affairs Select Committee.

She is an Alumnus of the London School of Economics and Political Science and the University of York.

Acknowledgements

I would like to thank the many people who have supported and encouraged me on my journey from student, to PhD, to full-time academic.

I would like to thank the Economic and Social Research Council for funding this research, under Grant ES/P000746/1.

I would like to extend my sincere thanks to my PhD Supervisors, Professor John Hudson and Dr Rachel Vipond, for being a constant source of support, encouragement, patience and good humour. I am a better person as a result of their guidance and unwavering friendship.

A number of amazing women academics have provided ongoing support, advice and challenge, and my warmest thanks are paid to Dr Lisa O'Malley, Professor Sharon Grace, Professor Carolyn Snell and Dr Kirsty Cameron, who have each helped me to overcome my feelings of 'impostor syndrome' at various points.

Finally, I would like to thank the 50 women in the occupations of academia, journalism, policing and politics, who took the time to speak with me. Their willingness to answer my many questions, and recount often distressing experiences, purely in the hope that by doing so they would help stop other women from having to experience similar abuse, was truly awe-inspiring. I hope I have told your stories well.

Chapter One

Introduction: The Problem of Gendered Abuse in the Online Space

Abstract

Chapter One introduces the themes of the book, before moving on to demonstrate how the online abuse of women communicated via social networking sites has increased significantly in recent years (Vera-Gray, 2017), with policy actors slow to respond to the immense change that has occurred as a result of the way that individuals interact in the digital space (Jane, 2017a). The chapter highlights how the emerging nature of this phenomenon has created a policy vacuum, with the lag in institutional responsiveness leaving victims without adequate protection or recourse (Jane, 2017a). This chapter also explains why the book focuses solely on the online experiences of women. Previous research has found that women's online experiences are underpinned by misogyny, violence and threat (Poland, 2016). The gendered characteristics of the online abuse received by women means that to include men in this investigation would risk creating a 'false symmetry between men's and women's experiences' (Krook, 2020, p. 107), whilst also ignoring the very real risks navigated by women on a daily basis (Lumsden & Morgan, 2017).

Keywords: Online abuse; misogyny; social networking; libertarianism; populism; public sphere; public facing occupations; trolling

Introduction

The online abuse of women communicated via social networking sites has increased significantly in recent years (Vera-Gray, 2017), and policy actors have been slow to

Gendered Online Abuse Against Women in Public Life: More Than Just Words, 1–7
doi:10.1108/978-1-83549-724-120251001

respond to the immense change that has occurred as a result of the way that individuals interact in the digital space. The emerging nature of these phenomena has created a policy vacuum, with evidence suggesting that a lag in institutional responsiveness leaves victims without adequate protection or recourse (Jane, 2017a).

One area where there is a noticeable dearth in robust investigation is in the online abuse that occurs in the public sphere, particularly of women who work in public facing occupations. The huge changes in communication brought about by the assimilation of social networking sites into everyday life provide the means for the public to interact directly with individuals in public facing occupations. However, such engagement is not wholly positive. For whilst it is true that social networking sites have provided a mechanism for the public to communicate with those working in the public sphere; whilst also offering feminist and other campaigning groups a useful platform (Banet-Weiser, 2018; Micalizzi, 2021; Weathers et al., 2016), this has also perpetuated online abuse.

The motivation for this research emanates from the author's experience of being a political staffer. Hearing first-hand stories from women holding public office, of the abuse and threats received as part of their engagement with online platforms, triggered both a personal concern for colleagues and friends, and an academic curiosity, which then morphed into scholarship. This concern occurred alongside a backdrop of increased political violence, horribly articulated by the assassinations of the Labour MP for Batley and Spen, Jo Cox in June 2016 and the Conservative MP for Southend West, Sir David Amess, in October 2021. Both Cox and Amess were murdered whilst holding advice sessions in their constituencies (Jones, 2019; Peele, 2022). The political and personal ramifications of these deaths continue to reverberate, with Parliamentarians and other public sphere representatives having to consider their safety and security whenever they are in public. These two heinous acts have raised awareness of the vulnerability of public servants, which frequently extends into the online domain.

However, it is not only politicians who are the target of online abuse. This research also investigates the experiences of academics, journalists and police officers. Receiving abuse of this nature is not an uncommon or noteworthy experience – rather, it has become a routinised part of the mundane communication exchange that occurs online. Furthermore, this abuse is increasingly difficult to escape, given the expectation from both employers and the wider public that those serving in public facing occupations maintain an active social media presence.

Research Context

There is no universally agreed definition of online abuse. However, the definition provided by Citron (2014, p. 3) is helpful, stating that online abuse 'involves the intentional infliction of substantial emotional distress accomplished by online speech'. Online abuse has been described in various different ways, including cyber bullying (Wagner, 2019), cyber harassment (Citron, 2014), cyber stalking (Southworth et al., 2007), doxxing (Lee, 2020), flaming (Jane, 2015), pile-ons (Thompson & Cover, 2021), swatting (Wu, 2015), trolling (Lumsden & Morgan, 2018) and Zoom bombing (Hernandez, 2020). For simplicity, in this book, these various terms are all assimilated into the phrase 'online abuse'. Where significant differences between the acts of abuse occur, these are discussed in the text.

The decision to focus solely on the online experiences of women is worthy of further explanation. Whilst there have been a number of studies focusing on the online experiences of both men and women in public facing occupations (e.g. Binns, 2017; Ward & McLoughlin, 2020), there is a robust rationale for excluding men from this research. Firstly, there is the finding that women's online experiences are overwhelmingly underpinned by misogyny, violence and threat (Poland, 2016), which is reinforced by a consistent underestimation of the scale of gender-based violence (both physical and virtual) from the (male) academy (Ahmed & Madrid-Morales, 2021; Walby et al., 2014). Secondly, as is illustrated in both existing literature and the empirical contributions gathered from participants in this research, there is a clear link between online abuse, gender-based violence (Salter, 2017) and the misogynistic aim to silence women's contributions in the public sphere (Mantilla, 2015). Whilst men in academia (Veletsianos, 2016), journalism (particularly sports journalism) (Binns, 2017) and politics[1] also experience threats of violence, they do not do so *because* they are men. Therefore, the gendered characteristics of the online abuse received by women in the four occupations selected for closer analysis means that to include men in this sample would risk creating a 'false symmetry between men's and women's experiences' (Krook, 2020, p. 107). Furthermore, insisting on a gendered comparison of male and female experiences risks drawing potentially misleading conclusions, whilst also ignoring the very real risks navigated by women on a daily basis (Lumsden & Morgan, 2017). Whilst not universally agreed upon (e.g. Gorrell et al., 2020), many working in this area would argue that most of the violent and aggressive online abuse is received by women (Kargar & Rauchfleish, 2019).

There is also a lack of quantitative data regarding the scale of online abuse, as these figures are not routinely collected. Nevertheless, there is a growing body of research from organisations such as the United Nations (2015), Amnesty International (2017) and the European Commission (Davidson et al., 2011), all of which has evidenced the growth in the amount of abuse disseminated online. Research has frequently been bolstered by high-profile incidents of abuse directed at public figures, some of which has been so extreme that it has gained significant notoriety (e.g. Criado-Perez, 2013; Dewey, 2014; Peele, 2022; Urwin, 2013). The aim of this research is to investigate the extent to which social networking sites have perpetuated a permissive climate towards gender-based violence and to identify and analyse the wider impact that such online abuse can have.

Outline of the Book

This book is organised into nine chapters that fall loosely into two separate parts. The first part, which consists of Chapters Two to Four, provides a theoretical

---

[1]The review of the literature has failed to find any published work specifically comparing the online abuse of male and female police officers.

underpinning to the empirical data that follow. By organising the book in this way, it is possible to gain a broad understanding of the key theories espoused in the diverse strands of computer-mediated communication, gender-based violence and the operation of the public sphere. The coalescence of these different theories is pivotal to the analysis of women's experiences that follows in the latter part of the book.

Following this introduction, Chapter Two explores the history of computer-mediated communication, revealing that when an interdisciplinary lens is adopted, it is possible to identify a number of theoretical explanations for the abuse that occurs online. The first scholarly investigations into the nature of technological communication emerged in the 1980s, straddling the disciplines of social psychology, culture and commerce (Jane, 2015). This early assemblage often determined that abuse in online communication was insignificant, infrequent or a source of entertainment (Jane 2015), with strong associations with wider libertarian and freedom of speech campaigns. More recent research has indicated a link between the hostility that occurs online between politically opposing groups and an increase in physical violence when parties meet in the offline space (Gallacher et al., 2021). At the same time, there is growing concern that social networking sites have increased the immutability of public opinion, with Sunstein's (2009a) work on echo chambers and group polarisation underlining the preponderance of people to adopt more extreme viewpoints or actions when gathered with others. Pariser (2012) has proposed the complementary theory of filter bubbles, created when online search engines and social media algorithms only show users selected content. It has been argued that when combined, echo chambers and filter bubbles lead to social homogeneity and group polarisation (Edwards, 2013; Harel et al., 2020), which have been enablers in the rise of political populism of the sort responsible for the election of Donald Trump in the USA and the Brexit vote in the UK (Bruns, 2019; Guo, 2020) whilst also being linked with right wing extremism (Kligler-Vilenchik et al., 2020) and an increase in online abuse (Ozalp et al., 2020). At the same time, online abuse has also become increasingly hostile (Founta et al., 2019), frequently containing misogynistic condemnation, threats and descriptions of sexual violence, moving from an individualistic, discrete activity, to a more generalised verbal violence that targets the individuals' personal or occupational life (Jane, 2015; Rohlinger & Vaccaro, 2021) – something that is followed up in Chapter Three.

Chapter Three provides a context for the span of behaviours falling within the definition of gender-based violence, which range from the mundane (Brown & Walklate, 2011) through to rape and homicide. By introducing the domestic abuse intervention programme (also known as the Duluth model) (Pence & Paymar, 1993); the continuum of violence (Kelly, 1988); the theory of coercive control (Stark, 2009) and the theory of cultural violence (Galtung, 1990), this chapter outlines four theories of gender-based violence that are integral to the understanding of gendered online abuse. This theoretical framework, predominantly associated with the domestic sphere, is then synthesised with theories of the gender-based violence that occurs in public, including workplace sexual harassment and sexual abuse. The theories introduced in Chapter Three intentionally position the issue of gender-based violence at the heart of the book, as it is the history, threat and manifestation of gender-based violence that situates the investigation into online abuse in context. This chapter illustrates how gender-based violence, whether it occurs in the home, the workplace, educational settings or in the street, serves to emphasise men's power over women (Stanko, 1990).

Chapter Four opens by providing a definition and description of the composition of the public sphere, highlighting that whilst women consistently make up more than half of public sector employees in the UK (Miller, 2009), the number of women holding senior roles in public facing occupations remains low. The discussion then moves on to consider the wider role of women in the public sphere and the challenges commonly faced. The potential consequences of the increased interaction with the public that has arisen as a result of the centrality of social media and other online communication mechanisms to the contemporary operation of the public sphere (Mellado & Hermida, 2021; Terren & Borge-Bravo, 2021) is also considered. In a wide-ranging discussion, this chapter also presents evidence on emotional labour (Hochschild, 2012) and safety work (Vera-Gray, 2017), which are highlighted as key issues for women in public facing occupations navigating online abuse. The chapter concludes by bringing together theories of the public sphere discussed in Chapter Four with the theories of gender-based violence introduced in Chapter Three, explaining how the two coalesce in the act of online abuse.

Chapter Five moves the focus of the book into the empirical phase. The chapter presents analysis of the research undertaken to better understand the online experiences of women working in academia, journalism, policing and politics. In doing so, it outlines seven pervasive elements of online abuse, which were found to be present (in whole or in part) in every instance of online abuse. These are defamation, emotional harm, harassment, threat, silencing women's voices, belittling and undermining women and the criticism of individuals' appearance and other physical characteristics. Each of these seven elements is further analysed using the empirical evidence provided in the testimony gained from 50 semi-structured interviews with women serving in public facing occupations. The power of this testimony comes from the examples and experiences provided by the women themselves, with an example of each element summarised in Table 1.

The gendered online abuse of women in the public sphere has not been categorised in this way before, particularly in regards to the discussion of defamation and the criticism of women's professional probity, honesty and behaviour. The richness of the interview data is complemented by data drawn from the qualitative analysis of a real-time Twitter data corpus amounting to some 10.4 million tweets. Taken together, these data provide an insight into the sheer scale of online abuse occurring on a daily basis.

Chapter Six explores two factors that are specific to online activity within public sphere occupations: the expectation that those holding positions within academia, journalism, policing and politics be always accessible online and that occupational seniority can act as an insulator from abuse, not by preventing pernicious communication, but by limiting exposure to it. The chapter then considers the consequences that can result for both the individual and their organisation

Table 1.   Empirical Accounts of Abuse Gathered from Interviews.

Element of Online Abuse	Example from Empirical Research
Defamation	*[I receive online abuse] basically challenging my ethics, or the way I operate, or… 'will the [role name] answer why she hasn't done anything about this', and neglected my duty.* (Karen, Senior Police Officer)
Emotional harm	*I knew that all that abuse would continue [after the election] and I was expecting my majority to go down to a couple of thousand, and I thought they'll keep coming, they'll smell blood and all I used to do was get bullied, permanently. It was absolutely horrendous.* (Phyllis, Member of Parliament until December 2019)
Harassment	*The people who do it know that they are chasing you to your very marrow. Everything you do, they are chasing you all the time and never leaving you alone. And the 'pile-ons', in inverted commas, are exactly designed to make an individual feel persecuted and overwhelmed. There's no question in my mind about that. Then when they think they've done their job, they back away.* (Patricia, Member of Parliament until December 2019)
Threat	*Somebody messaged me and said, it serves you right if your daughter gets raped in front of you. They made that physical threat to me and to my family.* (Agita, Member of the House of Lords)
Silencing women's voices	*I think a lot of what they do is to try and discourage you from doing the kind of reporting you do, rather than… I don't know, they may be personal in the stuff they say. Ultimately what they're trying to do is discourage you from covering the topic which is criticising them.* (Linda, UK-based journalist)
Belittling and undermining women	*We don't see this as a new phenomenon, it's just the newest iteration of an old phenomenon, all those things that continue to undermine and weaken women's protection in the physical space from violence and domestic partner violence, intimate partner violence, street violence, all of that, all those things are still at play in the digital world.* (Helen, Academic based in the USA)
Criticism of physical characteristics	*When pictures have been taken of me in Downing Street they try and zoom in on my badge and try and catch you out to see if you've exposed something that you shouldn't expose, either about your body or the post.* (Sarah, Senior Police Officer)

when they are targeted for online abuse. The chapter then identifies the elements specific to public facing occupations that make a sustained onslaught of online abuse particularly problematic. The chapter concludes by discussing the various benefits accrued from maintaining an online presence, highlighting why advising women to simply abandon their professional online activity is neither a realistic nor acceptable solution to online abuse.

Chapter Seven provides a topical overview of the policy landscape on gender-based violence and online abuse, assessing the numerous developments that have been proposed in this area. Policies have frequently been introduced on a sporadic basis, often emerging in response to public pressure; or, as Walby et al. (2014, p. 188) have vividly described (with reference to Jimmy Saville and Dominic Kahn), as a response 'to the violence that emerges into public view in the form of "scandals", when some famous man is accused of perpetrating gendered violence'. In the UK, in common with many other jurisdictions, there has been the lack of a comprehensive or structural approach to addressing online abuse. Consequently, Chapter Seven considers the emerging impact of the Online Safety Act which was finally entered into statute in October 2023; comparing the policy and legislative regime in the UK with other countries, highlighting the bifurcation in approach, with some places likely to prove better locations for women to work in public facing occupations than others, with the UK and USA being rapidly overtaken by more progressive online environments.

Chapter Eight presents a series of policy recommendations to tackle online abuse. These recommendations have been organised into a series of actions at an individual, organisational, legislative and structural level, reflecting a synergy with the levels at which the impacts of online abuse occur.

Chapter Nine brings together the various strands of the preceding chapters in order to summarise the content and consequences of the online abuse of women serving in the public sphere. The chapter revisits the seven elements of online abuse in order to further demonstrate how online abuse directed at women is misogynistic, frequently includes violent threats and dismisses women's contributions to online discussions. The chapter will emphasise how online abuse varies by occupation, with police officers most likely to receive abuse that denigrates their ability or appearance; politicians and journalists more likely to receive violent threats, and academics receiving abuse of all types. The chapter will also discuss how the consequences of abuse are felt at an individual, organisational and structural level, having a malign impact on women's contributions to public life in multiple ways, before revisiting the policy recommendations at the same three levels.

Finally, consideration will be given to the weaknesses of the research, its generalisability and the potential for further work in this area moving forwards.

Chapter Two

Charting the History of Abuse in Computer-mediated Communication

Abstract

This chapter explores the history of computer-mediated communication, revealing that when an interdisciplinary lens is adopted, it is possible to identify a number of theoretical explanations for the abuse that occurs online. The interdisciplinary underpinning to these theoretical explanations is unpacked, moving from the libertarian ideals that were influential in the early analysis of abuse in computer-mediated communication; through to the polarisation of public opinion in the present day. The persistent thread of misogyny that has been present in all stages of the development of the online space is also investigated.

Keywords: Computer-mediated communication; online abuse; filter bubbles; echo chambers; misogyny; libertarianism; freedom of speech

Introduction

This chapter explores the history of computer-mediated communication and considers how different theoretical perspectives have evolved over time in order to identify a range of different explanations for online abuse. Much of the scholarship in this area has been presented in a way that is discipline-specific, however, remaining in these disciplinary silos can create obstacles in understanding how online abuse proliferates. However, by adopting an interdisciplinary lens, it is possible to identify a number of theoretical explanations for the abuse that occurs online. The creation of Web 2.0 at the beginning of the 21st century (Blank &

Gendered Online Abuse Against Women in Public Life: More Than Just Words, 9–17

doi:10.1108/978-1-83549-724-120251002

Reisdorf, 2012; Herring, 2013) turned previously static web pages into virtual environments where users can interact with and contribute to the production of content and enabled the creation of social networking sites such as Twitter[1] and Facebook.

The History of Computer-mediated Communication

The first scholarly investigations into the nature of online interactions emerged in the 1980s, straddling the disciplines of social psychology, culture and commerce (Jane, 2015). This early assemblage largely determined that abuse in this form of communication was insignificant, infrequent or a source of entertainment (Jane, 2015), with strong associations with wider libertarian and freedom of speech campaigns. Broader research in this area can be traced back to the 1960s. During this decade, a significant shift occurred in the use of and attitude towards computers, as they became tools of communication rather than simple calculation machines (Abbate, 2000). Joseph Licklider, a psychologist and academic who was pivotal to technological developments in this period, due to his work on the human–computer relationship (Naughton, 1999), first described (what we would now recognise as) the internet as an 'intergalactic network' (Rheingold, 2000b, p. 151) in 1965 when his work at the Massachusetts Institute of Technology (MIT) convinced him that computing technology could be used to improve people's lives by broadening the opportunities for increasing knowledge and automating routine tasks (Naughton, 1999). Licklider was a founder (and funder) of ARPANET, the predecessor of the internet, described as 'the world's oldest computer mediated communication network' (Lea, 1992, p. 90). ARPANET was created by the US Defence Department in 1958, when innovative cooperation between the military and academia (Abbate, 2000) precipitated by the Cold War, led to a huge investment in the development of innovative technology by the US military (Wessels, 2010). ARPANET was developed specifically to decentralise command and control functions in the event of a nuclear attack (Wolfson, 2014), a concept that underpins the technical development of the internet; whilst Licklider's own innovations in the mechanisation of spoken language systems have directly influenced the development of contemporary technologies including Apple's Siri and Amazon's Alexa (Errity, 2016).

By the 1980s, ARPANET had developed to such an extent that bulletin boards and similar recognisable forms of computer-mediated communication began to emerge (Rheingold, 2000b). The myriad groupings that evolved as a consequence of the developments during this period were often described as 'communities' based upon their ability to bring together people from across the world using very rudimentary hardware (Naughton, 1999). The earliest of these, The WELL (The Whole Earth 'Lectronic Link') launched in 1985 in Sausalito, California. With

---

[1]Twitter was renamed X following its takeover by Elon Musk in October 2022. However, as the majority of scholarship in this area uses the company's former name, X will be referred to as Twitter throughout.

founders who were previously part of the Haight-Ashbury hippie community of the 1960s and 1970s (Rheingold, 2000a), named by Steve Jobs as his 'biggest influence' (Edwards, 2017, p. 26), The WELL is one of the world's longest continuously operating virtual communities (Edosomwan et al., 2011). It was unique at the time of its inception because it offered the opportunity for strangers to meet and connect with one another using text-based communication, organised into a series of groups (called 'chapters') on a wide range of topics (The Well, 2019). The multiplicity of sociological investigations that took place during the latter half of the 20th century was known as 'technological determinism', with technology viewed as a 'separate sphere, developing independently of society, following its own autonomous logic, and then having effects on society' (MacKenzie & Wajcman, 1999, p. xiv). To compartmentalise the growth of computer-mediated communication in this way is unhelpful, as it ignores the social and political implications of technology, and the vital role played by context (Spears & Lea, 1992). For despite early assertions that computer-mediated communication provided a neutral domain (van Dijk, 2013), it is now widely agreed that online activity is imbued with complex values (Beer, 2019) that are embedded in the social and historical contexts in which they are located (Dahlberg, 2007; Wessels, 2010).

Cyber Psychology

In 1951, Harvard Social Psychologist Robert F. Bales presented a theoretical explanation for the social elements underlying group behaviour (Spears & Lea, 1992), the antecedents of which would eventually evolve into cyberpsychology. Bales asserted that the social elements of group behaviour are defined in terms of the functional social roles that are held by individuals and the interactions between them (Báles et al., 1951). This work also provides an early example of interdisciplinarity, spanning as it does the boundaries of sociology, social anthropology, social psychology and psychology. Of interest when considering the future development of social networking sites is Bales' belief that the self is a social object engaged in social interaction that may occur in the past, present or future. Furthermore, Bales proposes that maintaining social and cognitive support within a group is an interactive and shared responsibility between participants and that the social processes that occur within groups reflect the underlying personalities, social systems and cultures that are in operation. The notion that group culture, which arises as a consequence of the behaviour of small groups, can provide a solution to the functional problems of interaction (Báles et al., 1951), reflects work undertaken half a century later, which explored the benefit derived from the membership of online communities (Finegold & Cooke, 2006).

As technical advancement hastened during the final decade of the 20th century, the discrete discipline of cyberpsychology emerged. The discipline began by building upon theories of social anonymity that originated in the 1960s and applying the notable traits that are recognisable today in internet technologies. These traits are that communication is asynchronous (Kirwan, 2016), can be undertaken anonymously (Christopherson, 2007) and has an absence of visual and auditory cues (Connolly, 2016). This discovery led to the development of two fundamental – but contradictory – theories. The equalisation hypothesis (Dubrovsky et al., 1991) and the social identity model of deinviduation effects emerged a little later (Postmes et al., 2002).

The equalisation hypothesis takes a largely positive view of computer-mediated communication. It asserts that the absence of social cues, which is a characteristic of online interactions, removes stereotypes (Connolly, 2016) and reduces differences in social status (Dubrovsky et al., 1991), making communication more equal. Dubrovsky et al. (1991) compared the differences in face-to-face and virtual exchanges that took place between individuals in asymmetrical power relationships, discovering that the absence of social cues reduced differences in status and made interactions more equal. The central findings of this research have been echoed by more recent investigations into how the absence of visual cues, anonymity and asynchronous communication offered by the internet can have positive benefits, such as giving more power to members of marginalised communities and freeing people from their traditional social roles (Christopherson, 2007). This builds upon earlier research by Rutter undertaken in 1987 into telephone communication, which found that the absence of social cues may actually increase the level of intimacy between individuals.

Similarly, research undertaken with LGBTQ+ communities has found that the disembodied nature of the internet offers individuals the chance to express their sexuality and gender in different ways, whilst simultaneously challenging the masculine and heteronormative approaches traditionally associated with technology (Karl, 2007).

In the latter part of the 20th century, the social identity model of deindividuation effects (SIDE) was developed further, to take account of advancements in computer-mediated communication and to explore how the theory related to online behaviour. Postmes et al. (2002) undertook a two-phase study in order to compare the effect of depersonalisation that occurs within computer-mediated communication. This study investigated communication between 24 groups from around the world, finding that the use of stereotypes was more prevalent amongst the anonymised participants, thereby contradicting the equalisation hypothesis advocated by Dubrovsky (1991) and others.

Results from the SIDE theory reveal that online communication can encourage anti-social behaviour and perpetuate negative social norms (Christopherson, 2007). A further text-matching study undertaken by Moore et al. (2012) found that anonymity in online forums was more closely linked with negative posts and established a link between anonymity and online abuse.

This finding complemented similar research that found that women are treated differently online (Herring, 1996). This study builds upon an experiment undertaken by Matheson (1992), which found that when an individual's gender was apparent in online interactions, gender stereotypes were maintained, with women perceived as compliant and men as more aggressive.

Whichever of the myriad of cyber psychological explanations proffered for abusive behaviour is adopted, it is widely agreed that there has been a significant increase in online abuse over the last 20 years. The growth in the popularity of social networking sites since the early 2000s has seen pejorative behaviour escalate exponentially (Sohn et al., 2019). In addition, the expansion of the internet into all parts of everyday life (Kutiš, 2014) has seen the perpetuation of abuse evolve from being a discrete online activity, to a more generalised verbal violence that targets the individuals' personal and occupational life (Jane, 2015; Rohlinger & Vaccaro, 2021).

Cyber Libertarianism

Those devising the technologies underpinning the early internet were often driven by a desire to build a communications network free from bureaucratic and hierarchical constraints (Wessels, 2010), influenced by the social changes and countercultural movements of the 1960s (Turner, 2006).

There was a belief that the advent of new communication platforms would herald a revitalisation in ideas of freedom of speech and democracy, enabling everyone to participate (Balkin, 2004; Taylor-Smith & Smith, 2019), with some going so far as to advocate complete anarchy online, with no constraints on behaviour whatsoever (Herring et al., 2002). This philosophy was famously summed up by technology journalist John Perry Barlow (1996, p. 6):

> We are creating a world that all may enter without privilege or prejudice accorded by race, economic power, military force, or station of birth. We are creating a world where anyone, anywhere may express his or her beliefs, no matter how singular, without fear of being coerced into silence or conformity.

Nevertheless, at the same time as Barlow and other cyber libertarians were advocating a community without limits (Kutiš, 2014), the US government was co-ordinating the establishment of protocols and technical standards that were to influence the way that data would be used on the various electronic networks that were emerging (Pohle & Voelsen, 2022). This illustrates the abiding dichotomy between freedom and control that remains across all forms of computer-mediated communication, where the anti-establishment mores of the hippy generation have coexisted in parallel with the neoliberal free market underpinnings of the big tech firms. This polarity was further entrenched by the Clinton Administration in the 1990s, when ARPANET and the National Science Foundation Network (NSFNET), which together managed these early electronic networks (Radu, 2019) were privatised (Pohle & Voelsen, 2022). It was this policy decision by the US government that transformed the virtual communities imbued with countercultural beliefs into the bulwarks of free market capitalism (Dahlberg, 2007) that exist today.

After a brief decline in the popularity of cyber libertarianism in the early 2000s (Dahlberg, 2007), largely prompted by the growth in the involvement of the private sector; the introduction of Web 2.0 and the emergence of large tech corporations such as Facebook, Google and Twitter (Pohle & Voelsen, 2022) led to a resurgence in cyber libertarianism. Supporters of neo-liberalism have used the online space particularly effectively, evolving from small groupings to become part of mainstream online activity as a distinct movement – the Alternative Right, or Alt-Right (Massanari, 2018). The Alt-Right have become particularly prominent since Donald Trump was first elected President in 2016 (Nagle, 2017), where they popularised use of the discussion-based websites 4chan and 8chan in order to reach over seven million users (Bernstein et al., 2011). The extent of the Alt-Right has since spread further, to platforms including Reddit and Facebook (Massanari, 2018).

The amorphous groupings that typify the Alt-Right are difficult to define, as they hold widely differing views, with pronouncements tending to centre on issues around race, sexuality and gender (Wendling, 2018). Others have asserted that the Alt-Right, rather than being a neo-Liberal grouping, are 'a polished, technologically adept strand of the far-right' (Koulouris, 2018, p. 750), a sentiment shared by Gallacher et al. (2021).

Whilst the Alt-Right are probably the most well-known of the various online libertarian political movements, there are also libertarian groups that emanate from the left of the political spectrum (Beltramini, 2020; Fuchs, 2020), as well as looser political groupings that focus on single-issue campaigns (Lance Bennett & Toft, 2009).

However, despite the resilience of these libertarian ideas, the most recent literature on the influence of cyber libertarianism in the development of computer-mediated communication has taken a slightly more sceptical view. Work by Mainwaring (2020) proposes that rather than promulgating the influence of libertarian ideologies within nation states, the internet instead centralises authority amongst state actors. This suggests that rather than the familiar imagery of the internet as a 'Wild West', where criminality and insurrection abound, there is instead a sophisticated system of control over many aspects of computer-mediated communication (Herrera, 2016), orchestrated by the actions of a complex mix of governments, transnational organisations and private corporations (Papacharissi, 2009; Puschmann, 2019).

Despite this divergence in perspectives, the primacy of cyber libertarianism has contributed to a growth in racist and misogynist behaviour within these technologies (Coleman, 2012). In many instances, a commitment to libertarian principles on the internet does not offer 'democratic, placeless cyberspaces... in which a worldwide repository of alternative propositions could be found' (Evans, 2013, p. 82). Instead, computer-mediated communication has facilitated the widespread dissemination of abusive, hurtful and vicious speech directed at users of the internet, undertaken under the guise of freedom of expression (Herring et al., 2002). This activity has historically been described as 'flaming'.

Flaming

Flaming emerged at the end of the 20th century (e.g. Gurak, 1995; Loader, 1997), describing 'hostile and aggressive interactions via text-based computer mediated communication' (O'Sullivan & Flanagin, 2003, p. 69).

Early scholarship in this area asserts that abuse in online interaction is insignificant and harmless (Suler & Phillips, 1998), advocating that instances of flaming serve to build group identity, are infrequent and are a source of entertainment (Jane, 2015). In the 1980s, uninhibited behaviour in online communities was often seen as little more than an expression of the computer subculture (Lea, 1992), which at the time was frequently described as little more than adolescent:

> Pranks, tricks and games are benignly tolerated when not actually encouraged. People are often impolite, unconventional, adventurous and irreverent. Mild larceny, such as faking accounts, breaking codes, stealing time, and copying proprietary software, is admired if not rewarded explicitly (Dubrovsky et al., 1986, p. 315).

Occupational culture of the 1990s upheld the belief that abuse in online interactions was insignificant, arguing that instances of flaming served to build group identity, were infrequent or provided a source of entertainment (Jane, 2015). Whilst this culture developed when the internet was in putative form, by ignoring and downplaying episodes of noxious interaction from the outset (or even denying its very existence), it reveals that the issue of online abuse has never been taken seriously.

In addition, the prevailing view at the time (Trottier & Fuchs, 2015; Wessels, 2010) was that flaming was integral to notions of freedom of speech (O'Neill, 2011; Rossini, 2021) and, therefore, that any attempt to regulate or limit computer-mediated communication would be a hugely retrograde step for individual liberty.

The perseverance of the libertarian theories that permit and even encourage flaming (Herring et al., 2002) has led to a situation where the issue of online abuse is all too frequently ignored (Jane, 2014a). For whilst the issue of flaming was once confined to the activities of fringe social movements such as 'Anonymous', who have as their aim 'to enable the free flow of ideas and communication without fear of third-party interception, monitoring, intimidation or coercion' (Trottier & Fuchs, 2015, p. 90); this is no longer the case. There is evidence that the Anonymous collective of individuals frequently – and randomly – targets individuals for abuse and harassment (Trottier & Fuchs, 2015), much of it misogynistic (Jane, 2017a). The random nature of this kind of abuse is important, as it has been suggested that for many individuals engaged in trolling, 'flamers or bullies may not see their "victims" as people but lines of text' (Tagg, 2015, p. 86).

The presence of abuse across multiple social media platforms has been intrinsically tied to a growth in political populism. Political populism – the view that 'political power rests with "the people" and not elites' (Norris & Inglehart, 2018, p. 5) – has become a feature of political campaigns in many countries across the world (Khosravinik, 2017). The phenomenon has occurred on both the right and the left of the political spectrum, leading to the election of Donald Trump – twice – in the USA, the Brexit vote in the UK and a surge in the popularity of populist figures such as Bernie Sanders and Jeremy Corbyn (Gerbaudo, 2018). For whilst social media has not *caused* political populism, the manner in which it operates clearly sustains it (Khosravinik, 2017), providing a means for populist parties such as Reform (in Great Britain) and Podemos (in Spain) to appeal to large groups of voters. Furthermore, where political populism is in the ascendancy, the online abuse of women politicians in particular is especially acute.

Echo Chambers and Filter Bubbles

In behaviour that frequently occurs as a part of a wider political populism, the most contemporary research has indicated a link between the hostility that is frequently a hallmark of online engagement between politically opposing groups and an increase in physical violence when these two sides meet in the offline space (Gallacher et al., 2021). At the same time, there is growing concern that social networking sites have increased the immutability of public opinion, providing a further illustration of the coalescence between social media activity and the growth in political populism. The twin theories of echo chambers and filter bubbles exemplify the development of this concern. Sunstein's (2009a) work on echo chambers and group polarisation highlights the preponderance of people to adopt more extreme opinions or actions when gathered with others who share similar views. The coming together of diverse groups of electors, who on the face of it share very little except the fact that they are 'both digitally connected and politically disgruntled' (Gerbaudo, 2018, p. 748), has been facilitated by the formation of echo chambers, which are created when the algorithms that underpin technology bring groups of people with similar views together by controlling the content that they see. Whilst it could be argued that choosing to seek out people with shared opinions is not unreasonable, what is causing concern is that this is being done deliberately for commercial gain (Khosravinik, 2017). Moreover, the creation of echo chambers frequently occurs without individuals being aware that their news feeds and other social media content is being orchestrated in this way, with priority being given to presenting information that is likely to be popular with a large number of people, rather than purely based on fact (Khosravinik, 2017). At the same time as this commercial selection of information is being diffused across different echo chambers, there has also been a growth in the promulgation of echo chambers by politicians and political movements, who have used sophisticated tools to segment the online space and target particular groups of voters to receive key electoral messages and attack adverts against their opponents. This was particularly prevalent in the 2016 Presidential campaign when the Trump campaign are believed to have spent in the region of $1 million per day on targeted online content in the last month of the campaign (Winston, 2016).

Work by Garimella et al. (2018, p. 219) has further highlighted the threat to political discourse posed by echo chambers, stating that 'there is growing concern that, as citizens become more polarised about political issues, they do not hear the arguments of the opposite side, but are rather surrounded by people and news sources who express only opinions they agree with'.

Along with the theory of echo chambers, Pariser (2012) has proposed the complementary theory of filter bubbles. Filter bubbles are created when online search engines and social networking sites use individuals' personal data to inform their algorithms, and in turn, algorithms then select the content that the platforms believe that they are most interested in (Khosravinik, 2017). The widespread manipulation of user data in this way has been described as 'surveillance capitalism' (Zuboff, 2015, p. 75) and has proven hugely financially lucrative for the big tech firms, whilst, at the same time, securing their dominance in the online space. It has been argued that when combined, echo chambers and filter bubbles create social homogeneity and group polarisation (Edwards, 2013; Harel et al., 2020). Taken together, these two processes have been enablers in the growth of political populism around the world (Bruns, 2019; Guo et al., 2020) whilst also being linked with right wing extremism (Kligler-Vilenchik et al., 2020) and the increase in online abuse (Ozalp et al., 2020). A notable example of the symbiotic relationship between echo chambers, filter bubbles, political populism and online abuse is provided in the study of Gamergate. In an event which has since become notorious, Gamergate occurred between 2014 and 2015. It involved the online release of the personal details of many women working in and writing about the computer gaming industry in the USA. This information was released deliberately and with malicious intent (now commonly described as 'doxxing') (Salter, 2018), for the purposes of harassment (Suzor et al., 2019). The event ultimately culminated in numerous misogynistic death threats and threats of sexual violence, with evidence that the main protagonists went on to form the alt-right networks behind 4chan and 8chan (Romano, 2020) that provided foundational support for the election of Donald Trump (Gerbaudo, 2018).

Conclusion

This chapter provides an interdisciplinary overview of the development of computer-mediated communication and the emergence of online abuse. In doing so, it has identified four contributing theories for the phenomenon, each of which contributes to the promulgation of online abuse: cyber psychology; cyber libertarianism; flaming and echo chambers and filter bubbles. When taken together, these different theoretical perspectives form a negative symbiotic relationship which further disseminates online hate.

In Chapter Three, a similar approach will be taken in order to consider the development of theories around gender-based violence in order to assess what this reveals about the dissemination of online abuse.

Chapter Three

Exploring Theories of Gender-based Violence

Abstract

This chapter provides a context for the span of behaviours falling within the definition of gender-based violence, which range from the mundane (Brown & Walklate, 2011) through to rape and homicide. By introducing the domestic abuse intervention programme (DAIP) (also known as the Duluth model) (Pence & Paymar, 1993), the continuum of violence (Kelly, 1988), the theory of coercive control (Stark, 2009) and the theory of cultural violence (Galtung, 1990), this chapter outlines four theories of gender-based violence that are integral to the understanding of gendered online abuse. This theoretical framework, predominantly associated with the domestic sphere, is then synthesised with theories of the gender-based violence that occurs in public, including workplace sexual harassment and sexual abuse. The theories introduced in this chapter position the issue of gender-based violence at the heart of the book, as it is the history, threat and manifestation of gender-based violence that situates the investigation into online abuse in context. This chapter illustrates how gender-based violence serves to emphasise men's power over women (Stanko, 1990).

Keywords: Gender-based violence; Duluth model; coercive control; continuum of violence; cultural violence; second wave feminism; intersectionality

Gendered Online Abuse Against Women in Public Life: More Than Just Words, 19–38
doi:10.1108/978-1-83549-724-120251003

Introduction

The term 'gender-based violence' has been adopted by public sector bodies and private sector organisations to describe a range of harmful behaviours perpetrated against women (Morales-Campos et al., 2009). The definition is deliberately broad in scope, recognising that these acts of violence are carried out within a variety of interpersonal relationships (or none), and by a range of perpetrators. Connections typically refer to domestic partners but can also be applied to parents, children and other family members or acquaintances and are certainly wider than the 'battered wives' first described by Dobash and Dobash (1980, p. 15).

However, irrespective of the relationship between the perpetrator and the victim, the type of behaviours falling within the description of gender-based violence ranges from the 'mundane and everyday' (Brown & Walklate, 2011, p. 7) through to rape and homicide.

The emergence of gender-based violence as a discrete topic for academic investigation is relatively new, dating back some 40 years. Similarly, whilst Mill (1992) highlighted the subjugation of women by their husbands back in 1869, an issue that was also identified by the first-wave feminists of the 19th century (Mooney, 2000), it was not until the emergence of feminist activism in the 1970s in the UK and the USA that the true scale and nature of gendered violence was brought to public attention (Stanko, 1988). In response, the criminal justice system slowly began to prosecute perpetrators of domestic abuse although it took until the end of the 20th century for the issue to be properly recognised (Holt et al., 2018).

Theorising Gender-based Violence

An early attempt at categorising the behaviours commonly found in incidents of gender-based violence was devised by the domestic abuse intervention program (DAIP), also known as the Duluth model (Bohall et al., 2016), in the early 1980s. Recognised by the Power and Control Wheel that forms an integral part of its theoretical framework, the schema was first devised in 1984 for use in a women's refuge located in Duluth, Minnesota (Pence & Paymar, 1993) as a response to the empirical evidence provided by the facility's service users (Pence & Paymar, 1993). The Power and Control Wheel (reproduced at Fig. 1) is a diagrammatic tool which seeks to illustrate common patterns of abusive behaviour committed by men in heterosexual relationships. The Duluth model has been continuously developed over the past 40 years and now offers a range of practitioner-based psychoeducational community-based intervention programmes for men who have been identified as perpetrators of gender-based violence (DAIP, 2022).

From its inception, the Duluth model utilised the details of abuse provided by survivors of violence to identify and categorise a range of different behaviours that typically occur within abusive relationships (Pence & Paymar, 1993). By articulating this information in a visual form in the Power and Control Wheel, it is possible to identify the relationship between power, control and physical abuse.

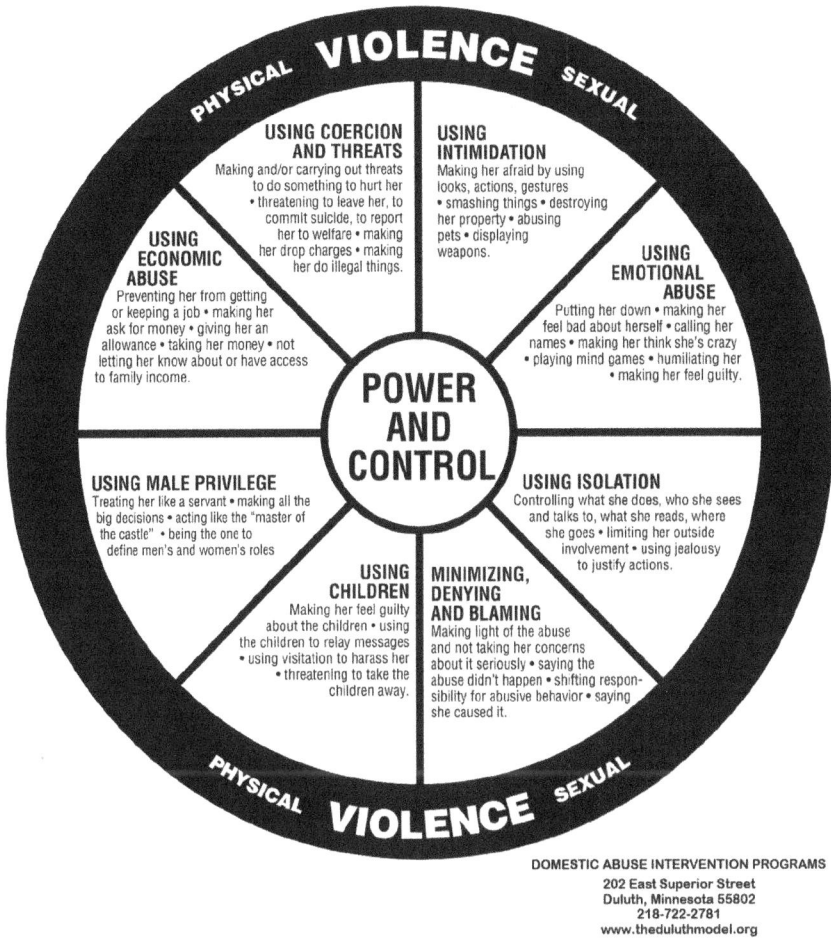

Fig. 1. Power and Control Wheel. *Source*: © DAIPs, used with permission.

During the same period, British academic Liz Kelly (1988) devised the continuum of violence, which provides an alternative way to consider gender-based violence. Kelly (1988, p. 41) describes the continuum as recording:

> Any physical, visual, verbal or sexual act that is experienced by the woman or girl at the time or later as a threat, invasion or assault that has the effect of hurting her or degrading her and/or takes away her ability to control intimate contact.

In common with the Duluth model, Kelly's continuum of gender-based violence similarly provides an empirically based schema of the range of abusive behaviours that women encounter. The 11 behaviours identified by Kelly are threats of violence, sexual harassment, pressure to have sex, sexual assault, obscene phone calls, coercive sex, domestic violence, sexual abuse, flashing, rape and incest. Kelly (1988) emphasises that no hierarchy is applied to the seriousness of the different offences and that the continuum applies purely to the prevalence of the behaviours experienced by research participants. Kelly further argues that the decision to identify offences without grading their seriousness 'enables a linking of the more common, everyday abuses women experience, such as leering, catcalls and verbal assaults, with the less common abuses such as rape and sexual assault which are officially labelled as crimes' (Kelly, 1988, p. 59). Furthermore, and with relevance to this research project, Kelly emphasises that the common characteristics emerging from her research are that each of these behaviours is applied by men in their efforts to control women and that they are so ubiquitous that they have been experienced at least in part by all women.

Work by Stark (2009) contributes a further theory to this corpus, with his work on coercive control. In a theory that has proven highly influential to the development of legislation on gender-based violence in numerous countries (Stark & Hester, 2019; Walklate & Fitz-Gibbon, 2021), Stark reframes the idea of domestic violence as a purely physical act into one where gender-based violence is a 'course of calculated, malevolent conduct deployed almost exclusively by men to dominate individual women by interweaving repeated physical abuse with three equally important tactics: intimidation, isolation, and control' (Stark, 2009, p. 5). Stark further expands on this, by stating that 'a victim's level of fear derives as much from her perception of what could happen based on past experience as from the immediate threat by the perpetrator' […] and that 'the cumulative harms inflicted by male partners explain why women are so much more likely to be entrapped by abuse than men' (Stark, 2009, p. 94). As well as providing a highly influential analysis of the realities of domestic abuse, Stark's work also illustrates the unequal role of male power in these relationships (Brennan & Myhill, 2022), something which is frequently replicated in societal inequalities of patriarchal power. The inclusion of the specific offence of coercive control into domestic abuse legislation in England and Wales in 2015 is discussed further in Chapter Seven.

Stark (and Hester) (2019) revisited the issue of coercive control a decade later, with this later work highlighting the growth in studies evidencing the repeat victimisation of many women experiencing domestic abuse, as well as adding financial abuse and gaslighting to the range of behaviours defined as coercive. Stark and Hester (2019) also used this paper to widen the scope of the theory to same-sex relationships and the coercive control of children and other family members.

In 1990, Johan Galtung published his theory of cultural violence. Building upon his earlier work on structural violence (1969), the concept of cultural violence brings together elements of structural and direct violence. In doing so, Galtung suggests that the merging of these two forms creates an environment in which both structural and direct violence are legitimised. When examined more closely, it is proposed that the use of violent speech and inflammatory language (whether written or spoken); along with the marginalisation of certain groups (e.g. women, or those from ethnically minoritised populations) that combine within cultural violence, in a way that makes physical violence appear innocuous, thereby changing the morality and permissibility of an act (Galtung, 1990). At its core, cultural violence allows certain violent behaviours to become permissible. One pertinent example of cultural violence useful in this discussion is the sanitation of language, where acts of physical violence are deliberately downplayed, particularly in the media. An integral part of the theory is the creation of a causal flow between cultural violence, structural violence and actual physical violence. In this process, cultural violence presents exploitation and repression as normal, making people immune to violent behaviour. This is then further manifested in structural violence, where violence is used or encouraged in order to break or maintain socially dominant structures, with victims blamed for the violence that occurs. The acceptance of forms of structural violence ultimately leads to the articulation of actual violence, which becomes endemic when overlooked by society as a whole. Galtung (1990) makes specific reference to gender-based violence in this typology, emphasising that whilst (on paper) women may have longer life expectancy rates than men, the risk of violence as a result of gender specific abortion, infanticide and familial violence continually imposes structural violence in order to maintain the dominance of the patriarchal system (Gardsbane et al., 2022).

Galtung's (1990) theory of cultural violence fits well within a theoretical domain that examines the wider role of patriarchy in gender-based violence. Over 40 years ago, researchers working in this field recognised that what differentiated gender-based violence from other acts of violence was that this behaviour was an explicit manifestation of patriarchal domination (Dobash & Dobash, 1980). This reflects the continued subordinate position of women across societies (Stanko, 1988), which most typically emerges when male power is perceived to be under threat (Dobash & Dobash, 1998).

However, whilst the theoretical explanations for gender-based violence outlined here are undoubtedly influential, they have each been the subject of criticism. For example, the original Duluth model has been criticised for focussing on a limited population (Bohall et al., 2016), concentrated on a cohort of largely white and wholly heterosexual couples. The model has also been accused of lacking a significant evidence base prior to being rolled out in other areas (Pender, 2012). Some of the most strident censure of the DAIP has come from Dutton and Corvo (2006, p. 457), who deem the Duluth model to be 'flawed research', believing it to have been developed and subsequently adopted by practitioners lacking a professional background and qualifications in either psychology or social work. Furthermore, whilst it is true that the Duluth model is avowedly feminist in approach, Dutton and Corvo believe that this has resulted in the widespread adoption of a wholly negative 'gender political model' (Dutton & Corvo, 2006, p. 457) towards gender-based violence. This is a heated debate that has lasted over a decade, as others, broadly supportive of the Duluth model (e.g. Gondolf, 2011), have weighed in to add their support for the model's core elements and to take issue with Dutton and Carvo's (2006) treatise.

In contrast to Kelly's non-hierarchical continuum approach, Wise and Stanley (1987) provide a model of gender-based violence that has a clear hierarchy of offence seriousness, with murder and rape at one end of the spectrum and patronising and uncalled for insults at the other. Kelly (2011) has produced a subsequent iteration of her continuum, in recognition of a wider awareness of both the presence of abuse in homosexual relationships, and a broadening of the understanding of gender-based violence, to add offences such as coercive control. Siddiqui (2013) has further revised the continuum, to include offences around (so-called) honour-based violence, including forced marriage, in recognition of the fact that Kelly's original work was based wholly on the experiences of white women (Rehman et al., 2013).

Feminist Theories of Gender-based Violence

Edwards (1990) emphasises that whilst the influence of both first and second wave feminism was vital to gender-based violence gaining public attention, there has always been more than one kind of feminism in operation, and each strand of feminist theory brings with it a slightly different explanation for gender-based violence. There are widely agreed to be four 'types' of feminism: liberal feminism, radical feminism, socialist feminism and post-modernist feminism (Jerath, 2021) although there remains significant divergence and nuance even within these different classifications (Davies, 2007).

Liberal feminism first emerged in the 18th century (Ackerly, 2001) and is epitomised by the first wave of feminism described by Spender (1982). Associated with pioneering women such as Mary Wollstonecraft, Virginia Woolf and Susan B. Anthony (Ackerly, 2001), liberal feminism adopts an equal opportunities approach (Davies, 2007). Liberal feminists first sought to highlight the position of women as a disadvantaged group, who were seeking equality in voting, divorce laws and access to finance and property (Ackerly, 2001). Described by some as 'feminist empiricism' (Hundleby, 2011, p. 29), liberal feminist philosophies are largely traditional in scope, adopting a cautious approach to social change. Liberal feminism has been criticised for excluding the views of Black feminists (Ackerly, 2001) and the wider intersectional feminist experience. When used as a lens to explore gender-based violence, liberal feminism relies on the role of institutions (and the men holding power within them) acting as agents for change (Gámez Fuentes et al., 2016).

In distinct contrast, radical feminism takes a revolutionary approach to feminist activism (Hundleby, 2011), roundly rejecting calls for the inclusion of men in the fight for female equality (Pretorius, 2018). Radical feminists argue that it is only through the dismantling of the institutions of marriage, patriarchy and labour that it will be possible to 'end the oppression of women, by creating awareness of and resistance not only to male-dominated or patriarchal institutions, but to the conceptual frameworks that sustain them' (Lee, 2001, p. 5513). This strand of feminism focusses on men's oppression of women through the actions of patriarchal institutions (Davies, 2007) and highlights what it regards as the lack of a structural response to gender-based violence (Walklate, 1995). The third (and somewhat related) strand of feminist theory is socialist feminism, which defines women as being oppressed by capitalism and dominated by men (Davies, 2007). Despite the disintegration of many socialist regimes that has taken place since the emergence of socialist feminism in the 1970s and 1980s, advocates of socialist feminism continue to highlight the convergence of capitalist and gender role models, most recently demonstrated during the multiple Covid-19 lockdowns of 2020–2022, when women were frequently left to undertake the majority of childcare and home-schooling activities, despite simultaneously juggling their own paid employment (Segalo & Fine, 2020). Socialist feminists assert that it is the iniquitous underlying structural and institutional conditions underpinning women's (and especially Black women's) experience that is the primary explanation for gender-based violence (Segalo & Fine, 2020). Adherents to this theoretical strand advocate that it is only by dismantling the existing systems that change will be achieved; or in the words of Segalo and Fine (2020, p. 9): 'there should be a refusal of normality... there shall be no going home until there is justice'.

In contrast, the more recent theoretical strand of post-modern feminism asserts that a post-modern feminist approach offers a degree of openness, plurality, diversity and difference (Walklate, 1995) that is absent from more traditional theoretical positions. Proponents of post-modern feminism believe that this new theoretical interpretation will lead to a 'socially transformative politics of emancipation and freedom from gender, race, and class exploitation' (Ebert, 1991, p. 887). It is further argued that post-modernist feminism has no policy agenda and that it instead seeks to break the traditional links that exist between science, rationality and policy making (Davies, 2007). Perhaps as a consequence of this approach, there is no body of literature offering a post-modern feminist explanation for either the causes of, or solutions for, gender-based violence, as the theory has not devised any such response.

The recognition of gender-based violence that materialised within the academy during the latter half of the 20th century was soon joined by a wider campaigning collective. In the 1960s and 1970s, pioneering work was undertaken by second wave feminists based both in the USA and the UK, to secure greater awareness and responses to gender-based violence. In the USA, the campaigning work of Gloria Steinem and Betty Friedan is central to this period. Friedan was an early second wave feminist activist, whose formative book, 'Feminine Mystique', highlighted the frustration felt by many women who found themselves obligated to fulfil traditional gender norms (Friedan, 1963). In 1971 (in partnership with Dorothy Pitman Hughes), Steinem launched Ms. Magazine, using it as a platform from which to campaign for women's rights, later coupling this work with her membership of the National Women's Political Caucus (Steinem, 2015). In the UK, notable second wave feminists of the period include Beatrix Campbell, Anna Coote, Tess Gill and Erin Pizzey (Lewis, 2020). Campbell was one of the founders of 'Red Rag', a Marxist feminist magazine of the period (The Barry Amiel and Norman Melburn Trust, 2021), whilst Coote and Gill won the right for women to stand at the bar in pubs with their male colleagues, under the new Sex Discrimination Act of 1975 (Rodrigues, 2012). Pizzey, whilst no longer a member of the feminist movement (Bell, 2021), introduced the first women's refuge in the UK in 1971, a ground-breaking initiative that was soon followed by the work of academics including Dobash and Dobash (1980), to highlight the pernicious and widespread nature of domestic abuse. Many of the same campaigners also highlighted the malign persistence of sexual harassment (David, 2016), campaigns that were often supported by trades unions (Dobash & Dobash, 1980), recognising that workplace sexual harassment was all too frequent, and often involved co-workers, managers and service providers (Croall, 1995).

Misogyny

The malign impact of misogyny has received academic scrutiny (e.g. Jones, 2019; Zempi & Smith, 2021), along with attention from social policy institutions (e.g. Cumming-Potvin, 2023) and the criminal justice system (e.g. Casey, 2023). A number of theoretical models reference misogyny as a contributing factor to online abuse (e.g. Jane, 2017a; Mantilla, 2015; Salter, 2017). Before analysing a selection of these models in greater detail, it is worth defining what misogyny actually *means* in the modern context, as otherwise it risks becoming a term that is widely promulgated without a clear understanding of what it signifies. Manne (2018, p. 47) defines misogyny as 'a systematic facet of social power relations', arising when women attempt to gain power and authority 'in a man's world... a patriarchy' (Manne, 2018, p. 34). Whilst theoretically useful, Manne's definition risks overlooking the sheer hostility of much modern misogyny. Banet-Weiser (2018) locates the hatred of women at the forefront of her definition of misogyny, whilst adding that 'popular misogyny is the instrumentalization of women as objects, where women are a means to an end: a systematic devaluing and dehumanizing of women' (Banet-Weiser, 2018, p. 2).

Theories of misogyny have a long history (Beard, 2017). The exclusion and subjugation of women both in public and private has had a negative impact upon the effective development of many facets of social and occupational life (Power, 2006). It is clear that even the most cursory of investigations reveal how men have been endeavouring to silence women throughout history, using whatever technology is available, creating what Gilmore (2009, p. 3) has defined as the 'male malady'. Analysis of literature in this area reveals that contemporary misogyny frequently contains four interrelated elements: silencing (e.g. Herring et al., 2002; Salter, 2017), the belittling of women's knowledge and opinions (e.g. Camp, 2018), the criticism of appearance (e.g. Backe et al., 2018) and threats of physical and sexual violence (e.g. Todd, 2017). Each of these elements will be considered in turn.

Silencing

The act of silencing women is integral to misogyny, with women frequently silenced, with their opinions ignored or appropriated by men (Spender, 1982). Women's voices are routinely muted, and this both enables and perpetuates the power of misogyny (Banet-Weiser, 2018). Misogyny is often perpetuated by the media, who refused to cover many activities of the first wave of feminist activism in the 19th century, including initial campaigns for women's suffrage (Spender, 1982); and who remain complicit in the silencing of women's voices, as evidenced by the treatment of the former Prime Minister of Australia, Julia Gillard (Worth et al., 2016). An examination of press coverage following her speech on sexism discovered that Gillard's accusations were 'dismissed, minimised and under-mined' (Worth et al., 2016, p. 52); whilst 'silence [was] privileged over speaking up against sexism' (*ibid.*).

When considering the act of silencing within the online space, there is clear evidence of online abuse attempting to silence women (Barlow & Awan, 2016; Lewis et al., 2018), confirming it as both an aim and function of wider misogyny (Carson, 2018). Silencing may also prove to be the consequence of online abuse, for example, when law enforcement agencies advise women to withdraw from online activity for their own safety, which is also seen by some as an example of a wider institutionalised misogyny (Yardley, 2021a). The act of silencing women in this way, necessitating their retreat from social networking sites (Bliss, 2019), has the potential to wreak huge financial damage upon the women targeted for abuse. Computer-mediated communication is now firmly embedded in social and economic participation (Henry & Powell, 2015), particularly since the Covid-19 pandemic precipitated a shift in patterns of working into the online space. The cost of such silencing is so substantial that Jane (2018, p. 576) has termed it an act of 'economic vandalism'.

Belittling

Another way in which misogyny seeks to undermine women is to question or belittle their skills, knowledge and experience (Farrell et al., 2019). Chapman (2014) suggests that this behaviour is central to both misogyny and gender-based violence. In the domestic sphere, belittling is often used as part of a wider sys-tem of shaming (Camp, 2018). In the public sphere, women frequently have their authority undermined in a deliberate attempt to halt their activity (Phillips, 2019).

There is evidence that misogynists have habitually employed techniques designed to belittle and undermine women's professional competence, in an attempt to remove them as potential competition in the public sphere (Mantilla, 2015), whilst also perpetuating their economic dominance (Spender, 1982). As Spender (1982, p. 95) explains: 'we have 300 years of evidence that men *do* dis-credit and bury women's work on the basis of their sex' (italics in original).

Focus on Appearance

Misogynistic abuse frequently focusses on women's appearance. In the corpo-real realm, this is often articulated as a dimension of coercive control, where an abuser will use criticism of clothing or body shape as a means of asserting their malign intent (McCauley et al., 2018). Research undertaken into police culture has identified a focus on appearance as being integral to the negative percep-tions of gender (Brown et al., 2019), a finding that echoes work from two decades earlier, which highlighted that some 60 per cent of women police officers had received comments from male officers that criticised their appearance (Brown, 1998). In the political realm, there was a considerable discussion about Hillary Clinton's appearance (particularly in relation to her age) both before and during the Presidential campaign of 2016 (Hayes et al., 2014; Jennings & Coker, 2019).

It is likely that such coverage was exacerbated by her Republican opponent engaging in the negative portrayal of women as 'fat', 'dogs' and 'pigs' (Banet-Weiser, 2018, p. 173). This emphasises once again how media coverage frequently amplifies misogynistic behaviour occurring in the public sphere.

Threat

The threat of physical and sexual violence is a perpetual presence within misogyny (Ging et al., 2020). Anthropological studies record the widespread use of gang rape for minor transgressions across many countries (Gilmore, 2009), and threats of violence are a common feature in warfare (Krook, 2020), as well as in religious, historical and fictional works (Gilmore, 2009). However, despite its constancy, violent misogyny is often perceived as a private matter (Tomkinson et al., 2020). This echoes attitudes towards gender-based violence discussed earlier in the chapter, which highlighted that spousal violence was frequently ignored by the police and social policy agencies for much of the 20th century (Radford & Stanko, 1991). There is some evidence that the rise in violent offending by followers of misogynistic men's groups (Wright et al., 2020) including the so called involuntarily celibate or Incel movement (Banet-Weiser, 2018) has increased public awareness of the threat implicit in misogyny, making action from criminal justice agencies more likely (Tomkinson et al., 2020). The multiple shooting that took place in 2014 in Isla Vista, California, when six people were killed and 14 others were injured (Manne, 2018), emphasised how the violent misogyny exhibited by Incels poses a threat to both women and men (Tomkinson et al., 2020). The murder of four men and two women (Manne, 2018), corroborated evidence linking the propensity to engage in gender-based violence, with wider acts of violence and terrorism (Johnston & True, 2019). In the UK, there is some evidence that the mass shooting carried out in Plymouth in August 2021 was at least in part motivated by an adherence to Incel doctrine (Bengtsson Meuller, 2024; Townsend, 2021). Meanwhile, research by Smith (2019) found that the men responsible for terrorist attacks in London and Manchester each had histories of committing acts of gender-based violence. Whilst such acts are thankfully rare, and present the most extreme examples of misogynistic threat, they do illustrate how contemporary misogyny emanates from 'a much more antagonistic politics of sexual entitlement, disenfranchisement and revenge' (Ging et al., 2020, p. 852). The change of government in July 2024 appeared to provoke an increased discussion of the level and perpetuation of gender-based violence in society, with the National Police Chiefs Council describing the amount of gender-based violence in the UK as an epidemic, and calling for a 'whole-system approach that brings together criminal justice partners, government bodies and industry, in a new partnership that seeks to reduce the scale and impact of violence against women and girls' (NPCC, 2024, p. 1). This research reveals how this behaviour is frequently intertwined with activity on social networking sites (Ging, 2019) and the perpetuation of online abuse (Wright et al., 2020).

Consequently, the literature on online abuse frequently contains examples of threats made via electronic communication, some of which have already been quoted in this study. However, as Tulip Siddiq, the Labour MP for Hampstead and Kilburn in London explained, the fear that online threats could manifest physically is constantly felt, most recently in the wake of the murder of Sir David Amess MP in October 2021:

> It's constant on Facebook and Twitter. I only report it when it's extreme. It distracts from my casework – I could be helping a woman who has become homeless rather than spending energy reporting abuse. But now I'll be vigilant once again (Urwin, 2021, p. 12).

Reminders of the presence of online threats are important, as they provide evidence to policymakers of the extent of abuse and allow them to formulate regulatory and legal responses (Husnain et al., 2021), something that will be discussed in more detail in Chapter Seven. Publicising threats made online may also provide succour to victims who have experienced similar online encounters, allowing them to find comfort in the knowledge that they are not alone. This was demonstrated in the '#BeenRapedNeverReported' hashtag campaign of 2014, where women shared their experiences of sexual assault with others on Twitter (Teotonio, 2014), as one woman explained:

> I got an overwhelming awesome response the night I posted ... There was one ... all she said was, 'we stand with you, friend'. And that one made me cry. I'll admit it, that one made me cry. And then there was one that told me I was incredibly strong and brave for doing what I did.... there was six or seven comments like that. Which, for me, was overwhelming because I didn't really think that anyone would say these things, you know, it was just I was helping the hashtag understand why things weren't being reported. And I didn't really expect any response at all. And next thing you know, I got likes and favourites and comments, and I was just, like, oh, my gosh, what is going on here? (Mendes et al., 2018, p. 238)

This brief review of the underlying features of misogyny illustrates how prejudice against women is not unique to the internet. Indeed, Mantilla (2015, p. 132) asserts that online abuse is 'a reflection and embodiment of long-standing cultural patterns of misogyny'.

However, as both academic and journalistic investigations in this area (e.g. Cranston, 2015; Jane, 2017a; Jones, 2019) have highlighted, the additional communication mechanisms offered by social networking sites have both normalised and amplified sexism and threats of violence towards women (Vera-Gray, 2017), leading to a disproportionate amount of gender-based abuse directed at women active in the online space (Ging & Siapera, 2018).

In addition to explorations of the nature of misogyny, most recently in the online space, there has also been an attempt by the academy to theorise about more broader aspects of online abuse. Whilst obviously not as prolific or enduring as theories exploring the gender-based violence that occurs in the physical space, there has nonetheless been a growth in the theoretical explanations for the abuse that occurs online.

The first of these theoretical explanations is 'e-bile', which was introduced by Jane in 2014. This theory provides one of the first detailed attempts to define the nature of online abuse:

> The term e-bile…describes the extravagant invective, the sexual-ized threats of violence, and the recreational nastiness that have come to constitute a dominant tenor of internet discourse. My case is that a new descriptor is required in order to gather under one heading a variety of denunciatory forms that share characteristic, signal features and so demand a broad field of inquiry – one that is able to gather ostensibly variegated speech acts into a specific yet widely conceived theoretical reflection (Jane, 2014a, p. 531).

As Jane (2014a) explains in this passage, what makes online abuse conspicuous is its violent invective that is imbued with misogyny. By adopting this theoretical explanation for online abuse, it is possible to broaden the academic understanding of such abuse and to develop an evidence base of its occurrence. Integral to the theory of e-bile is a recognition that, for many years, the seriousness of online abuse and the damaging nature of this type of communication upon both individuals and institutions have been downplayed and ignored (Jane, 2014a). Jane (2014a) is reluctant to provide an overly rigid definition of online abuse, believing that to do so risks excluding important facets of this emergent discourse. Instead, she provides a 'loose framing' (Jane, 2014a, p. 540) of the likely elements of e-bile. These elements include overt misogyny, sexualised and violent threats, a vitriolic and extravagant invective that frequently includes the use of obscenities, recreational nastiness (e.g. highlighting aspects of a woman's appearance), victim blaming and the belittling of women's knowledge and achievements.

A similar theory that has been devised to better define online abuse is gender-trolling (Mantilla, 2015). Mantilla (2015) uses this theory to differentiate between the misogynistic abuse that is promulgated online and other forms of techno-logical communication. In doing so, she asserts that gendertrolling is 'a new kind of virulent, more threatening online phenomenon' (Mantilla, 2013, p. 564), further arguing that this manner of invective is 'specifically and dramatically more destructive to its victims' (Mantilla, 2013, p. 564). The theory of gendertrolling, which is comprised of seven key elements, provides a deeper analysis of online abuse than the theories summarised thus far, as it articulates *how* the abuse is delivered, and not just the format that it takes. Mantilla (2015), therefore, highlights how an aim of online abuse is to silence women in the online space, typically precipitated by women voicing an opinion. This abuse commonly involves gendered and sexualised insults that are designed to belittle and demean their chosen target and frequently make sexualised and violent threats. Mantilla (2015) further recognises that online abuse occurs over multiple online platforms and at a high level of intensity/frequency. Finally, online abuse can be perpetuated for a long duration and often involves multiple attackers – characterised as a 'mob' (Citron, 2020).

Mantilla's typology (2015) has echoes of the different strands of misogyny discussed above, whilst Citron (2009) has similarly highlighted the frequent attempt to silence women in the online space, emphasising that the perpetrators of online abuse 'directly implicate their targets' self-determination and ability to participate in political and social discourse' (Citron, 2009, p. 406). Furthermore, Citron (2009, p. 415) provides a reminder that 'any silencing of speech prevents us from better understanding the world in which we live', which should act as a catalyst for policy makers in this area, something discussed further in Chapter Seven. In a more recent study, McCarthy (2022) draws parallels between the belittling that is synonymous with sexual harassment in the physical space, and the attempts to delegitimise professional women online, confirming that online abuse shares many similarities with this enduring gendered persecution, as first highlighted in the Duluth model (Pence & Paymar, 1993).

A complementary theory to the concepts outlined above is the continuum of image-based sexual abuse, devised by McGlynn et al. (2017). This theory adds the visual dimension to the analysis of online abuse, using as a catalyst the increase in legislation implemented by governments across the globe to tackle the issue of so called revenge porn. Drawing on Kelly's continuum of violence (1988), the continuum of image-based sexual abuse (McGlynn et al., 2017) includes a range of behaviours that it is argued should all be viewed as types of sexual violence. When taken together, these behaviours are much broader than the offence of revenge porn (commonly understood to mean 'the dissemination of nude, intimate and sexualized images of individuals (overwhelmingly female), without the consent and against the wishes of those pictured' (Yar & Drew, 2019, p. 579) that has become a familiar part of everyday discourse. Instead, this continuum aims to bring together a 'range of gendered, sexualised forms of abuse which have common characteristics' (McGlynn et al., 2017, p. 25). McGlynn et al. (2017) provide a set of six broad examples of image-based sexual abuse. These are a threat to distribute private sexual images online, the online distribution of stolen (hacked) private sexual images, the non-consensual creation of private sexual images, the taking of private sexual images in public (e.g. up-skirting), sexualised extortion and the filming of sexual assault and rape. In addition, McGlynn et al. (2017) seek to go further than providing this definitive list of injurious activities, and instead seek to future-proof their continuum by providing a theoretical definition for image-based sexual abuse. This definition is: 'the abuse experienced predominantly by women arising from the non-consensual creation and/or distribution of private sexual images' (McGlynn et al., 2017, p. 26). The scope of this definition means that it is possible for behaviours to be added (or removed) as technology develops and new types of offensive behaviours emerge. An advantage of this approach is that it offers the potential for policy and legislation in this area to keep pace with future technological innovation, something which is incredibly challenging in this area. At a conceptual level, the theoretical continuum 'illuminates the abusive nature of the practices and the commonalities between seemingly disparate phenomena' (McGlynn et al., 2017, p. 28), whilst confirming that *all* such behaviours involve gendered harassment and abuse (Citron, 2014) and lead victims to equate their experiences as being 'akin to sexual assault' (Wittes et al., 2016, p. 4).

When considering the different theoretical explanations underpinning online abuse and gender-based violence, it is crucial to recognise that the abuse received by women of colour, disabled women and LGBTQ+ women who are communicating in the online space is more extreme than that received by heterosexual white women. This difference occurs when women who are members of numerous demographic groupings find their multiple identities intersecting, creating myriad levels of discrimination and/or deprivation (Beckman, 2014). In a wide ranging examination of the gendered inequality that pervades the digital sphere, Galpin (2022) uses the theory of intersectionality to consider how women who are already marginalised due to existing demographic characteristics become the target for online abuse. As a consequence, Galpin (2022) defines online abuse in two ways. Central to the first of these classifications is the recognition of 'participatory inequality' (Galpin, 2022, p. 164), which highlights the way that women who already face discrimination in the physical world find their marginalisation perpetuated, and indeed, exacerbated in the online space. This is often done by men employing techniques to silence the contributions made by such women (Galpin, 2022). Galpin then goes further, identifying how the actions and policies of social media companies themselves contribute to this discrimination, by determining whose voice is heard in the online space, and as a consequence 'reinforcing capitalist structures' (Galpin, 2022, p. 167). The second strand of Galpin's theory examines the role of 'subaltern counter-publics' (Galpin, 2022, p. 164), which she proposes as an explanation for the ways in which online platforms can create 'spaces of resistance' (Galpin, 2022, p. 164) for feminist activists. However, Galpin also highlights the way that marginalised women are frequently excluded from these campaigning settings, due to the actions of white, middle-class feminists, whose needs and identities are often more highly valued than those of black and transgender women, thereby creating an alternative locus for discrimination. This echoes the foundational work of Crenshaw (1989), which highlights how women with intersecting identities are 'theoretically erased' in the conceptualisation of oppression within 'single-axis frameworks' of either gender, race or class (Crenshaw, 1989, p. 57). Galpin concludes by asserting that the intersectional identities of *all* women must be included in any analysis of online abuse in order to acquire a true understanding of the phenomenon. Galpin's theory of gender inequality in the digital sphere echoes ideas around the role of filter bubbles and echo chambers in perpetuating online abuse, first discussed in Chapter Two.

Consolidating Theories of Gender-based Violence and Online Abuse

Examining the literature on gender-based violence alongside scholarship on online abuse enables the identification of a number of areas of overlap between the two domains. Highlighting these synergies is pivotal to understanding how online abuse is another form of gender-based violence.

The discussion of the different theoretical explanations of online abuse in this chapter began with an examination of Jane's theory of e-bile (2014a), which emphasises the need to record and report the obscene nature of online abuse in order to communicate the extent of the harm it can cause. When compared with Galtung's theory of cultural violence (1990), there is a connection between the two theories, as Galtung's work (1990, p. 295) asserts that the 'sanitation of language' is a fundamental aspect of cultural violence, as it downplays the seriousness of cumulative episodes of structural violence. By positioning these two theories together, it is possible to gain a clearer understanding of how the use of language is an integral facet of the perpetuation of violence in the online space.

Nevertheless, despite the similarities between Jane (2014a) and Galtung (1990) and the importance of identifying the unexpurgated nature of online abuse in order to recognise its seriousness, Galpin (2022) takes issue with some aspects of this. For whilst agreeing with the need to recognise the true nature of online abuse, including its use of violent invective and threatening obscenities, Galpin stresses that the academic understanding of online abuse must go further and assess the impact that receiving such communication has on individual women and society as a whole.

The theory of technology facilitated sexual violence and harassment, devised by Henry and Powell (2015) synthesises many of the points identified in the literature on both gender-based violence (e.g. Kelly, 1988; Pence & Paymar, 1993), as well as more recent scholarship on online abuse (e.g. Mantilla, 2015; McGlynn et al., 2017), to devise a definition of sexual violence and harassment against adult women that encompasses the malign creation and distribution of sexual imagery, with broader themes of violence, harassment and structural misogyny. Similarly, another theory that combines both the older and newer scholarship is provided by Dragiewicz et al. (2018) in their theory of technology facilitated coercive control. This theory builds upon Stark's original (2009) work on coercive control, by highlighting the way that online platforms work to exacerbate existing coercive behaviours, whilst also introducing new methods of abuse. Dragiewicz et al.'s (2018) study confirms the presence of harassment as integral to the theory of technology-facilitated coercive control, whilst also demonstrating that the most likely perpetrators of gendered online abuse are current and former partners (Lenhart et al., 2016). Of relevance to this discussion is that in addition to detailing the behaviours that exemplify technology facilitated coercive control in the private sphere, such as the use of technology to stalk a partner's movements, the unauthorised sharing of sexual images (revenge porn), and the electronic control of financial affairs, Dragiewicz et al.'s (2018) work begins to explore the proliferation of such behaviour beyond the domestic sphere. For instance, Dragiewicz et al. (2018) provide the example of perpetrators of domestic violence using the opportunities presented by online networks to join together with wider misogynistic groupings, in order to perpetuate the impact of abuse beyond the original target and impinge upon women in the course of their professional lives, using the 'Gamergate' episode as an example.

The theory of technology facilitated coercive control is one that concurs with more traditional scholarship in this area, confirming the presence of both misogyny and structural discrimination against women in the abusive behaviour that extends domestic violence from the physical world into the online space (Dragiewicz et al., 2018). Integral to the theory of technology-facilitated coercive control is the question of the role played by the social media companies as both facilitators of abuse and as crucial to its prevention (Dragiewicz et al., 2018). This stands out as one of the few theories to consider how online platforms fail to tackle the abusive behaviour that occurs on their sites.

The theoretical framework that considers technology-facilitated domestic abuse in the political economy (Yardley, 2021a) has the concept of omnipresence at its heart. First identified by Woodlock (2017), omnipresence in technology-facilitated domestic abuse describes the motivation of an attacker to remain 'omnipresent' in a woman's life, which is achieved by utilising everyday surveillance technology to be omnipresent in ways not previously possible. Yardley (2021a) has further developed ideas of omnipresence, identifying four distinct types of omnipresent behaviour that are found in episodes of domestic violence that are deemed to have a technological component. These are establishing omnipresence, overt omnipresence, covert omnipresence and retributive omnipresence (Yardley, 2021a, p. 1484). In work that concurs with the findings of Dragiewicz et al. (2018), Yardley (2021a) highlights how perpetrators of domestic violence are harnessing the emergence of new technologies to commit enduring harms. For example, Yardley's (2021a) theory highlights how 'smartphones, text messaging, social media and GPS location tracking are all examples of technologies repurposed for abuse' (Yardley, 2021a, p. 1479) and used to undertake campaigns of harassment and stalking.

Whilst identified by Stark (2009) as a central tenet of coercive control, there is also evidence that as surveillance devices become more ubiquitous, this behaviour has become more acceptable (Dragiewicz et al., 2018).

This theory of technology-facilitated domestic abuse clearly positions the combined malign patriarchal influences of sexism and misogyny at the heart of explanations for such behaviour. It confirms that the underlying impact of these tenets of patriarchal power has evolved and endured alongside the development of new communications technology, with the growth of neoliberalism adding to the pernicious online environment experienced by many women. Of particular relevance is the dimension of retributive omnipresence, which usually occurs once the intimate relationship has ended, and the perpetrator seeks to regain control over their former partner. With the intention to cause maximum humiliation for the woman concerned, retributive omnipresence will frequently threaten to undermine an individual's professional reputation and economic security, for example, by using fake accounts to spread disinformation about their qualifications, or by accusing them of malfeasance in public office (Yardley, 2021a). When women attempt to report such activity to the police, they are often told to change their mobile numbers or delete their social media accounts. This further institutionalises misogyny and has links with victim blaming, whilst also making women individually responsible for their own safety. Yardley's theory of technology-facilitated domestic abuse in political economy has strong parallels with Vera-Gray and Kelly's (2020) theory of safety work, which makes similar points about the individualisation of gender-based violence and Lewis et al.'s (2017) links with online abuse, public shaming and victim blaming (Lewis et al., 2017).

Bailey and Burkell (2021) build upon the structural and institutional weaknesses highlighted by Yardley (2021a) in their assessment of the scholarship in online-gendered violence, devising a theory of technologically facilitated violence that is based on structural and intersectional perspectives (Bailey & Burkell, 2021, p. 531). In echoes of the work of Galpin (2022), this theory of technology-facilitated violence similarly recognises the role of gender in this behaviour, as well as the greater impact on women from marginalised communities, as their different identities intersect to make their treatment worse. This is a particular problem when theoretical explanations of violence consider the issue from an individualised perspective, as this ignores the structural siting of multiple spheres of exclusion, harassment and harm (Bailey & Burkell, 2021). In contrast, the theory of technologically facilitated violence devised by Bailey and Burkell (2021) emphasises the need for wholesale structural change to societal systems and institutions, including the composition of the social media companies, which are overwhelmingly run by those who are wealthy, male and white, in order to offer genuine solutions to technologically facilitated violence. Furthermore, this theory also recognises the need for a collegiate approach to devising solutions to online abuse, one that involves 'governments, platforms and online communities' (Bailey & Burkell, 2021, p. 537). This theoretical approach to the issues of gender-based violence, intersectionality and online abuse is wider in scope than some of the other theories discussed in this chapter and as such provides an interesting rubric to consider the approach of policy makers, online platforms and legislation, which is considered further in Chapter Seven.

By exploring scholarship in both gender-based violence and online abuse, it is possible to draw a number of important conclusions. Firstly, there is little doubt that online abuse is overwhelmingly gendered and, as such, can be categorised as a form of gender-based violence (e.g. Galpin, 2022; McLachlan & Harris, 2022; Rogers et al., 2022). For whilst not universally agreed upon (e.g. Gorrell et al., 2020), the majority of scholars working in this area agree that most violent and aggressive online abuse is received by women (Kargar & Rauchfleish, 2019).

The prevalence of online abuse directed at women discussed in this chapter confirms that misogyny is a crucial factor in its production and dissemination (Barlow & Awan, 2016), with social networking sites providing a major platform for misogyny. Indeed, there is some evidence that the emergence of the online space has created new manifestations of misogyny (Ging & Siapera, 2018). By enabling those who share similar views to connect and, therefore, maximise the dissemination of hate and hostility, the preponderance of such views has been significantly amplified (Harris & Vitis, 2020; Khosravinik & Esposito, 2018). Rather than being an individualised phenomenon, online abuse frequently contains several core elements, namely, being highly aggressive, labelling women as weak and often containing rape threats (Doyle, 2011). This reinforces online abuse as a structural problem (Yardley, 2021a) that has the potential to affect all women. This finding has important ramifications, as it should remove the application of blame from individual victims of online abuse, negating any discussion of what they may or may not have done to deserve such vicious invective (Jane, 2017a). Instead, online abuse should be conceptualised as a broader societal issue, a finding supported by the theoretical models provided by both Galpin (2022) and Yardley (2021a). There is also the potential for a wider negative impact, affecting women's very equity and citizenship (Jane, 2017a), as the online abuse received by women in the public sphere causes them to withdraw completely from their roles in public facing occupations. This concurs with the 'economic abuse' dimension found in the Wheel of Power and Control (Pence & Paymar, 1993), which identifies the malign financial and economic impact of gender-based violence.

Interestingly, on the rare occasion that men are the targets of online abuse, this abuse is itself gendered, with attacks focussed on the female relatives of male targets (Jane, 2014b). This is illustrated in the case of journalist Jon Stewart, who reported how a photograph of his wife published online was described as 'She's a liberal. They only come in ugly', and 'Looks like a trip to Auschwitz might do her some good' (Jane, 2014b, p. 11). In the UK, journalist Stig Abell has vividly recounted how his Twitter feed filled with rape threats directed at his wife and young child, following the publication of his first book: 'they were really graphic, and he was saying he knew where we lived' (Llewelyn Smith, 2018, p. 19).

Furthermore, on the few occasions when women have been convicted of perpetrating online abuse, the threats have been sexual as well as violent, leading Lewis et al. (2017) to describe the online space as one that perpetuates online misogyny, or masculinised violence, rather than simply male violence.

This exploration of a multi-dimensional corpus has confirmed the centrality of misogyny as an integral element of online abuse. By adopting theories of gender-based violence originally advocated by second wave feminists to define and then record violent behaviour (e.g. Galtung, 1990; Kelly, 1988; Pence & Paymar, 1993), it is possible to gaining a deeper understanding of this most contemporary demonstration of gendered harms. Furthermore, by bringing together these different theoretical strands, and combining them with more recent scholarship on computer-mediated communication and the facilitation of online harms, it is possible to identify six elements of online abuse, namely, emotional harm (Dragiewicz et al., 2018), harassment (Bailey & Burkell, 2021), threat (Jane, 2014b; McGlynn et al., 2017), belittling (Camp, 2018), silencing (Galpin, 2022) and criticism of appearance (Backe et al., 2018). An element of misogyny that does not map discretely onto the Wheel of Power and Control (1993) is the criticism of a woman's appearance. However, this dimension does appear in Jane's theory of e-bile (2014a). Furthermore, this aspect of misogyny frequently appears in first-hand accounts of online abuse, as evidenced in numerous tweets sent to Professor Mary Beard (Mantilla, 2015):

> After a 'Question Time' appearance... she was repeatedly vilified on an internet message board. One user described her as 'a vile, spiteful excuse for a woman, who eats too much cabbage and has cheese straws for teeth'. Less creatively, another commenter posted a doctored photograph in which an image of a woman's genitals was superimposed over Beard's face (Mead, 2014, p. 2).

Beard describes the abuse she receives as 'truly vile' (Dowell, 2013, p. 1), noting that it occurs whenever she speaks publicly (Boseley, 2017), frequently describing her as 'old, clapped out and obsolete' (Lewis, 2020, p. 310).

Despite this thorough investigation of the different interdisciplinary perspectives on online abuse, there remain a number of issues that the existing literature fails to consider. Crucially, there is very little attention paid to the consequences of online abuse being directed at women working in the public sphere, which is of critical importance given the centrality of social media and other online communication mechanisms to its operation (Mellado & Hermida, 2021; Shirky, 2011; Terren & Borge-Bravo, 2021). For whilst a small amount of research has considered the experiences of women working in *some* public sphere occupations (e.g. Krook, 2017; Marshak, 2017; Salin & Hoel, 2013; Veletsianos et al., 2018), this issue is much wider than the withdrawal of women from holding political office, around which much of the discussion is currently centred. Up to now, there has been a lack of research to consider the experiences of women working across public sphere occupations, and how these women are targeted online as a result of undertaking their occupational role. Consequently, there is a gap in the understanding of the impact that such abuse has on the individuals who receive it. At the same time, there is also a lack of knowledge around the reporting of abuse, and the decisions women make around choosing when (or if) to report the abuse that they receive, and the consequences of doing so. These issues are directly addressed in the forthcoming chapters.

Conclusion

The majority of the literature discussed in this chapter defines online abuse as a structural and gendered issue. This is in contrast to the very early (pre-2010) literature on online abuse, which adopted a range of individualised explanations for the phenomenon (Henry & Powell, 2015), often informed by libertarian theories of free speech (Dragiewicz et al., 2018). This change in approach appears to have been driven by research that has shown that women receive the majority of abuse perpetuated online (Backe et al., 2018), much of it sexual (Antunovic, 2019). The detailed examination of online abuse by feminist academics (e.g. Citron, 2014; Jane, 2017b; Mantilla, 2015) has revealed that the nature of this communication both reintroduces and reinforces traditional gender stereotypes and thereby reconstitutes gender role models from a bygone era (Barratt, 2018). The utilisation of the technological advances instigated by social networking sites to extend the patriarchy in this way (Campbell, 2017) has links with other forms of sexism (Carson, 2018) and reflects the social and sexual inequality that persists in the physical space (Dragiewicz et al., 2018). The empirical evidence that is presented in forthcoming chapters confirms that sexual harassment in the workplace has found a new mechanism for dissemination in the online space and that the presence of gendered abuse is not a new phenomenon. Crucial to the future direction of this research is the identification of six elements of online abuse, namely emotional harm (Dragiewicz et al., 2018), harassment (Bailey & Burkell, 2021), threat (Jane, 2014b; McGlynn, 2017); belittling (Camp, 2018), silencing (Galpin, 2022) and criticism of appearance (Backe et al., 2018). Using the theoretical structure provided by the model of power and control first devised by Pence and Paymar (1993), it is possible to illustrate how these six elements of online abuse align with existing theories of gendered violence. Ultimately, whatever theoretical explanation is adopted, this misogynistic behaviour continues to have profoundly deleterious effects on the lives of women around the world, wreaking trauma and devastation on the physical, emotional and mental health (Garcia-Moreno & Stöckl, 2017) of those who experience it. Furthermore, it is not just in the context of intimate partnerships or other familial relationships that women encounter acts of violence. The perennial presence of malign behaviour in the workplace, which frequently includes sexual harassment and sexual abuse, represents a pernicious combination of 'patriarchal control with organisational power' (Croall, 1995, p. 242) and is something which the growth in computer-mediated communication has, if anything, further entrenched.

Chapter Four

Technology and the Public Sphere

Abstract

This chapter explores the public sphere and assesses the impact that the introduction of digital technologies has had on its operation. The chapter opens by providing a definition and description of the composition of the public sphere, highlighting that whilst women consistently make up more than half of public sector employees in the UK (Miller, 2009), the number of women holding senior roles in public facing occupations remains low. The discussion then moves on to consider the wider role of women in the public sphere and the challenges commonly faced. The potential consequences of the increased interaction with the public that has arisen as a result of the centrality of social media and other online communication mechanisms to the contemporary operation of the public sphere (Mellado & Hermida, 2021; Terren & Borge-Bravo, 2021) is also considered. In a wide-ranging discussion, this chapter also presents evidence on emotional labour (Hochschild, 2012) and safety work (Vera-Gray, 2017).

Keywords: Public sphere; sexual harassment; safety work; emotional labour; Habermas; Hochschild

Introduction

The growth and application of technologies to complete tasks that were traditionally undertaken away from the public gaze has significantly altered the operation of the public sphere. The potential consequences of increased interaction with the public that has arisen as a result of changes made to the contemporary operation of the public sphere (Mellado & Hermida, 2021; Terren & Borge-Bravo, 2021) are

Gendered Online Abuse Against Women in Public Life: More Than Just Words, 39–46
doi:10.1108/978-1-83549-724-120251004

central to this chapter. In a wide-ranging discussion, this chapter also presents evidence on emotional labour (Hochschild, 2012) and safety work (Vera-Gray, 2017), which are highlighted as key theories in exploring the experiences of women in public facing occupations managing episodes of online abuse.

Assessing the Public Sphere

Women consistently make up more than half of public sector employees in the UK (Miller, 2009), a statistic that is reflected across many OECD countries (OECD, 2015). However, whilst the inclusion of women in all levels of public service is crucial for 'the achievement of both transparent and accountable government and administration and sustainable development in all areas of life' (Commonwealth Secretariat, 2016, p. 1), the number of women holding senior roles in public facing occupations remains low. Less than half of senior civil servants (Cabinet Office, 2023) and 40 per cent of Members of Parliament are women (Cracknell & Baker, 2024), whilst making up 29 per cent of the members of the House of Lords (Buchanan, 2024). In academia, only 30 per cent of Vice Chancellors are women, whilst only 20 per cent of social media CEOs and 21 per cent of national newspaper editors are female (Kaur, 2020). In policing, 19 women currently hold the position of Chief Constable in England and Wales (Hymas, 2023). Work by Silvestri and Tong (2020) highlights the relative absence of women in leadership roles within policing across Europe, one of many studies to confirm the presence of perennial barriers blocking women's advancement to senior levels in public sphere occupations (e.g. Al-Rawi et al., 2021; Sobande, 2020; Veletsianos et al., 2018; Walby & Joshua, 2021). Analysis of statistical data reveals that the number of women in positions of power in the public sphere remains in flux. For example, membership of the House of Commons elected in July 2024 has the highest level of female representation in history (Cracknell & Baker, 2024). However, despite this increase in parliamentary representation, the level of female leadership at the top of universities has declined over the same period (Brooks, 2019). Across all sectors being investigated in this research, the representation of non-white women is even poorer (Tariq & Syed, 2018).

Theorising the Public Sphere

A key benefit proposed for the widespread adoption of digital technologies is the opportunity it provides to bring opinion formers and members of the public together, in ways not previously possible (Heiss et al., 2019; Lee et al., 2020). It has been argued that the expansion of technology extends traditional notions of the public sphere and strengthens the concept that there is a space between society and the state where the public can organise and opinion be formed (Barker & Jane, 2016).

Public sphere theories can be traced back to the 18th century when the concept of a platform for debate with opinion formers was initially proffered (Habermas et al., 1964). More recent definitions centre around the notion of an online public sphere that 'facilitates discussion that promotes a democratic exchange of ideas and opinions' (Papacharissi, 2002, p. 11). The huge changes in communication brought about by the assimilation of social networking sites into everyday life provide the means for members of the public to interact both easily and directly with individuals in public sphere occupations, including academics, journalists, police officers and politicians. At the same time, the widespread adoption of the use of social media platforms facilitates greater political debate, offering the potential for a new form of policy making that transcends traditional boundaries (McLaughlin, 2004; Papacharissi, 2009). Taken together, this represents an opportunity to reshape the public sphere, making it more responsive to grassroots concerns (Dey, 2019). Bohman (2004) identifies the role of mutual obligation as being at the heart of these new political relationships. He suggests that the benefits of citizenship emanating from online participation can only be secured when such engagement occurs within an institutionalised public sphere backed by state institutions. However, it is arguable whether the widespread implementation of such a model is possible given the dominance of the large privately financed corporate institutions responsible for the operation of social media platforms. Just as in discussions around freedom of speech mechanisms within computer-mediated communication, there is a perennial concern that the increasing reliance on technology to facilitate debate in the public sphere has led to an inequitable dominance by technology companies (Castells, 2009; Habermas, 2004).

More recent analysis of the presence and function of the public sphere has highlighted a concern that the commercialisation of the mass media and the overtly capitalist motives of social media corporations has led to the commodification of the public sphere (Gane & Beer, 2008), concentrating its ownership amongst a wealthy few (Salter, 2017). Taken together, all argue that there is 'nothing truly public about the public sphere' (Rheingold, 2000b, p. 379).

Initially, there were hopes that the widespread use of social media platforms would blur the separation that exists between the public and their public sphere representatives and that this would herald the creation of a more open and responsive society (Harel et al., 2020). In reality, this has not occurred. Instead, concern has grown that the advent of social networking sites has increased the polarisation of public opinion (Guo et al., 2020; Kligler-Vilenchik et al., 2020; Newman, 2018) and contributed to a wider lack of trust in public institutions, most notably in the political realm, but present throughout the public sphere (Dubois et al., 2020). The increased immutability of public opinion is highlighted in the work of Sunstein (2009a) on group polarisation. For whilst, Sunstein's (2009a) treatise fails to consider in any detail the role of social networking sites, which with the benefit of hindsight seems a glaring omission; it does underline the preponderance of people to adopt more extreme viewpoints or actions when gathered with others (Sunstein, 2009a). Sunstein (2009a) uses this hypothesis to explain multiple social and political changes that have occurred throughout history, including the rise of fascism in the 1930s, the growth of student radicalism in the 1960s and the global collapse of the financial markets in 2008 (Sunstein, 2009a). Furthermore, Sunstein (2009a) proposes that social segregation, where individuals actively seek out others who share their opinions, both encourages and exacerbates group polarisation. Such a proposition has clear parallels with the activities of the users of online platforms. Sunstein (2009a) speculates that online social networks bring with them the risk of creating 'polarisation machines' (Sunstein, 2009a, p. 25), with people's opinions not only reaffirmed by involvement with others sharing similar views but potentially made more extreme. Sunstein's (2009b, p. 12) further work on the creation of 'echo chambers' first introduced in Chapter Two identifies the tendency of people to organise themselves into self-selecting groups sharing the same opinions. However, there are concerns that scholarship in this area frequently fails to appreciate the nuances that exist between different online platforms (Kligler-Vilenchik et al., 2020), and indeed, in the way that different political candidates choose to conduct their presence on social networks, as these factors may affect the way opinion leaders influence voters (Guo et al., 2020). An alternative to the echo chamber hypothesis is offered by Taylor-Smith and Smith (2019), whose study of the social formations made on Facebook, instead suggests that defining such groupings as 'boundary objects' (Taylor-Smith & Smith, 2019, p. 1866) better describes the coming together of people with a wide range of views for non-polarised discussions within an online community space.

Feminist Critiques of the Public Sphere

Feminist critiques of the public sphere assert that claims of equality of opportunity cannot be viewed as valid until there is an end to the pervasive discrimination endemic across the public sphere (Carver & Chambers, 2011). Other work in this area has sought to highlight the role of feminists in expanding the public sphere to include women more fully, as evidenced by the Suffragists of the first wave feminist movement, and the campaigns against sexual harassment led by second wave feminists in the 1970s (Vera-Gray & Kelly, 2020).

Just as the internet was hailed as offering the opportunity 'for the sharing of multiple views and public opinions' (Harel et al., 2020, p. 2), it was similarly posited that the growth in online platforms would provide a mechanism to advance women's equality, with the internet 'hailed as a place where offline prejudices and abuse could be negated and destroyed' (Poland, 2016, p. 159). As this volume has already highlighted, the reality is rather less egalitarian, with research confirming the online perpetuation of traditional (offline) gendered differences in political engagement. Men remain more politically active online than women, a difference resulting from an enduring gendered inequality in economic, educational and technical resources (Ahmed & Madrid-Morales, 2021) that the internet has failed to overcome. Whilst it is true that social networking sites have offered feminist and other campaigning groups an effective platform upon which to operate (Banet-Weiser, 2018; Micalizzi, 2021; Weathers et al., 2016), this has come at a substantial cost, in the shape of online abuse. When considering the impact of online abuse on women's involvement in the public sphere, there is evidence that the barrage of abuse is causing women to withdraw entirely from the public arena (Lewis et al., 2017; Watson, 2019; Yelin & Clancy, 2021), thus precipitating the opposite of what was intended. Furthermore, there is also the potential for online abuse to affect women's very equity and citizenship (Jane, 2017a), as the online abuse received by women in the public sphere causes them to eschew a career in public facing occupations altogether (e.g. Thomas et al., 2021).

When evaluating the impact of the growth in social networking sites on women working in the public sphere, there is a multiplicity of issues to consider. The changes in working style and access, facilitated by the removal of barriers traditionally present between the public and those employed in public facing occupations, have led to other pressures on women holding such roles. These issues are considered using the lenses provided by the two key theories of emotional labour and safety work.

Emotional Labour

The theory of emotional labour first emerged in the 1970s, in relation to analysis of women's experiences of employment, particularly in the service industries (Hochschild, 2012). However, there are several key messages that can be taken from the concept and applied to the use of social networking sites, particularly in relation to the use of online platforms such as Facebook and Twitter, which have become an integral part of communication with the public (Williams et al., 2019).

The theory of emotional labour describes the process that occurs when the 'trained management of feeling' becomes an intrinsic part of an individual's employment, with 'women…more likely to be presented with the task of mastering anger and aggression in the service of "being nice"' (Hochschild, 2012, p. 24). Whilst Hochschild's original study, published in 1983, investigated the feelings and experiences of women working in the airline industry, the theory provides an important insight into the multiplicity of emotional support tasks that are currently demanded of women in the course of their employment (Fessler, 2018), and the 'emotion regulation that occurs within work contexts' (Zammuner & Galli, 2005, p. 251). Research exploring the link between emotional labour and social media has highlighted how the use of Twitter 'means that boundaries become blurred, and discussions can cross between the professional and the personal with no clear distinction between the two' (Bridgen, 2011, p. 3), with the line between 'work' and 'non-work' are increasingly indistinct (Smith Maguire, 2008).

Research by Wajcman et al. (2008), which details how women often use technology to break down barriers between work and family life, makes a similar link with emotional labour. This study suggests that whilst women are largely successful in maintaining the multiple necessary boundaries between the roles of caregiver and employee, the presence of technology, such as mobile phones, means that employees are always 'on duty' and that the separation between work and leisure time is increasingly amorphous. The huge changes in work patterns, originally necessitated by the Covid-19 pandemic (Akande et al., 2020; Kong et al., 2022), now seem to be firmly entrenched (Vyas, 2022). Amongst the many alterations to routines post-Covid is the shift to 'working from home', which was originally the consequence of numerous enforced lockdowns, but which now has become the norm for employees in both public and private sector organisations across the globe (Vyas, 2022; Williamson, 2022). The growth in hybrid working has seen an increasing reliance on online tools, hastening the process by which the internet becomes further ingrained in daily life (Wessels, 2010), with the delineation between online and corporeal activity rapidly disintegrating (Harris & Vitis, 2020). This emphasises the view that 'you don't do things on the internet – you just do things' (Patel, 2014, p. 1) and that the completion of tasks using technology cannot logically be separated from other activities.

It is worth remembering that the growth in computer-mediated communication precipitated a change in how people worked, even before the rapid restructure of working patterns necessitated by Covid-19. The phenomenon of 'peer production' provides a useful illustration of this change (Mandiberg, 2012). Peer production is the term used to describe the co-creation of technical innovation, journalistic content and political activism online (Kreiss et al., 2011). The system has been applauded for operating outside traditional power relationships (O'Neil, 2014), providing some credence to the libertarian ideals that advocate that the internet should continue to be organised outside of traditional rules or regulation (Wessels, 2010).

However, work by Kreiss et al. (2011) has shown that the changed occupational patterns associated with the growth in peer production has negatively blurred the boundaries between work and home that traditional bureaucracies create for employees, adding to the emotional labour demands within these occupations and methods of workplace organisation.

Furthermore, it is not just within the shift to online working that emotional labour is a factor. When women in public facing occupations become the target of online abuse, this further exacerbates the weight of emotional labour that must be managed (Lewis et al., 2017). In their study of women academics, Veletsianos et al. (2018) showed how female scholars often face an expectation from university management that they actively engage in the online space. However, in common with employees in other public facing occupations (Todd, 2017), this frequently leaves them open to abuse:

> I said something about women in science (I am a chemist). I got a barrage of abuse targeting both me and my daughter (not my sons, whose photos are also on my feed – they were never mentioned) – it was mostly variations of 'fuck off back to the kitchen'. It went on for months and every time it started up again men would encourage others to join in (Lewis et al., 2017, p. 1471).

The need to not just navigate online abuse but to actively manage online vitriol and threats necessitates a new form of emotional labour, where energy must frequently be invested, during a typical working day, to protect, respond or ignore (often multiple) instances of abuse (Kerr & Lee, 2021; Veletsianos et al., 2018). Indeed, the very act of 'coping' with online abuse and harassment requires recipients to manage their emotions in order to lessen its potential to cause harm (Lewis et al., 2017):

> It's something I experience quite often, and just for being a feminist. On an almost daily basis I have to deal with messages

from men, many of which contain pictures or content that's sexual and unwanted. It upsets me greatly, but I've gotten used to it and I can't afford to let it upset me (Lewis et al., 2017, p. 1474).

Safety Work

The different strategies that women in the public sphere engage in, in order to successfully navigate a way through the online abuse they receive, is a manifestation of a range of measures that women employ to protect themselves in the public space. Coming under the term 'safety work' (Vera-Gray, 2017), this description details the activities that women employ on a daily basis to protect themselves from the risk of sexual harassment, sexual assault or rape. Such measures enacted in the offline world may include avoiding public transport after dark, taking a different route home from work, or wearing sunglasses or headphones to avoid attracting attention (Vera-Gray & Kelly, 2020), all taken in a bid to evade the persistent threat of habitual gendered violence (Stanko, 1990). Whilst some have claimed that such strategies serve only to increase women's fear of crime (e.g. Ferraro, 1996), it has been argued that rather than presenting a futile overreaction, such safety work actively protects women from victimisation (Vera-Gray & Kelly, 2020). Kelly (2013) defines the online space as one conducive to abuse, citing a lack of regulation, the reduced status of women online and a large pool of potential targets, echoing the finding that as activity on social networking sites has grown, so too has the incidence of online abuse (Jane, 2017a). The expansion of abuse from the corporeal public sphere into the online space has provided a new location for abuse (Iudici & Girolimetto, 2020), which is causing women to employ similar safety work measures to protect themselves. What is striking here is just how visible the parallels are with the explanations provided for the gender-based violence of the 1970s and 1980s, discussed in Chapter Three. For the historical battles that second wave feminists fought to win recognition of the malign treatment of women some 50 years ago echo resoundingly with experiences of the treatment and reporting of online abuse in the present day. At the same time, there are also corresponding similarities between women's experiences of sexual harassment in public spaces during the same period and the sexual harassment that women now encounter online (Vera-Gray & Kelly, 2020).

By adopting the definition of sexual harassment as a 'spatial expression of patriarchy' (Valentine, 1989, p. 309), it is possible to view the online space as a hostile environment that women are overwhelmingly likely to find 'cold and threatening' (Christopherson, 2007, p. 3052). This is deliberate, as it is the explicit intention of those who engage in acts of online abuse to actively reinforce women's exclusion from the public sphere (Vera-Gray & Kelly, 2020). Furthermore, Vera-Gray (2017) suggests that for those researching the issue of online abuse, including women academics and journalists, the emotional labour invested in such investigations is doubled, as 'not only is there work to be done in managing the research subject (and our own position in relation to it), but we have to conduct both work to manage our responses to our own experiences and histories of men's violence, as well as safety work, that is the work of managing one's own safety in relation to men's practices' (Vera-Gray, 2017, p. 73).

Conclusion

This chapter provides a contemporary description of the public sphere, and the role that women play within it; which will be used to underpin the empirical chapters that follow. It highlights how, whilst consistently making up more than half of public sector employees in the UK (Miller, 2009), the number of women holding senior roles in public facing occupations remains below parity, with consequences for women who undertake these roles. The coalescence of theories of the public sphere and gender-based violence seeks to actively reinforce women's exclusion from the public realm (Vera-Gray & Kelly, 2020). This chapter is the last of the three theoretical chapters in this monograph. Moving forwards, the different interdisciplinary lenses provided by this analysis of the combined corpora of computer-mediated communication, gender-based violence and the public sphere will be applied to the empirical evidence provided by women working across the public sphere occupations of academia, journalism, policing and politics.

Chapter Five

'Keep Your Head Down and Shut Up' – Exploring the Seven Elements of Online Abuse

Abstract

This chapter introduces the empirical research undertaken with women working in academia, journalism, policing and politics. It outlines the seven elements of online abuse, which were found to be present (in whole or in part) in every instance of online abuse. These are defamation, emotional harm, harassment, threat, silencing women's voices, belittling and under-mining women and the criticism of individuals' appearance and other physical characteristics. Each of these seven elements is further analysed using the empirical evidence provided in the testimony gained from 50 semi-structured interviews with women serving in public facing occupations.

Keywords: Defamation; emotional harm; harassment; threat; silencing; belittling; appearance; age

Introduction

This chapter introduces empirical evidence of online abuse gathered from women working in the public sphere. There are two types of research material presented here: 'traditional' qualitative data drawn from 50 semi-structured interviews carried out with women working within academia, journalism, policing and politics and the qualitative analysis of a Twitter corpus that was collected in real-time between January and June 2020. Combined, these data provide a detailed account of the realities of engaging professionally in the online space.

Gendered Online Abuse Against Women in Public Life: More Than Just Words, 47–93

doi:10.1108/978-1-83549-724-120251005

Chapter Three established a coalescence between theories of gender-based violence and online abuse, leading to the identification of six pervasive elements of online abuse: emotional harm (Dragiewicz et al., 2018), harassment (Bailey & Burkell, 2021), threat (Jane, 2014b; McGlynn et al., 2017), belittling (Camp, 2018), silencing (Galpin, 2022) and criticism of appearance (Backe et al., 2018). This chapter provides further evidence of the presence of these six elements in every episode of online abuse and, crucially, adds a seventh – defamation. These seven elements accurately portray the experiences of women working across the public sphere interviewed for this research and can be further mapped onto the Twitter dataset.

Outlining the Empirical Data

The empirical evidence is drawn from 50 semi-structured interviews held with women employed in academia, journalism, policing and politics. These interviews were held both in person and via Zoom during the spring of 2020, with women based in the UK, the EU and the USA.

Twitter Data

Data were also gathered from tweets directed at women employed in the four occupational groups. This captured three 'Twitter storms' experienced by a Member of Parliament[1], an academic and a journalist, as they occurred in real time.

A Twitter storm is described as 'a sudden spike in activity surrounding a certain topic on the Twitter social media site' (Technopedia, 2013, p. 1). As Morello (2015) has highlighted, such storms often arise from nowhere and can have protracted consequences, being swiftly disseminated across the social media platform as a result of multiple tweets and retweets (Pfeffer et al., 2014; Vasterman, 2018). By focusing on these storms of communication, it was possible to illustrate the scale and ferocity of the tweets that are frequently sent to high-profile figures as a result of their engagement in public discourse. By performing a word frequency search across the dataset, it was possible to gain an insight into the tone of the tweets found in each of the storms. When viewed in isolation, these words and phrases often appear unremarkable. However, when read together, these tweets convey a wider derogatory culture that frequently denigrates women's appearance, experience, knowledge and opinions.

API research is 'a type of investigation based on the information collected by social media platforms and made available through standardized commands to query, filter, format and download such information' (Venturini & Rogers, 2019, p. 533). Following the takeover of Twitter by Elon Musk in October 2022 (Rohlinger et al., 2023), free access to the Twitter API for research purposes was

---

[1]At the time of data collection.

withdrawn, leaving this manner of data analysis now financially beyond many academic researchers.

Much of the social science research conducted using an API has been quantitative in nature, focused on analysing the volume of tweets on a given issue (e.g. Gorrell et al., 2020; Micalizzi, 2021). Whilst acknowledging the contribution made by this approach, this study provides a qualitative examination of the content of tweets sent during three separate storms of activity, recognising the benefit to be gained from an in-depth analysis of this data (Humprecht et al., 2020).

Software was employed to collect the tweets that named any of the women contained within a sample frame of 200 individuals who had (a) an active online presence and (b) who belonged to any of the four occupational groups being investigated. Data were collected between 1 January 2020 and 30 June 2020. Compiling the data in this way made it possible to identify and analyse three 'Twitter storms'. The software used to interrogate the Twitter API simultaneously tagged the tweets sent to the sample frame that contained obscene or unpleasant terminology, as defined by Ofcom (2016). During the six months that API data were harvested, over 25 million tweets were collected, creating files amounting to some 2GB in size. The data were then output as text files and analysed using NVivo data analysis software.

Storm 1: Politician – 3 February 2020

The first storm scrutinised involved Tracy Brabin MP. On 3 February 2020, the then Shadow Secretary of State for Culture, Media and Sport raised a point of order about Brexit at the Despatch Box (Rawlinson, 2020). As she did so, the broken ankle that she had sustained the previous day caused her to stumble, and her dress to fall forwards, exposing her left shoulder (PA Media, 2020). The image was captured on camera and prompted the tweet, as shown in Fig. 2. This tweet was sent at 18:00 on the day of the incident.

Tweet text: "Is this really appropriate attire for parliament? @TracyBrabin #DressStandards.

Image included in tweet: *A screenshot of the BCC Parliament broadcast showing British politician Tracy Lynn Brabin speaking in the House of Commons, wearing a black top that shows her right shoulder.*

Fig. 2.   Tweet Sent to Politician, 3 February 2020. Link to image: https://theweek.com/105540/tracy-brabin-what-are-the-conduct-rules-in-the-commons

This tweet generated a total of 55,368 tweets over the following three days. In contrast, the MP's Twitter feed normally received an average of 90 tweets per day. In response to the growing storm, at 15:55 on 4 February, Brabin tweeted the comment, as shown in Fig. 3.

Tweet text: "Tracy Brabin MP @TracyBrabin: Hello. Sorry I don't have time to reply to all of you commenting on this but I can confirm I'm not....
A slag
Hungover
A tart
About to breastfeed
A slapper
Drunk
Just been banged over a wheelie bin.

Who knew people could get so emotional over a shoulder... [eye rolling emoji]"

Fig. 3.   Politician's Response on Twitter.

This gave rise to yet more tweets, many of which were retweets of Brabin's comment, in support of her stance. Many of the negative tweets coming after 15:55 on 4 February were sexualised, suggesting that Brabin's robust response unleashed a gratuitously sexual invective, as illustrated in Fig. 4.

Tweet text: "It's not the shoulder. It's the fact it hangs over showing off your breast area. It is not appropriate and unprofessional. Look like you've just had a quickie and rushed to get dressed

Fig. 4.   Sexualised Tweet Sent to Politician.

Storm 2: Academic Commentator: 21 February 2022

The second storm occurred between 21 and 23 February 2020 and targeted the US academic and writer, Jude Ellison Sady Doyle[2]. Doyle is a prolific user of online platforms and has been the target of online abuse on several occasions (Doyle, 2011). They are also a prominent supporter of the Democratic Party and have in the past championed both Hillary Clinton (Crockett, 2016) and Elizabeth Warren (Doyle, 2020) in their respective Presidential bids. On 21 February 2020, they tweeted about their experience growing up with an aggressive father, and how this made them fearful of verbal hostility, as a reference to their dislike of the then candidate for the Democratic Party nomination, Bernie Sanders. The tweet is provided in Fig. 5.

---

[2]At the time of this analysis, Jude Ellison Sady Doyle was known as Sady Doyle.

Original tweet text: "I'm sorry you don't like it when Bernie yells, but not all of us grew up in frigid WASP homes!!!"

Reply tweet: "Sady Doyle @SadyDoyle: Once, my dad spent a few hours making a pot roast, and when he thought it was slightly overdone, he picked up each plate on the table and flung it at the wall. We didn't get to eat that night. Yeah, I guess you were lucky that your associations with men yelling are positive."

Fig. 5.   Tweet Sent by Academic, 21 February 2020.

The tweet generated a total of 14,485 tweets over three days. Doyle usually received an average of 355 tweets per day.

Storm 3: Journalist: 25 April 2020

The third storm occurred between 25 and 27 April 2020 and targeted the journalist Naga Munchetty. On 25 April, she was presenting the television show 'BBC Breakfast', between 06:00 and 09:15. At 10:01, she was sent the tweet in Fig. 6.

Tweet text: "I'm not known for my own sartorial elegance but why would anyone like Naga Munchetty feel the new to wear high-heeled shoes like these on a BBC TV breakfast news programme? Discuss...

Image in tweet: A screenshot of the BCC Breakfast Show, showing presenter Naga Munchetty on set wearing stiletto heels.

Fig. 6.   Tweet Sent to Journalist, 25 April 2020.

This tweet (Fig. 7) generated a total of 32,929 tweets over three days. In contrast, the journalist's Twitter feed normally receives an average of 150 tweets per day.

At 17:07 on the same day, Munchetty replied with the tweet, as shown in Fig. 7.

Tweet text: "Naga Munchetty @BBCNaga: Because I want to."

Fig. 7.   Journalist's Response on Twitter.

In a repetition of storm one, Munchetty's response gave rise to yet more tweets, and, in common with the support shown to the politician, it is likely that the retweets of Munchetty's response occurred in support of the journalist.

The pivoting of both these loci for abuse into (somewhat) supportive environments has strong parallels with the work of Micalizzi (2021), and the identification of Twitter as a possible site for the advancement of public discourse on the sociocultural construction of the role of women. Additionally, a considerable amount of abusive language was used to criticise the individual who sent the initial tweet. This highlights how abuse storms can become multi-directional.

Adding Defamation to the Typology of Online Abuse

The opening chapters of this book have illustrated how receiving online abuse has multiple impacts. Nevertheless, one consequence that has attracted limited consideration thus far is the effect that online abuse can have on an individual's professional standing within their chosen occupation and the wider community. Having a strong professional reputation is important for all those working at a senior level. However, there is evidence that this reputation building is particularly crucial for *women* as they seek to break through the 'glass ceiling' (Palmer & Simon, 2010, p. 22) that persists in many occupations (Aaltio et al., 2008). To achieve a position of power and then risk having that standing undermined by online abuse is both personally and professionally damaging. For the purposes of this discussion, the definition of defamation that has been applied is the one provided by Marwick and Miller (2014, p. 9), namely that 'defamation is the communication of a false statement of fact that harms the reputation of a victim, and includes libel, which covers written published statements, and slander, which covers spoken statements'. The three most common professionally damaging defamatory attacks recounted by interview participants were attacks on their integrity, their abilities and the accusation that an individual was a 'traitor'. The women targeted in the three Twitter storms were similarly subjected to abuse that denigrated their professional reputation. Angelotti (2013) highlights the challenges presented to existing laws on defamation by computer-mediated communication, emphasising how Twitter has 'increased the pressure of being first to publish, often to the detriment of truth and accuracy' (Angelotti, 2013, p. 432). In addition (in one of the few articles to reference defamation in the context of online abuse), Watts et al. (2017) suggest that the level of harm caused by 'cyber-bullying' may lead victims to seek civil redress although Marwick and Miller (2014) confirm that such cases are rare. However, in an indication of the lack of consensus on this issue, Lidsky (2000) warns against the use of defamation law in an attempt to stop the spread of online falsehoods, expressing concern that to do so risks endangering the public's right to free speech. This work has clear echoes of the wider debate on internet freedoms first discussed in Chapter Two.

Women interviewed for this study confirmed that the questioning of an individual's integrity occurs both as direct accusation and as an implied slur. The articulation of allegations was frequent and often felt relentless.

> *[I receive online abuse] basically challenging my ethics, or the way I operate, or that I have neglected my duty.* (Karen, Senior Police Officer)

An academic working in biological sciences spoke of the unexpected consequence of winning a large research grant:

> *I got some blow back [online] saying ... what a horrible use of money ... suggesting that I would use the money irresponsibly.* (Eileen, Academic at a European university)

Politicians often found their integrity being impugned in relation to financial impropriety, particularly if they had expressed an interest in supporting external organisations:

> *They said I was taking money from the [utilities] industry, which was nonsense. I was a water company shrill; I was this, I was that, and it just went on and on and on.* (Patricia, Member of Parliament until December 2019)

Whilst occurring over a decade (and five parliaments) ago, the parliamentary expenses scandal of 2009, when the Daily Telegraph newspaper discovered a web of illegal claims for public money made by MPs (Crewe & Walker, 2019), continues to negatively affect the way that politicians are perceived. This is often expressed in the online abuse they receive, with their financial integrity frequently questioned. One former MP illustrated this:

> *When they talk about, expenses, I never coined anything other than accommodation and my train fare, but when they talk about MPs expenses, if you count the fact that you've got to rent an office and buy equipment and all the rest of it, then if you count that as expenses, it can come to like a huge amount, but it's actually running two businesses if you've got two offices. But the abuse doesn't recognise that.* (Lauren, Member of Parliament until December 2019)

This echoes the work of Bishop (2014), who found that the then Conservative minister Esther McVey MP received a considerable amount of online abuse relating to expense claims:

> *In the case of the person who posted about Esther McVey, they used it as an opportunity to express their dissatisfaction of her as a Conservative Party politician, such as references to her completing 'expenses' forms and pejoratively calling her a 'Tory'. In fact such allegations were unfounded as McVey entered Parliament after reforms had been made to deal with the 'expenses scandal'* (Bishop, 2014, p. 120).

The Twitter storm involving politician Tracy Brabin included 33 separate references to financial integrity over the purchase of the dress she was pictured wearing. A summary of these is provided in Fig. 8.

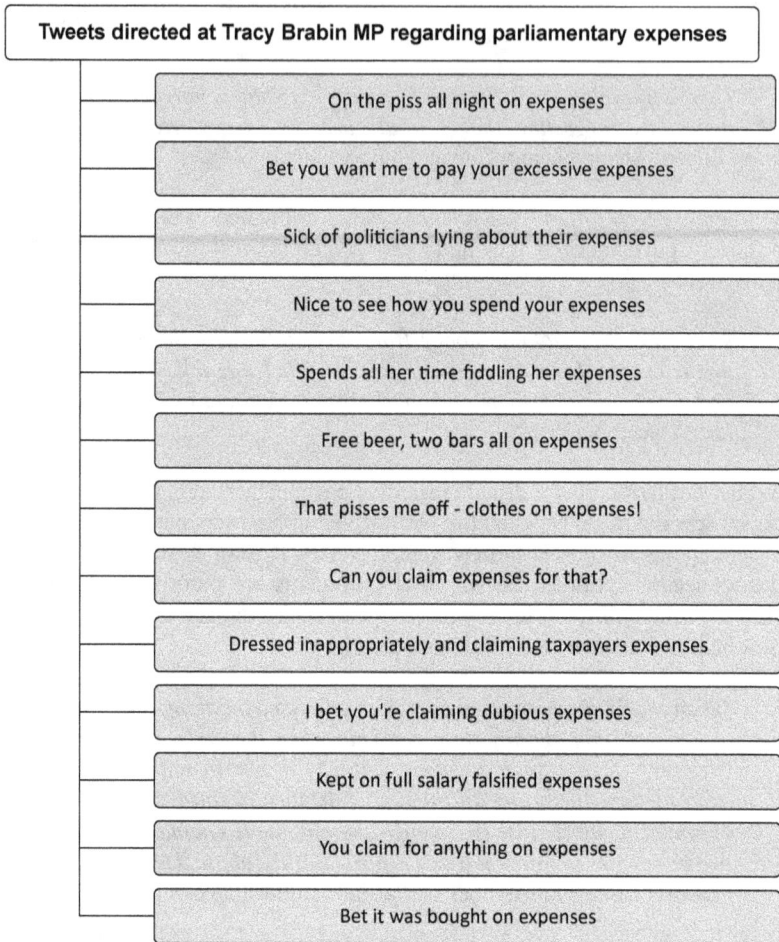

Fig. 8.   Anonymised Summary of Tweets Referencing the Expense Claims of Tracy Brabin MP.

The analysis of the Brabin storm identified a wider range of potentially defamatory tweets, many of which focused on Brabin's previous occupation as an actor. Almost nine thousand of these tweets also referred to prostitution. This illustrates the enduring notion of acting as a profession akin to sex work, which dates back to the 17th century (Rosenthal, 2007). An example of four of these tweets is provided in Table 2.

As well as questions about their integrity, women also found their professional abilities under constant scrutiny:

Table 2. Tweets Referencing Prostitution.

Tweet Time Stamp	Tweet Contents
04/02/20 10:07:05	She looks like a 50p whore
04/02/20 10:54:02	Put some clothes on love, you look like a tart!
04/02/20 12:06:52	You look like you've been in a broom cupboard with Bercow's wife! Is it really appropriate to go to Parliament dressed as a veteran hooker?
04/02/20 12:11:08	Actresses and prostitutes were once much the same thing. Some would say they often still are. Still, the old tricks come in handy when she has to go and pick up the postal votes. She's 50 years too old for that crowd but they're not fussy

> *A number of accounts, all of them anonymous, literally every time I say anything, say I'm stupid, I'm naïve, that the comments I make on behalf of the organisation are inaccurate. So there's that very targeted abuse: every time you say anything, we're going to say you're wrong.* (Sarah, Senior Police Officer)

Sarah's contribution confirms the enduring nature of sexism within policing (Brown, 1998). Long before the advent of online abuse, Berg and Budnick (1986) highlighted how the traits of competence and technical proficiency are more commonly attributed to male officers. Similar experiences were shared by women in other professions:

> *A stream of stuff that comes through ... undermining me in my role, telling me I'm stupid or don't deserve to be in the role I'm in, that kind of stuff.* (Wendy, Local Councillor)

Several participants recognised that the treatment that they had received had parallels with gender-based violence experienced in the offline space:

> *People on message boards started suggesting that I made up ... the incident for attention. That there was this huge attention seeking merit around it, which is of course the same kind of narrative used when women voice sexual assault offline.* (Christie, Academic at a UK university)

> *Spreading lies and misinformation is a form of abuse as well, because that is bringing to that person's door even more anger.* (Constanta, Political Staffer)

A specific epithet that arose repeatedly was the use of the word 'traitor', which was frequently directed at politicians during the various Brexit debates in Parliament. Many politicians felt that this exacerbated the febrile atmosphere that they were navigating prior to Britain's exit from the European Union in 2020. This word, which does not appear on the Ofcom list of offensive terms (2016), nevertheless had a deleterious impact on those to whom it was targeted, as three women explained:

> *The tone and the nature of the aggression [of the online abuse], the far right, the use of terms like traitor and betrayal.* (Phyllis, Member of Parliament until December 2019)

Patricia, who was a Member of Parliament until the General Election of 2019, made a direct link between the abuse that she received online and the abuse she faced in the street:

> *There's a lot of online abuse, like in that period outside of Parliament when we had all those demonstrators and it got very difficult at one point to walk down the street without people shouting after me, and being told I was a traitor.* (Patricia, Member of Parliament until December 2019)

Whilst Patricia's evidence is compelling, such an assertion should be treated with a certain amount of caution, as there is no direct evidence linking the two. Similar evidence was provided by a political staffer:

> *She got an email Christmas card and when I opened it up it said you're a traitor to your race, the white race is rising, Brexit has arrived.* (Constanta, Political Staffer)

Obviously, the term 'traitor' is not in and of itself, an abusive one. However, when weaponised in a politically febrile environment, and combined with racist jibes, as is evidenced here, many of the participants felt that it contained a potentially dangerous message. This was presciently explained by the daughter of a serving politician, writing at the height of the Brexit debate in Parliament:

> *I am scared. I am scared when I scroll through the replies to her tweets calling her a liar and a traitor. I am scared when our house gets fitted with panic buttons, industrial-locking doors and explosive bags to catch the mail … Even if we disagree with our politicians, when was this something we actively wanted to hurt them for?*
>
> *This whole thing has gone too far. When people start getting hurt, that is the moment we should step back and ask if any of this is even worth it. All the anger and the screaming and the taking sides. The traitors and the liars and the surrendering* (Cooper, 2019, p. 1).

What Cooper (2019) describes is the concern that many women in public facing occupations feel, namely that the changes to the nature of public debate, the switch from robust discussion to violent invective, contains within it a threat to the safety of women that mirrors the threat posed by gender-based violence in the private sphere.

Whilst there is clear evidence that defamation is a recurring element of the online abuse directed at women in public facing occupations, there have been very few cases of defamation brought before the courts (Marwick & Miller, 2014).

Emotional Harm as an Element of Online Abuse

Emotional harm is another element of online abuse and is by far the biggest consequence of such communication. The variety of issues raised under this topic have been grouped into three themes: the effect on an individual's wellbeing, the wider impact of emotional harm on the person targeted and the repercussions of the emotional harm as it relates to others, such as family members, friends and staff.

> *I don't know anyone who's trying to do socio-political activism who's not utterly ground down to a paste from having to deal either from active abuse or the fear of abuse and having to tie themselves into knots and take elaborate measures to avoid it.* (Sophie, Academic and Journalist, USA)

> *I knew that all that abuse would continue [after the election] and I was expecting my majority to go down to a couple of thousand, and I thought they'll keep coming, they'll smell blood and all I used to do was get bullied, permanently. It was absolutely horrendous.* (Phyllis, Member of Parliament until December 2019)

These interviews reveal the scale of harm caused by online abuse, echoing earlier literature (e.g. Hodson et al., 2018; Jane, 2017a; Mantilla, 2015). Once again, there were considerable similarities shared by the four occupational groups. Reiterating the quote from Phyllis, many women described online abuse as a form of bullying:

> *It really is bullying. A lot of my abuse is from people that are not my constituents. I actually can't think of another way of describing it. They're bullies. And I think the traits of a bully are very cowardly.* (Jill, Member of Parliament)

Other women spoke of their bemusement regarding online abuse and questioned the motivations of those sending it:

> *Why do people have this desire to do this to strangers, to insult, harass and bully strangers? Is that just innate in humanity and has the internet just created a process to finally let it out, or is it something about the internet that encourages it? Why do they do that? What are they getting out of doing that? It's just bizarre.* (Jacqueline, Academic at a UK university)

Wendy felt that often, the sending of abuse was an end in itself:

> *People don't want me to reply, they don't expect a reply, it's just abuse. And I think that's changed. Before, even if it was like something at a level I would consider abuse, it would be in anticipation of a response. Whereas now, I don't think these people even want a response, they just want to fling mud.* (Wendy, Local Councillor)

Another participant wondered if there had been a change in the social or political climate that had led to a greater tolerance of abuse:

> *I think it has become more permissible to talk about stuff that has previously been less acceptable, and it's more socially acceptable to say something really nasty. Now I think people feel that open permission to say more stuff.* (Karen, Senior Police Officer)

Sometimes, the motivation for online abuse was political.

> *There was an attempt … in 2013, when a Liberal Democrat councillor who'd gone to UKIP, started trying to bully me and undermine me online, because of council cuts, as though that was my fault.* (Patricia, Member of Parliament until December 2019)

Politically motivated abuse is a particular problem for women politicians, and crucially, the abuse is not restricted to one specific political party or ideology.

Another characteristic of online abuse discussed was the sheer nastiness of many of the comments:

> *There were some who almost pretty much any time I put a tweet out, would give me some sort of sneering comment and wind people up.*

> *The abuse was more misogynistic, it would be absolutely vitriolic … it was so horrific.* (Stacey, Senior Police Officer)

Sometimes, abuse sent via online platforms was consolidated with abusive emails:

> *I definitely got emails that said things like you're a stupid bitch, you should kill yourself.* (Jacqueline, Academic at a UK university)

The abusive tone of much online abuse was similarly raised by others:

> *When I started looking at the online abuse, I was really shocked and dismayed at the amount of swearing, huge amounts of negativity, political criticism, insults, rudeness, just nastiness, that were on my profile.* (Beth, Member of Parliament until December 2019)

I don't expect to receive absolute, misogynistic, homophobic, absolute hate of my sheer existence. (Karen, Senior Police Officer)

There's one guy in particular who essentially told me to burn in hell, where at least I'll see my dead dad again. So that was nice. (Simone, Member of Parliament)

A significant factor in the emotional harm engendered by online abuse is the fear that it generates. This seemed to be a particular issue for politicians who had lost their seats in the General Election of 2019. This is unlikely to be coincidental, as these constituencies were often the areas where debate was most polarised, and consequently, where levels of online abuse were highest. The women in these seats often had little protection afforded to them in terms of a litany of staff and extra security, leaving them feeling more vulnerable than those holding Front Bench positions.

I got to the point where I was genuinely fearful about going on the train, fearful of walking my dog, fearful of going to events ... social media had made me feel unwanted in my home, it made me feel that I couldn't go to the pub because I didn't know who was sitting at the table next to me. I didn't want to go anywhere on my own. (Phyllis, Member of Parliament until December 2019)

So, there was about three months where I didn't go to the constituency on my own at all. I just didn't go there because I was too nervous about staying overnight in the house. And it was at that point that we had all the panic alarms installed, which was being done as part of a parliament security upgrade, but that was my absolute priority, to get the panic alarms in that house. (Beth, Member of Parliament until December 2019)

I would have a wobble about my security, probably once a year, when I'd see something online that really scared me ... there'd be that one day a year I'd just need to hide from the world because I was scared about someone hurting me. (Caroline, Member of Parliament until December 2019)

Issues around safety were not confined only to women involved in national politics and affected politicians serving at a local level. Kerry spoke of her fears as a Muslim woman representing a local council ward in an inner city:

I have seen people online, saying things like 'what's [NAME OF CITY] doing, electing you know, people', and using the 'n' word. But if that became physical then I would be really worried. I do actually worry that if someone attacks me and says, you know, that woman,

> *or 'n' woman that lives there is a councillor. And if the EDL[3] comes to me where I live, then if they do find out that it's a politician that's Black, why have they elected her, then they could attack somebody in the street, that looks just like me.* (Kerry, Local Councillor)

It is worth noting, however, that fears around personal safety were not solely limited to politicians. Police officers, academics and journalists had all received threatening online abuse as a result of their role:

> *My role as Hate Crime Coordinator and the abuse [I received] ... I was fearful of further abuse.* (Anna, Police Officer)

Christie spoke about the abuse she received as a consequence of researching the growth of the involuntary celibacy (Incel) (Ging, 2019) movement in the UK:

> *That was the first time I was properly made to feel scared and that there was a real concern for my physical safety.* (Christie, Academic at a UK university)

Similar fears were expressed in regard to activity in the USA:

> *And then really with the rise of Trump ... the anti-Semitism online has been ... fucking terrifying but it's also been fucking terrifying offline.* (Sophie, Academic and Journalist, USA)

The emotional fallout of receiving online abuse was highlighted by Beth:

> *Certainly in the last year it became quite physically threatening, and the spill over between the Twitter threats and abuse and what was going on outside our workplace ... those lines became blurred, and we felt under psychological and physical siege.* (Beth, Member of Parliament until December 2019)

A consequence of the fear discussed here is that women begin to make choices about the sort of work they will be involved in, limiting both their own career choices (and potential advancement) and the coverage of socially important issues, as Ann, an academic and journalist based in the USA, explained:

> *Right now, in the United States ... women journalists who I've spoken to really would love the opportunity to write about white supremacist extremism. But they don't, because of their profound worries about their own personal safety.* (Ann, Academic and Journalist, USA)

---

[3] *English Defence League, a Far-Right political organisation.*

Being exposed to violent invective has an impact on many aspects of an individual's life. These long-term psychological consequences were discussed by two women who had been involved in particularly high-profile political campaigns:

> *I think that one of the reasons I burnt out was my experience that being in politics, in particular in politics in an age of social media, is that you are required to have a persona ... and that online persona always has to be ready for the battle and the fight that is involved online. I felt like the person that I was having to be was further and further away from who I really was, and that the person the people saw was not the person that I really was. But I didn't have any choice in it.* (Klaudia, Politician in Scotland)

> *Every time I did go into Twitter, which I had to do for work, I would be faced with this absolute wall of abuse. All designed to make you feel crap about yourself and your abilities. You have to build far greater resilience to deal with that, and I talked quite openly about this at the time, that my fear was, as much as I was able to give myself the emotional armour to protect myself, what was the price of that? Was it empathy, were you less willing to feel other people's experiences because you'd built up so many barriers to protect yourself from it?* (Julia, Politician in Scotland)

The theory of emotional labour, where the 'trained management of feeling' (Hochschild, 2012, p. 24) becomes an intrinsic part of an individual's employment, is evident in the experiences detailed here. Indeed, this evidence suggests that the effort expended on managing the emotional response to online abuse is even greater than the emotional labour demanded in the workplace described by Hochschild (2012); with it subsuming many parts of an individual's existence.

Sophie highlighted the degree of emotional labour that women in public facing occupations undertake, both individually and collectively, to manage the onslaught of online abuse that is received. An important part of Sophie's contribution is the assertion that, just like in the forms of emotional labour Hochschild (2012) discussed in her original study, there is very little recognition of this work.

> *Somebody needs to be doing this work and the [tech] companies aren't doing it, and so we're all just picking it up and no one even notices it's getting done ... it's just another form of unpaid women's labour.*

Sophie then discussed the inequity of this situation:

> *We need to acknowledge that it is unfair that we have to think about this ... we never talk about the emotional experience of this, we are individually left to be alone with our experiences.* (Sophie, Academic and Journalist, USA)

One malign aspect of the barrage of online abuse is the relentlessness of the situation, which adds to the emotional harm that it causes, as it feels inescapable.

> *It's constant and exhausting and that's even when you're not engaging.* (Sophie, Academic and Journalist, USA)

> *It affects my partner, who wanted to take on everybody who was threatening me. We couldn't get away from it … No. We just can't get away from it.* (Karen, Senior Police Officer)

> *Oh my God, it's twenty-four-seven … I think it's too much. It's really too much.* (Jill, Member of Parliament)

In addition to the emotional effort of managing online abuse, it is also hugely time consuming:

> *Often I just don't gravitate toward it because I'm like 'do I have the energy to deal with the bullshit today?' … it's exhausting.* (Sophie, Academic and Journalist, USA)

> *It was relentless. I think there was something like seven or eight thousand responses, most of which were negative.* (Samantha, Senior Police Officer)

> *It absorbed so much time and energy, it was so difficult to do anything else.* (Patricia, Member of Parliament until December 2019)

As Patricia expressed, many women in public facing occupations feel that the need to monitor their online activity is hugely time consuming and creates a substantial burden, particularly for those with no support staff (Ward & McLoughlin, 2020). In addition, the fatigue caused by the constant surveillance of social media sites was linked to staff sickness and feelings of 'burn out'. The impact of online abuse is not just felt by the individual being targeted. The consequences of this frequently violent invective can spread to family members, staff and even the wider community. The fear is often felt most around the threat that is posed to women's friends and family members, as Peggy explained:

> *I took my son to an event in the constituency and … I noticed he was standing with his back to the wall by the door and I said, come over here. And my son said, 'I'm just going to stand here', and I said why, and he said, 'because if I've got my back to the wall people can't harm me from behind, and if I'm by the door I can escape'. And I just wanted to burst into tears that he feels that way.* (Peggy, Member of Parliament)

The fear [I had] for my mother was just awful, truly, truly awful. My stepfather dealt with it by learning self-defence. Because he was scared, they were scared. (Caroline, Member of Parliament until December 2019)

Somebody messaged me and said, it serves you right if your daughter gets raped in front of you. They made that physical threat to me and to my family. (Agita, Member of the House of Lords)

Some felt that the threat posed to their family was so great that they put in place safeguards to protect them:

I spoke to my daughter if I ever had to leave her alone because I was popping out for something, I would say stay in my room, lock the front door, lock the bedroom door and if anyone bursts in, lock the bathroom door and jump out the window. You know, I drilled her into how to escape. (Beth, Member of Parliament until December 2019)

One guy said, 'protect your child, it would be a shame if something happened to him in a few years when he's going to school or something', which was obviously horrible. The fact that he threatened my child … resulted in us having to go and have a conversation with my son's head teacher and my other son's nursery manager, that's not a conversation we wanted to have. So, even if the guy didn't intend to do anything … he had an impact on us in the physical world. (Charmaine, Member of Parliament until December 2019)

Threats to family members, whilst more common amongst politicians, were not restricted solely to this group, with academics, police officers and journalists recounting similar episodes:

They've made so many comments about my ethnicity, they've written about my family, my husband, my son … what really bothered me was to see family and friends mentioned on these white supremacist sites, because obviously they didn't ask for any of that … (Linda, UK-based journalist)

He sent WhatsApp messages … And the day after he started writing stuff about my mother, that my mother was a horrible person, stupid like me, he threatened my father a lot. I can never listen to those audio messages from that night. But my lawyer said a lot of actual death threats were to me and my father in those audio messages. That was the final incident. That's when the police intervened, and they sent him a formal restriction order. (Ranjit, Academic at a European university)

> *It does have an impact, a really big impact, on my family, particularly on my daughter. She literally searches my Twitter account every day. She doesn't just look me up, she looks up what people are saying about me and … she really worries. The long-term effects on people like her are really profound.* (Sarah, Senior Police Officer)

Several women felt a sense of responsibility for their loved ones being exposed to online abuse:

> *I chose to enter public life. I chose to stand for Parliament. They didn't. None of them have chosen to do that. My kids, my grandkids, my staff aren't public figures.* (Loretta, Member of Parliament)

In July 2017, in a speech which brought the online abuse received by politicians to the forefront of public attention, the Labour MP for Hackney North and Stoke Newington, Diane Abbott, read out a sample of the abuse received by her office, during a debate on abuse and intimidation in UK elections (Hansard, 2017). One of the most striking observations that she made was when talking of the impact of online abuse on her staff:

> One of my members of staff said that the most surprising thing about coming to work for me is how often she has to read the word 'nigger'. It comes in through emails, Twitter and Facebook …. I accept that male politicians get abuse, too, but I hope the one thing we can agree on in this Chamber is that it is much worse for women. As well as the rise of online media, it is helped by anonymity. People would not come up to me and attack me for being a nigger in public, but they do it online. It is not once a week or during an election; it is every day. My staff switch on the computer and go on to Facebook and Twitter, and they see this stuff. (Hansard, 2017, Column 159WH)

The experiences Abbott recounted in this debate were familiar to contributors in this research, who felt a sense of both concern and responsibility for their staff:

> *I get really protective. I go really mamma bear about our team. I'm probably more protective of them.* (Souad, Academic at a UK university)

> *I worry about the wellbeing of my staff and actually that's the thing that will break me. The fact that I wasn't there when this bloke broke into the office. It's the only time that I've sat in my office in Westminster and wept because it's me, they're conscripts to this life.* (Peggy, Member of Parliament)

Once again, the most vitriolic and potentially dangerous attacks were directed at the staff of politicians based in the more marginal constituencies, where debate was the most heated.

> *I've always felt really worried … because of social media, more fearful for their sake. But also the impact on them for having to trawl through it, having to see it all the time, I didn't see half of what they did.* (Phyllis, Member of Parliament until December 2019)

> *We put in place a system where my staff would read my notifica-tions, and it got to the stage where they stopped that because of what it was doing to their mental health. We probably should have stopped it earlier than we did. But because I wasn't seeing it, I wasn't aware. I think that for people that have never seen it, it's a shock … and to wade through it was taking hours.* (Charmaine, Member of Parliament until December 2019)

Charmaine, Caroline and Beth each expressed concern about the impact of online abuse on new or younger staff members, providing the following illustrations:

> *For most of my staff, this was their first job in politics. So, they aren't necessarily used to that and so it's hard for them. I think that some of the people who probably end up bearing the brunt of the impact of online abuse, are the staff of those in leadership or who are in senior roles like being an MP.* (Charmaine, Member of Parliament until December 2019)

> *So, my staff who were amazing, incredible, and protective, they saw all of that [the online abuse]. We never published my office address, after we saw what happened with Jo Cox[4]. My staff were always with me, and therefore, they were potentially vulnerable. Their emo-tional wellbeing [was being jeopardised]. In order to protect me, they were seeing things that were just awful.* (Caroline, Member of Parliament until December 2019)

> *I was most concerned about my staff in the constituency office because they're the most vulnerable, and that's where the attacks tended to take place.* (Beth, Member of Parliament until December 2019)

---

[4]*The assassination of Jo Cox, the Labour MP for Batley & Spen, in June 2016.*

The feelings of being overwhelmed and exhausted were shared by political staffers, who often found themselves in the front line when dealing with online abuse:

> *It was just, it was relentless, it really was relentless.* (Constanta, Political Staffer)

> *Once she was elected, it was absolutely impossible, because ... at that point there were hundreds of comments every couple of seconds.* (Svetlana, Political Staffer)

Svetlana also revealed the impact that the role working for a high-profile politician had:

> *I think it's the fact that it was every single day, it was draining ... and I know, for my colleagues, it really did affect their mental health.* (Svetlana, Political Staffer)

Concern about the impact that receiving online abuse had on others was not limited to family members and staff. An academic working in the field of sexual violence felt a sense of responsibility towards her research participants when the website set up for their use was infiltrated by men's rights activists:

> *A bunch of comments came through from men ... who were saying things like 'this research is a waste of time', to things like 'this bitch has no idea' ... 'what a cunt'. They even created a YouTube video that seeks to make fun of the research, it was just so odd.*

> *And then under the YouTube video there were then all of these comments ... making fun of the research, making fun of the institutions, and then just going off on a bit of a rant about how feminists have lost the plot and are dirty and we bleed everywhere.*

> *But then I [had] ... to disable the comments, because what started to happen was that women who had previously left comments saying that they wanted to participate or they were interested in the project ... men started posting underneath their comments, and so those women were being notified. The abuse wasn't only directed at me, it started to become directed at the other women who had chosen to participate.* (Jacqueline, Academic at a UK university)

An MP in Scotland spoke about the responsibility she felt towards a company in her constituency that became the target for online abuse as a consequence of appearing in a social media post with her:

I did feel terrible because I thought, here's a local business, who's facilitated a visit, and that's what they've got for it. (Esther, Member of Parliament)

Another MP reported a similar online attack directed at a volunteer at a local food bank:

There's this lovely guy who runs the food bank, and he's like eighty-six or something, and he's not a [name of party], but he does go in to back me. They'll say, she's done fuck all, blah, blah, blah, and he'll say oh, no, no, no, she's done X, Y and Z. And then someone will say, what do you know, I've looked at your profile, I could do what you've done in fifty years in a year. You know, just really nasty. So, this poor old man, and he's lovely. So, I phoned him just to check he was ok. (Jill, Member of Parliament)

Sometimes, simply being tagged by a politician caused a member of the public to become the target of online abuse:

So, there's a woman that I met at a mental health event … and she'd written this brilliant thing about how to cope with anxiety and so I retweeted it and said this is brilliant, and she got back to me and said, I'm so flattered that you have retweeted it and what you've said, but could you remove it please because I'm just getting all this abuse … online abuse doesn't just affect me, it's very much like classic violence against women and girls, the first thing that they have to try and do is to isolate you, to stop other people talking to you, to stop people interacting. And that's literally rule one of a domestic abuser. It's very, very similar. (Peggy, Member of Parliament)

As Peggy emphasises, the repercussions faced by women interacting with politicians on Twitter, evidenced here by an individual requesting to be removed from prominence, provides another parallel with the silencing and ostracisation that is a recognised feature of gender-based violence (Camp, 2018). This type of harm is pernicious and enduring and illustrates how detriment can be caused to others.

Peggy expressed concern for the wellbeing of members of the public who engaged with the online abuse that was directed at her. Recounting the experience of meeting a constituent who was under the mistaken belief that she had called a section of voters 'stupid', an accusation that she had proved to him was incorrect:

He said, well that's not what I was told. I was told this, this, and this … and I read this on the internet, I read that. He was harmed by that, because he is not a well person. So, it's not just harming me, it is harming vulnerable people who, the people who are doing it claim to represent. Whereas all I want to do is help people. On a number of occasions I have dropped all charges against people who have literally threatened the life of me and my family, because I can see that they are not the root of the harm. They are a product of it, just as I am, and they are a victim of it just as I am a victim of it. (Peggy, Member of Parliament)

When viewed as a whole, the testimony provided here reveals the scale of harm being experienced by women across public facing occupations. The following quote from Kerry encapsulates the feelings of many of the women spoken to about the emotional harm inflicted by online abuse:

It doesn't really matter who you are, as long as you're a woman and a politician, people tend to forget that you're a mum, you're a wife, you're a sister, you're a cousin, you're a friend. (Kerry, Local Councillor)

Harassment

Whilst equally responsible for causing the sort of emotional harm to the individual and wider community that is discussed above, harassment is nevertheless subtly different. The accounts of online harassment provided here reveal a systematic campaign of intimidation targeted at an individual, which is frequently perpetrated by one person or group. In this way, it has clear parallels with theories of gender-based violence outlined in Chapter Three. The harassment dimension of online abuse outlined here uses the framing provided by Walklate (1995), which defines sexual harassment as a public manifestation of gender-based violence. Whilst not always overtly sexual, the harassment described here certainly fits within Walklate's (1995) typology, as a form of violence that is precipitated by gender and occurs within public gaze.

One way in which online abuse becomes harassment is when multiple attacks on an individual take place, orchestrated by either someone acting alone, or by a group. Such attacks are increasingly common and had been experienced by women across the four professions analysed. Tiprat, an Academic in the USA, described what this means in reality:

Hordes of men, sometimes thousands, coordinate with each other on various online forums, come together to attack a woman. (Tiprat, Academic based in the USA)

Tiprat's description certainly applies to the situation described by Linda, a journalist in the UK, who finds herself the focus of orchestrated campaigns of harassment whenever she has a book published.

When my first book came out, in 2017, which is on gender, I did get some sexists and misogynists who targeted me. But it was when my latest book came out last summer that I got a huge amount of racist abuse. A community of people online started to mobilise. One of them made a YouTube video of me, where he pretended to be Indian and tried to imitate me. That got taken down because there were a lot of complaints. But he put it back on to BitTube, another platform, not YouTube. (Linda, UK-based journalist)

Linda was not the only participant to have been the focus of such malign activity. Sarah recounted her experiences of harassment, both experienced by her personally, and those that she had been made aware of in an operational capacity:

At a countrywide level, whereas before there was social media … you could have an instance where somebody would abuse somebody in the street it would be a one on one, or a one on five, or a one on ten intervention, when it happens online, so many more people can see it and therefore it becomes a much bigger thing more quickly. So, I think it has a bigger impact on victims because they think they've been more widely humiliated. (Sarah, Senior Police Officer)

The people who do it know that they are chasing you to your very marrow. Everything you do, they are chasing you all the time and never leaving you alone. And the 'pile-ons' are designed to make an individual feel persecuted and overwhelmed. Then when they think they've done their job, they back away. (Patricia, Member of Parliament until December 2019)

The phenomenon of multiple people orchestrating an attack was similarly experienced by Linda, this time via a website for supporters of white supremacy:

The community of people who organise around this kind of intellectual racism, they are quite small and they're very global, so they all know each other. In my last book, I did write about the rise of the far right and some of these individual figures, so they targeted me as a result of that … then there was a lot of stuff on white supremacist websites, mainly in the US, and that doesn't really stop, that seems to be ongoing. (Linda, UK-based journalist)

The perpetrators of orchestrated campaigns of harassment were not only drawn from Far-Right organisations. They also emanated from small, local groups, particularly in marginal parliamentary constituencies, where election campaigning was especially intense.

What was really damaging, and I regret never really getting a handle on … I don't know if I could, was community groups. So, there would be like [village name] Uncensored, a community, gossip Facebook site, and a similar group that covered [local town] and the admin on those would be horrendous and if any of our members went on to defend me or push back, they got blocked, their comments were deleted, and they were blocked. So, all this stuff was going to thousands of people. I've never met these people. All I've done is try and help people with their casework, try and be a good local MP. (Phyllis, Member of Parliament until December 2019)

Sometimes things got to such a level of vitriol, so then you think there's probably some forum somewhere where somebody's posted the link and they almost agree to gang up, that is what the behaviour is like. And I don't know what was on those horrible forums, but I can't help but feel that people are being radicalised and egged on by others in a way that is much more than a random group of friends that meet down the pub. People gravitate towards others that are like them, so the people who are most extreme find others who are extreme. (Charmaine, Member of Parliament until December 2019)

There would be insults, so, if I did a media appearance, there would be orchestrated troll armies, so people would put the message out on their Facebook and then everyone would come off Facebook and pile on to Twitter to attack me. Some of which were accounts that only had two followers and had literally been set up in order to harass me. (Beth, Member of Parliament until December 2019)

Whether orchestrated by groups within a well-financed and well-organised network, or more organically created, where individuals sharing similar viewpoints 'pile on' to add to the abuse being directed at an individual, the one thing that these activities share is the ability to mobilise at speed, use multiple platforms and exert a significant amount of pressure and distress upon an individual (Thompson & Cover, 2021):

A video on Facebook doesn't stay on Facebook. It goes to Instagram, and it goes to WhatsApp, and then it went to Twitter. (Souad, Academic at a UK university)

There's also a kind of abuse that I think is the hardest to get people to pay attention to, which is a relentless deluge of negative content from lots of accounts. Each person can look at their individual tweet and claim 'I am just criticising you', but when you experience it from hundreds and hundreds of people, and it's organised online … it's harassment. (Sophie, Academic and Journalist, USA)

There's certainly good evidence that online people … at the really nasty end, find other people, someone who before the internet may have just sat in their bedroom and thought dark thoughts, now they find other people around the world thinking in similar ways and are affirmed and strengthened by that ... it probably does create more of a physical risk. (Maria, Member of the House of Lords)

It [the abuse] was clearly organised, that was the thing that made it worse, the organised nature of it. That was what changed. (Patricia, Member of Parliament until December 2019)

Peggy described the scale of a typical campaign of harassment:

It's not just abuse, it's harassment because it's thousands of messages.

[...] I have a man who has sent me thousands and thousands of emails. Originally, when I reported that to the police they went and told him not to do it ... and it made it worse. And it is deeply misogynistic, deeply racist stuff that this man sends me It is just horrendous. Absolutely horrendous. And, when I say thousands, I mean it ... on one occasion he sent me a hundred and twenty emails in twenty minutes. (Peggy, Member of Parliament)

Wendy and Simone each provided examples of orchestrated campaigns of online harassment, illustrating how politicians at both a local and national level are targeted for abuse:

He routinely posts screenshots of my profile and tells people to go and give me abuse. And he's got hundreds of thousands of followers. What he did, the thing that I reported ... he had screenshotted my profile on the tweet I put out, he blocked me so I can't see it, I just notice a spike in abuse ... and then I'll ask someone to go check his profile and yeah, he'd screenshotted me. (Wendy, Local Councillor)

It doesn't necessarily bother me if someone swears at me. That I can take. But it's when it's a sustained and repeated tirade, that I think it becomes abuse. There has been ... there's one guy in particular who responded to every single tweet I put out, with something incredibly derogatory. (Simone, Member of Parliament)

Rose described how some pile-ons can emerge from nowhere, seemingly sparked by a throwaway comment.

I got a massive pile on, to the point where I did something I've never done before: I protected my [Twitter] account for a few days. There wasn't a sustained trolling or a sustained campaign. It wasn't coordinated. It was just a massive pile on of people, a lot of them repeating things that had already been said. If you dare say, [something is] not as clear cut as that, then they'll pile on and start. And otherwise rational people tell you you're just like cruel and heartless and what harm can it do. (Rose, Academic based in the USA)

Contributors felt that such attacks were harmful, and had a detrimental impact upon the individual, because they demanded time and energy, and were ultimately a distraction from existing workloads:

> *We need an understanding of what this is, this is why this is not benign, this is why this seemingly non-abusive pile on is in fact abuse.* (Rose, Academic based in the USA)

> *On certain topics, people pile on, and I've had that happen to me a couple of times, groups of racists from across the world. It can happen at any time. You look at something you posted ages ago and suddenly one very influential person on Twitter picks it up and suddenly all their followers are piling on and there's nothing you can do about it.* (Linda, UK-based journalist)

The experiences of women of colour are frequently the most extreme (Tariq & Syed, 2018). This was certainly the experience of Kerry, who felt that her intersecting identities made her a target for harassment.

> *Because I'm a woman, because I'm Black, because I wear a hijab, if you escalate it then they would just come out from all over the place and I fear these great boxes I'm ticking. One of them is going to be the target, and then obviously the other two would come on board as well.* (Kerry, Local Councillor)

It is important to acknowledge the difference between the sending of individual malicious tweets and an orchestrated campaign that may involve many people from across the world. This is a differentiation that is not always made, and consequently, the seriousness of attacks of online abuse can be overlooked, or incorrectly described as a 'spat', rather than an organised hate campaign (Salter, 2018).

'Doxxing' is the term that describes a form of 'online abuse where a malicious party harms another by releasing identifying or sensitive information' (Snyder et al., 2017, p. 432). Whilst originally a hallmark of the Gamergate scandal in the USA, which saw the personal details of many women working in and writing about the computer gaming industry released with malicious intent (Salter, 2018), doxxing has become an all-too-common feature of online abuse.

The following contributions relate directly to the experience of being 'doxxed', illustrating that geographical boundaries prove no barrier to those intent on perpetrating online abuse:

> *A couple of years ago … I was doxxed … by an account in the States, and they thought they'd put my home address, but it was actually our old address … they published it on a website in the States.* (Michelle, Journalist based in the UK)

> *Women are doxxed collectively. People [are] sharing our private information for the purpose of malice and using that in a threatening way.* (Ann, Academic and Journalist, USA)

The literature confirms that the aim of orchestrated attacks, 'pile ons' and doxxing, is to silence women, whether by prompting them not to comment on controversial topics, removing their social media accounts or shutting down their blogs (e.g. Citron, 2014; Searles et al., 2020). Removing the opportunity for women to engage in free speech, risks ensuring that the only voices that are heard are those that are white, male and privileged (Phillips, 2012).

Just as women have long had to employ various measures to protect themselves against they have faced in the physical world (Wise & Stanley, 1987), similar measures are frequently necessary online. Sophie described the measures that she had to take to protect herself against doxxing attacks:

> *We actually delayed the launch of the project so that we could take some time to lockdown our information online. It took an entire weekend to scrub my address from the internet. One of the things people don't understand is the amount of labour that is required ... Like the tax. Like if you want to speak online and not be threatened, the amount of labour that it requires. And money: I pay an annual service to keep scrubbing my address from the internet.* (Sophie, Academic and Journalist, USA)

Linda, who discovered that her personal information had been distributed across several white supremacist websites, attempted to safeguard her privacy in order to reduce the risk to her safety. However, she found this an impossible task:

> *It's quite difficult. There's not really anything I can do about it. When the white supremacist website listed my family background and my parents' names and my old address and my husband's name and my son's name on their website, I did ask Google to get that page taken down, but they wouldn't take it down, so there's not really anything I can do.* (Linda, UK-based journalist)

The work that Sophie and Linda describe having to undertake to protect themselves has clear parallels with the safety work that women are obliged to take against public sexual harassment (Vera-Gray, 2018).

This appears to be a particular problem for academics. This group of women may have been more aware of their need for safety work because they are less likely to have the protective barrier provided by a staff team. This often left them feeling at risk. Numerous examples of safety work undertaken to alleviate both the likelihood and impact of online abuse were offered by the contributors to this study. These examples broadly fit into two categories: the safety work undertaken to protect oneself and one's work and the safety work undertaken to protect children and other family members:

I hid my pregnancy. I was on the news at eight and a half months pregnant and I hid my belly under a table. I entirely hid my pregnancy on social media. (Christie, Academic at a UK university)

I try very hard when I do any media. Like I don't do it at my house. You won't believe how many journalists have said, can we interview at your house, can we film you at home? I'm like, no! (Souad, Academic at a UK university)

There's filters on my website ... on my emails ... even my Twitter account has muted certain words, so I won't see it. Most of us have taken our own protection levels seriously. (Emma, Academic at a UK university)

Emma felt that the safety work she employed was an inevitable consequence of speaking out. This has parallels with the notion of a 'tax' being paid by women to use their voices, described earlier in this chapter.

If it means I can continue my online presence, continue to live my online life without seeing stuff on a regular basis, that's something I can live with. Is it enough? Of course not. (Emma, Academic at a UK university)

I don't have my personal account linked into my work accounts. So I've got a Twitter account, I've got an Instagram account which is with friends, but I don't share those two things. Because of what I work on, I try and keep my personal life off the internet. (Jacqueline, Academic at a UK university)

Jacqueline went on to explain how the safeguards women employ in their online activity mirrors the actions taken in the offline environment, a point echoed by Ann, which emphasises the global nature of this kind of protective toil:

Women must behave online in the same way that they adapt to threats offline, to the degree that we don't even think about it. Most women don't think about it, it's just part of their daily routines. They don't do certain things, and I hate that, I understand the costs of that level of vigilance, whether it's conscious or not. (Ann, Academic and Journalist, USA)

The sort of thing women are doing online when they're having to use these platforms to communicate messages around feminism or violence or anything that's going to be likely to encourage, this kind of [abusive] behaviour. We do that work online, habitually without even thinking about it. (Jacqueline, Academic at a UK university)

Some women felt that the measures that they had to employ to protect themselves and their loved ones from online harm were explicitly undermined by their employer or by others within their occupational sphere:

> *You're just constantly negotiating. If you are speaking publicly at a conference, you then ask can you take this photo in a certain way, and the amount of times I was at a public engagement and said please only photograph me straight on.*

> *And then, they put it on their social media feed, and I have asked people to take things down and then I've also had to negotiate this weird space where some people say, well what if I post it as an Instagram story, so it won't be traceable either, and if we also cut off part of your baby's face. With the kind of work that I do[5], people want to almost exploit the fact that I'm working and have a baby attached, because it reflects well on them.* (Christie, Academic at a UK university)

Just like academics, local politicians mostly work alone and rarely have a staff team to support them or to triage their social media activity. The measures that Wendy had taken to protect her young family were similar to those taken by Jacqueline:

> *I've just had a baby. I won't put my child's picture online. I'll make sure that her face is always hidden. I'm very specific about not tweeting my location and things like that.* (Wendy, Local Councillor)

As discussed in Chapter Three, social media platforms and other technological resources are often harnessed in order to facilitate or perpetuate a campaign of gender-based harassment that originates in the offline space. Ranjit shared her experience:

> *He started with the insults, very early, with name calling. Then I started receiving hundreds of messages, initially only WhatsApp, and then he moved onto other platforms. There were messages most nights, saying that I was horrible, and he wanted to get rid of me and I was a prostitute. On the nights he didn't do it I felt wonderful in the morning because I didn't wake up to a hundred messages of insults. And when he realised that I wasn't answering his messages, I wasn't paying attention … that's where the real abuse started. So I had two violations of my personal data, my email and my Twitter account. In my Twitter account he found private conversations, took screen shots*

---

[5] *Research on Incels.*

> *of those, and published them on his Facebook.* (Ranjit, Academic at a European university)

Ranjit's account illustrates how perpetrators often use multiple platforms to disseminate online abuse (Rohlinger & Vaccaro, 2021), causing the maximum amount of emotional harm:

> *It was a continuous, with a growth of these messages every night. The final episode was on 16 July when I woke up to twelve new voice messages. I never listened to them. There were also eighty-six written WhatsApp messages. Because I had blocked him on Facebook a long time before … WhatsApp was the only possible way to harass me.* (Ranjit, Academic at a European university)

Threats

The majority of threats made online are overt and are specifically designed to provoke fear. It is within this dimension that online abuse most closely aligns with gender-based violence. In an echo of the gender-based violence that occurs in the physical space, the threats made online can take a multiplicity of forms. The different types of threat received ranged from blackmail to stalking and also included swatting, threats of physical and sexual violence, rape and death.

> *I've had threats saying … we have your private password information and will be hacking your accounts unless you do X. I had a very persistent series of messages that were very threatening, 'why aren't you answering me, I have access to your accounts, I'm sorry but now we're going to have to take over your accounts'.* (Ann, Academic and Journalist, USA)

A reference to the offence of blackmail also appeared in one of the abusive tweets sent to the politician Tracy Brabin and collected as part of the analysis of Twitter storms. Blackmail also features in the literature on online abuse, with Henry and Powell (2015) including blackmail as one of the range of behaviours in their typology of technology-facilitated sexual violence and harassment, explaining how 'email, the internet and mobile phone technologies are being used as a tool to harass, intimidate, humiliate, coerce and blackmail women' (Henry & Powell, 2015, p. 115). Whilst Henry and Powell's (2015) focus is, like this research, on the role of online abuse in gender-based violence, their findings relate to intimate partner violence, specifically revenge porn; as opposed to women who receive online abuse as a consequence of their occupation, and the risk of blackmail appears smaller amongst those interviewed in this study. Similarly, work by Jane (2017a) reports the growth of blackmail related to revenge porn from former male partners; and the emergence of rape video blackmail, where a woman is subjected to sexual violence which is filmed, and with the victim then blackmailed with the threat of the video being released on the internet.

For some women, using social media in the course of their work had led to them becoming the target of behaviour that is akin to stalking:

> *On Facebook I was posting issues surrounding social justice and racism and a guy contacted me privately ... and then he Googled me, found my office phone number from the department website ... And then called me a couple of times just to chat about race. And that was, that was bad. I almost completely stopped answering my office phone because of it. It wasn't a face-to-face thing, but that was the first time that I've felt threatened, felt that my safety was threatened because of what I had said online.* (Eileen, Academic at a European university)

> *The worst situation I had was with one particular man who was prolific on social media within my area of interest, and I started receiving inappropriate messages privately, and pictures and ... at the time, I didn't realise that what was happening was abusive and ... exploitative, and manipulative. I slowly unravelled what was going on ... what made me really upset was I found out he was also doing it to other women, who were far more vulnerable than me. It was really unpleasant, and quite targeted, and because his account was anonymous, he got away with it.* (Carol, Academic at a UK university)

> *I've had a couple of problems with stalkers. When I was working in Wisconsin in 2011 – I had a couple of right-wing folks, who knew I was working on the ground during protests, who set out to find me, to find my home ... to find me in a crowd to harass me.* (Judith, Journalist based in the USA)

Some participants based in the USA recounted their experiences of 'swatting'. Swatting is the term applied to a crime which is relatively unheard of in the UK. It describes the act of 'falsely reporting people to the police so that SWAT teams descend on their homes' (Lukianoff, 2015, p. 48) and is most commonly used as a tactic in intimate partner violence (Wu, 2015). Whilst the incidence of swatting events occurring in this study was rare in comparison to other threats meted out online, the act contains such a huge potential for harm that it is worth recording here. Furthermore, and analogous to other forms of online abuse, there is evidence that the threat posed by swatting is greatest amongst women of colour and other minority groups:

> *I have called my police department to say there is the chance that I might be swatted. And that can be very dangerous and violent. If you are in a neighbourhood where most of the people are Black, swatting a target can get many people potentially hurt, killed or jailed. It's just the way the bias works. It's much more dangerous in a neighbourhood marginalised already.* (Ann, Academic and Journalist, USA)

Despite the danger posed by swatting, the participants who were most concerned about becoming a target for the offence had found it hard to make their local police departments take their concerns seriously:

> *I called them up [the police] and I explained the situation and they literally said ... we have nowhere in our system to record this! I wanted to say to them if you get a call trying to send a SWAT team to my house ... ask some questions. Right? (laughs)* (Sophie, Academic and Journalist, USA)

> *When I called the police, I had to explain to them what swatting was, and why if someone made a distress call with my address, they needed to understand that's what may be happening.* (Ann, Academic and Journalist, USA)

In contrast to the discussion on swatting, threats of physical violence remain an all-too-common feature of online abuse and were similarly the most common threat experienced by participants in this study:

> *The landscape of online misogyny and the real threat of violence moving off screen and on to the streets has heightened in the last couple of years. So, although I [now] get less abuse, I'm also more scared about my physical safety.* (Christie, Academic at a UK university)

> *Over the last three years or so, I've had all of these attacks, malicious communications, and I think there's been four cases of people found guilty. Suddenly they've got a platform so, they post a picture of a gallows with somebody hanging and my name next to it. There's been threats with guns ... one person was trying to incite people to find out where I lived, it's just absolutely horrendous.* (Loretta, Member of Parliament)

> *Depending on whatever they're focused on at the time, the harassment is varied from Islamophobic because my name sounds like it's Arab, ... if I write about race, it might be about hanging or lynching ... a lot of pornography, which takes the form of either images or video.* (Ann, Academic and Journalist, USA)

> *During the election [of December 2019] I received some of the worst abuse of anyone. Someone said they wanted to poison me with Ricin. And then they threatened to lock me in my house and bomb me and film me.* (Jill, Member of Parliament)

> *There's a fella that got three month's suspended sentence a few months back for making a threat on private messenger to me. He sent me a private message on Facebook, calling me a fucking*

tramp, and a slapper, and then threatened me ... he said something else, he called me a couple of sentences of abuse and then he said, 'you're fucked'. (Sherrie, Member of the Northern Ireland Legislative Assembly)

One example that stands out was when somebody said they wanted to see me on the end of a bayonet. That made me feel very uneasy. (Julia, Politician in Scotland)

As the awareness of the online abuse targeted at women in public facing occupations has grown, those most intent on causing harm via the distribution of online threats of violence appear to have become more circumspect in their use of the various platforms. Many perpetrators are now careful not to use overtly violent terms, as they realise that the use of such language can attract the attention of filters or more formal regulatory sanctions from the various online platforms:

Abuse is ... a lot more violent, a lot smarter, so they probably don't use words anymore, right, because they know we'll get them banned off the platform. (Souad, Academic at a UK university)

Some of the most dangerous offenders do not use violent terminology at all, as Sue explained:

One of our biggest challenges with social media is context, because within the domestic violence space, often the threat is only really understood if you know the partner and you know the history. So, for example, an abusive partner might say 'on the day that I kill you, I'm going to deliver you roses'. And so, they might post a picture of roses on her Facebook page or tag her on Twitter. She's terrified. But that doesn't violate any of the terms and conditions of the social media platforms, because it's a picture of roses. (Sue, Academic based in the USA)

This reiterates the importance of context, and why it is essential to have increased awareness of the potential for harm widely communicated to those responsible for online platforms, law enforcement and legislation.

Arguably, the clearest manifestation of misogyny in online abuse is exhibited through the making of threats of rape and sexual violence (Jane, 2016), which have become an all-too-common feature of online interaction for many women in public facing occupations. The research undertaken by Amnesty International (2017), coupled with testimony from the likes of Diane Abbott MP (Hansard, 2017), was echoed in the empirical research undertaken for this study:

The first time that I ever really felt that I suffered from it [online abuse] was very, very, very graphic descriptions of how people would harm and rape me. Going into really specific details about how they would do that, as if they'd really thought about it. And it's never really gone away. (Peggy, Member of Parliament)

Depending on what I'm working on, I get a lot of threats. I should be explicit that that includes rape threats and death threats. (Ann, Academic and Journalist, USA)

I get rape threats … I have no tolerance of them. (Agita, Member of the House of Lords)

Once again, the issue of race and gender intersects in the abuse that is generated when women speak out in the public sphere:

[Four years ago], I wrote an article in a newspaper … that article has been shared a hundred thousand times. It's been quoted, picked up etcetera by press across the world. It was about a movie … but within twenty-four hours … I was inundated with rape threats and death threats. Frankly, most people who write for newspapers don't have to worry about it. I do. And that's not because I'm writing for a newspaper, it's because I'm a migrant woman of colour in Britain, daring to criticise a British film. And that's the reality of it. (Emma, Academic at a UK university)

The presence of online abuse is viewed as so predictable by some that they have mechanised routines to manage it:

It's almost funny because I have this standing joke with my literary agent, that I keep a file on my computer. It's my standard death threats and rape threats file. (Emma, Academic at a UK university)

Whilst still the rarest form of threat made against women in politics (Krook, 2020), and despite being an offence under section 16 of the Offences Against the Person Act (1861), the Protection from Harassment Act (1997), section one of the Malicious Communications Act 1988, and section 127 of the Communications Act 2003 (CPS, 2016); several contributors to this study had received death threats via online channels:

I got stuff saying, 'she should be hung up', 'she should be in a body bag'. There was a stupid article [in a national newspaper] about how Brexit was going to lead to a crisis in body bags because they were made in the EU, so they were saying 'perfect for our MP' and all that sort of stuff. (Phyllis, Member of Parliament until December 2019)

I haven't reported it [online abuse], even death threats. It's quite normal for journalists, and I've had death threats in the past, even before I became an author, when I was working for the BBC. (Linda, UK-based journalist)

> *There's someone who wanted to ... threatened to kill me with a machete.* (Caroline, Member of Parliament until December 2019)

Whilst the women speaking here showed an enormous degree of resilience when faced with threats of abuse, violence and death, there is no doubt that receiving communication of this nature had an impact, which often endured long after the event:

> *There are certain things that I now associate with that first death threat ... I wore an Apple watch up until that point and my Twitter notifications came through on my watch. I haven't had my watch on since that weekend, because death threats flashing up at you is not really something that ... I don't want to wear that watch again.* (Caroline, Member of Parliament until December 2019)

The death of Jo Cox was a recurring topic in the interviews. Every participant without exception (including those based outside the UK) discussed the assassination of the Labour MP for Batley and Spen in West Yorkshire, by neo-Nazi Thomas Mair on 16 June 2016. Whilst evidence given at his trial showed that Mair had used the internet to both gather information about Cox and to plan his crime (Liem & Geelen, 2019), there is no indication that Mair targeted Cox with online abuse prior to killing her. Nevertheless, for all the women interviewed, the death of Jo Cox remains a shocking reminder of the vulnerability that they share. This was best summed up by Phyllis, who was a close friend and Parliamentary colleague of Jo's:

> *Listen ... there was a reason it was Jo that was killed, you know. They didn't pick on a strapping six-foot bloke, did they? They went for a woman who dared to be strong and ferocious and brilliant and brave. They silenced her the only way they could. Misogyny runs through absolutely all of it.* (Phyllis, Member of Parliament until December 2019)

The threat of significant physical harm remains an ever-present danger for women in many public facing occupations. Despite this, women are still prepared to hold public office, irrespective of the risks that they face:

> *I'm much more scared of a world where this [online abuse] stops people coming forward than I am scared of a world where people come forward and might suffer it. I'm much more frightened of the bullies winning and taking over the playground. I'm willing to give my life to that. I'm much more frightened to sit down than I am to stand up because what sort of world would my kids grow up in if people don't keep putting themselves forward?* (Peggy, Member of Parliament)

Criticism of Physical Characteristics

The Twitter storms that were analysed for this project demonstrated that a significant amount of the abuse women receive online focuses on their appearance and other physical characteristics. The dominance of physical characteristics as a focus for the content of online abuse is further corroborated by interview evidence. This denigration is most pronounced in three areas: physical appearance, voice and age.

> *I get gendered hate speech; I get anti-Semitic hate speech and I get fatphobic hate speech.* (Judith, Journalist based in the USA)

The literature on online abuse confirms that appearance is frequently central to the abuse that women receive (e.g. Backe et al., 2018), primarily as a consequence of sexism and a wider misogyny (Jennings & Coker, 2019). This behaviour endures within public facing organisations with a strong occupational culture, such as policing (Steinþórsdóttir & Pétursdóttir, 2022). This appears to be particularly applicable to women in public facing occupations, whose occupational roles routinely expect them to interact with the media, or to have their image featured on publicity materials for their employer:

> *It's just an obsession with commentating on how you look all the time. I've had a group of trolls who became really obsessed with my front teeth. I've got really wonky front teeth, and every time I posted anything, they zoomed in on my teeth and circled them and commented on them. It was really quite bizarre.* (Sarah, Senior Police Officer)

> *I did something on ITV, and someone commented on my makeup. It seems minor, it's not really minor.... I think it's just a reality that people feel they can make a comment on your life, twenty-four-seven.* (Jill, Member of Parliament)

> *People who have a track record of disagreeing with you, criticise your appearance ... I bet there wasn't a single word about a man and what they were wearing.* (Loretta, Member of Parliament)

As with other forms of online abuse, the targeting of women in public facing occupations for criticism or ridicule of their appearance was both frequent and unpredictable:

> *Just last night I had a guy email me insults about my weight, and then a really offensive picture, I didn't look at it.* (Judith, Journalist based in the USA)

One contributor mused that some women were targeted for online abuse more than others, drawing on her own experience:

I haven't had much. Well, apart from the odd comment telling me I'm ugly, or that I'm stupid. But I'm not like the others, like Jess Phillips or Diane Abbott. I don't know how some people get chosen as the target for abuse. Is it because they are younger and prettier than me? (Agnes, Member of Parliament)

Sometimes, the focus on a woman's appearance has malevolent intent, driven by a desire to discredit or humiliate:

There are groups that focus on my appearance … when pictures have been taken of me in Downing Street they try and zoom in on my badge and try and catch you out to see if you've exposed something that you shouldn't expose, either about your body or the post. (Sarah, Senior Police Officer)

They got [a photo] where I'm kind of looking down, and they took a screenshot that's all blurry, and made it look like I'm asleep in the Chamber, and then spread this thing that I was. And of course, other people start picking stuff like this up … it was horrific. (Phyllis, Member of Parliament until December 2019)

I didn't think it possible that my hair would be discussed as much as it was. And then it manifested in that people felt the need to complain about me, make a complaint about me to the Police and Crime Commissioner. The bit that I remember more than anything else was that people said I've got no standards and I was letting the police down by the way I was dressed. (Karen, Senior Police Officer)

The abuse that Karen referred to was also mentioned by other police officers in their discussions about online abuse:

How dare they judge her by her appearance when she's utterly capable and able? I felt very indignant about that. It was further evidence to me of the venom that there is and the incapacitating nature of that type of trolling. (Stacey, Senior Police Officer)

The outrage articulated by Stacey on Karen's behalf evidences both the existence and benefit of mutual support networks frequently created by women in public facing occupations; an issue that is discussed further in Chapter Six.

A gendered focus on appearance was not limited to the UK:

I will never necessarily be acknowledged for who I really am, … I've lived in several different countries so I feel like my identity will always be pegged at that level of how I look rather than who I am. (Nicole, Academic at a UK university)

Once again, the experiences of women of colour and minoritised groups were likely to generate even more abuse of this kind. Kerry frequently finds herself receiving racist abuse, instigated by her appearance, as she explained:

> *I think I've received more due to the fact that ... I'm a woman and Black ... and for wearing a hijab, I have as well. Something I tweeted came up and there was a xenophobic thing going on. It was nothing to do with people who care about anti-Semitism or xenophobia. It was just somebody picking on someone with a hijab on.* (Kerry, Local Councillor)

Smita, who like Kerry, is also a local Councillor, described how, as a Muslim woman, she felt that she had to deal with criticism of her appearance from all sides. Within hours of being elected in a marginal seat, she found herself on the receiving end of unpleasant comments from men purportedly within the Muslim community:

> *It [online abuse] got all negative because of me and my appearance. So, I wear my headscarf as a turban ... and ... I wear makeup. And the pictures that were going round, suddenly there was a huge amount of abuse from men, saying that I'm not covered enough. This was before I'd even started, before I'd even gone into the council to do any official work. The hate abuse that I got ... just because of what I was wearing, with some people having the view that I was showing my face and I was wearing far too much makeup it was horrible, it was a really, really difficult time.* (Smita, Local Councillor)

In an example that highlights the multi-faceted nature of misogyny and that criticism of appearance can often hint at a more malign threat, Peggy offered the following example:

> *There was a bloke recently, sort of left-wing bloke who said to me that I need fucking to get my teeth fixed, that ... a good fucking would fix my teeth.* (Peggy, Member of Parliament)

One interesting finding to emerge from the interviews was that even positive online interactions often focused wholly on a woman's appearance, rather than what she was saying or the role she was fulfilling, which the individuals concerned found frustrating:

> *I had a comment on the back of my telly appearances ... people saying, oh, you've had a haircut, why don't you get something more girly and flattering.* (Beth, Member of Parliament until December 2019)

> *She would write a policy post, but the tweets and responses would be about how they didn't like her hair, or her dress, or her earrings, or her makeup, or the shoes she was wearing.* (Svetlana, Political Staffer)

This empirical evidence echoes the work of numerous studies that have emphasised how women politicians find their clothing and other aspects of their appearance the focus of much greater scrutiny than their male counterparts (e.g. Hayes et al., 2014).

Caroline recalled her experience of speaking in the emergency Parliamentary debate on the use of force in Syria, which took place in April 2018:

> *Obviously, it was very challenging, and I was in favour, and someone wrote to me asking where my dress was from. I've just given a speech about whether we should deploy troops, and one lady wants to know where my dress is from. So, really? You're not going to ask where a man's suit's from. And they think they're being really supportive, and you're like really?! Did I not actually make a difference to what you're paying attention to?* (Caroline, Member of Parliament until December 2019)

When considering the online abuse related to physical features that is received by women in public facing occupations, their voice is a prominent target. This has echoes with older (pre-internet) research, with Beard (2015) highlighting how public speaking has been viewed as the very essence of masculinity since (at least) the Second Century AD, emphasising how a deep and powerful voice was frequently perceived as a 'defining attribute of maleness' (Beard, 2015, p. 812). Similarly, the criticism of Margaret Thatcher's voice, which was described as 'shrill' (Wilson & Irwin, 2015, p. 23) when she was elected Leader of the Conservative Party in 1975 (Blundell, 2008), precipitated the now famous intervention by her advisors that led to her undertaking a series of lessons to make her voice seem 'firmer and more powerful' (Coffè, 2020, p. 423). Some have argued that the efforts that were made to modify Thatcher's voice to make her sound 'more like a man' (Grebelsky-Lichtman & Katz, 2019, p. 701) were an integral part of her election success (Wilson & Irwin, 2015), with others believing that the distinctive nature of her voice acted as a clarion for the many organisations and individuals who were vehemently opposed to her political agenda (Shaw, 2018). Whilst the modification of Thatcher's voice is now an integral part of her narrative, few male voices have been subjected to such detailed and enduring public scrutiny.

The intervening decades have not done much to alter the criticism of how women's voices sound. A number of politicians recounted their own experiences:

> *People would comment on my voice being too high, or [that I] speak too fast.* (Julia, Politician in Scotland)

Agita identified a very gendered difference in the way that women's articulation is perceived:

> *There is a difference in what you get called ... a man is strong, and a woman is sort of breathy or shouty ... and it's like very subtle use of language that I really worry about.* (Agita, Member of the House of Lords)

As an aside, it is interesting to note that in their analysis of mixed gender presidential campaigns, Grebelsky-Lichtman and Katz (2019) found that if women are perceived as too masculine (like Hillary Clinton), voters think they are competent, but dislike them; whilst if they are perceived as too feminine (like Sarah Palin), voters like them but do not believe them to be competent. The explanation offered by this study is that institutionalised misogyny means that women in public facing occupations, whether in politics, policing, journalism or academia, are criticised – on both social media platforms and in traditional media outlets; however they present themselves.

Age and ageing were also weaponised by perpetrators engaging in online abuse, as the criticism of older women became yet another target for the opprobrium of physical characteristics.

> *Something about being a woman in a senior position, I think is one thing, rarely do you see that abuse directed at men who just happen to be grey and wrinkly. If there was a senior policeman who was grey and wrinkly, I don't think it'd get mentioned. yet women who are in senior positions, it seems ok to either go, 'cor, she's hot stuff', could be at one end of the spectrum couldn't it, and that would seem appropriate, or at the other end, you know, whatever amount of abuse you want to dish out, as to how somebody looks.* (Samantha, Senior Police Officer)

This is consistent with the work of Pickard (2020) and Lewis (2020), who both highlight the castigation of older women as an essential component of modern misogyny; whilst also echoing the ageist abuse directed at the politician Tracy Brabin uncovered by the analysis of the Twitter data corpus. Research by Steinþórsdóttir and Pétursdóttir (2022) adds a further dimension to this area of abuse. In a study that considers the attitudes of serving police officers in Iceland, they discovered that young men, especially those newly recruited, were the group most likely to hold sexist attitudes towards female colleagues. It is proposed that this occurs as a consequence of these officers seeking to reassert male dominance within policing, fearing that any move towards greater equality could pose a threat to their own occupational advancement (Steinþórsdóttir & Pétursdóttir, 2022). It may also be the wider consequence in the growth in popularity of openly misogynistic online figureheads such as Andrew Tate (Ging, 2023).

Caroline's experience neatly emphasises how the different facets of physical appearance are frequently weaponised in online abuse. She highlighted how the anti-Semitic abuse that she and three parliamentary colleagues had received had targeted different aspects of their appearance for denigration:

> *[Individual One] … got horrendous abuse, awful, awful abuse, and out of everybody got the worst out of all four of us … but [Individual Two] and [Individual Three] get ageist gendered abuse. So, they get a three-level hit, and [Individual Three] is very upfront about that.*

So, mine will be sexualised; [Individual One's] really was, you know, she's a beautiful woman, so hers would be sexualised, and gendered, but much more sexualised, and racist, but they would bring [Individual Two and Individual Three's] age into it.

The men [male Jewish MPs] never got any of it. It was very much about the four women ... (Caroline, Member of Parliament until December 2019)

Camp (2018) demonstrates how the belittling of victims is an integral part of gender-based violence within the domestic sphere. This study has confirmed that this is similarly evidenced in the online abuse that women serving in public facing occupations regularly receive.

You know nothing, you're just a dafty lassie who couldn't hack it in politics ... (Julia, Politician in Scotland)

Julia provides a striking example of the online abuse she received, the purpose of which was to undermine and belittle her work as a politician. This type of online abuse is different from other examples provided in this chapter, as it contains no obscenities, or any other overtly discriminatory tropes that can be identified as abuse by either text filters or human moderators. Nevertheless, this type of malign communication has the clear purpose of undermining public confidence in women tasked with making important decisions, and consequently, it can be hugely damaging. As more than one participant remarked, this type of abuse is pernicious and is rarely directed at men:

Take sexism. All the obvious stuff we can deal with, all the obvious bullying, you can deal with that. But the problem with social media abuse is that so much of it is really low level. Just grinding sexism. When you see women on Twitter and they're in positions of authority, or positions of expertise and then some fucking bloke will pop up and go, well yes, but really .... and that's a form of abuse. (Rose, Academic based in the USA)

You have to balance the benefit of tweeting out and informing people about what we are up to as an organisation, against being the subject of ridicule and abuse. I think there's this army of armchair warriors, mainly looking out for women who are opinionated and intelligent ... looking to comment in a negative way. (Stacey, Senior Police Officer)

I think there is more of an attempt on Twitter to humiliate women than men. Absolutely humiliate them by making them feel worthless. (Patricia, Member of Parliament until December 2019)

> *Something I've been subjected to is, and this has been offline as well as online, is 'God this is what happens when you put a woman in charge'.* (Sarah, Senior Police Officer)

Agita summed up what she believed were the potential consequences of the incessant belittling and undermining of women were:

> *It's like women are worthless, that they have no value, so they can just be raped and abused and just calling them a fucking cunt online is ok.* (Agita, Member of the House of Lords)

Silencing Women's Voices

The silencing of women's voices as a demonstration of misogyny has a long history (e.g. Banet-Weiser, 2018; Beard, 2017). One example of how online abuse is used in an attempt to silence women – through criticism of the sounds of their voices – has already been discussed. In addition, there are three further ways that silencing can be exhibited. These methods may be overt and unmistakable, as Kerry demonstrated:

> *Because I have an opinion, he's trying to shut me up. But what happened was, in that panic, you feel helpless, you know? His motivation [for the abuse] was to silence me, to scare me, to say that you're weak.* (Kerry, Local Councillor)

However, sometimes, the bid to silence is more implicit, with the pressure exerted on an individual to moderate their contribution in the online space:

> *I think the structural impact is similar to the ways that women have been silenced throughout history. It creates an effect where women are more afraid to speak out, more afraid to stick their necks out, more afraid to give opinions, more afraid to occupy political office or positions of authority. And I think that this effect is in tandem with what happens in women's real life lives, where women are not heard.* (Tiprat, Academic based in the USA)

> *I think a lot of what they do is to try and discourage you from doing the kind of reporting you do. Ultimately what they're trying to do is discourage you from covering the topic which is criticising them.* (Linda, UK-based journalist)

> *To me there's no difference between online and real life, I mean, all our cities, all our villages, all our roads, all our public spaces are meant to exclude women. So, any space therefore we occupy is despite the best efforts and despite the design. It's not because they were made for us.* (Emma, Academic at a UK university)

As has been illustrated elsewhere, the impact of being silenced is not experienced equally, with women of colour and other disadvantaged groups more likely to be targeted, replicating their experiences in the offline environment:

> *This is something that I think most of us – especially a lot of women of colour – were very aware of from day one, and we have been arguing about it and writing about it. Unsurprisingly, nobody listens to us. Nobody listens to women, and women of colour even less.* (Emma, Academic at a UK university)

> *The structural impact is very clearly that women, people of colour, trans folks, Jews, all of us are hesitant to speak when folks in the majority are not hesitant … and so structurally, it has a silencing effect.* (Sophie, Academic and Journalist, USA)

> *It ultimately drives women and people of colour offline and out of the conversation. So much of our political and social discourse takes place online, but for so many people, harassment just reaches a point where it's just not worth it, so they end up taking their voice out of the conversation. Which, by the way, is generally the intention. The idea is to drive women and people of colour offline.* (Judith, Journalist based in the USA)

The data also identified a feeling that women are less likely to be asked to contribute to online discussions: yet another way that women are being excluded:

> *One thing I think can be tricky with social media, is the bias by omission, which is tricky to prove as they've not actually had a go at you, but you're cut out of the conversation. Or you're cut out of the coverage. And I think that happens to women more often.* (Lauren, Member of Parliament until December 2019)

> *Women are much more circumspect around their activity, about what they are prepared to share … and what they're prepared to comment on. In my experience, women's voices are quieter.* (Imogen, Senior Police Officer)

The silencing of women has a greater consequence than simply removing the voices of influential women from the online space. For the act of silencing may also prevent women from forming the networks that are essential to both tackling online abuse and successfully progressing on their chosen career path:

> *It absolutely keeps us from entering public conversations or exerting our full power in public conversations, but it also keeps us from connecting with each other. And it stops us using these tools to connect*

> *with each other … to organise, or just to get social support and build connections. Structurally, this kind of harassment keeps us afraid of connecting. Or it creates high costs to pay for attempting to connect.* (Sophie, Academic and Journalist, USA)

> *My concern is that there are obstacles, multicultural barriers to women in authority, and this level of hostility intensifies everything. And we already know that girls who have been watching are inhibiting themselves.* (Ann, Academic and Journalist, USA)

The women participants in this study revealed how the abuse that they had received, and that they had witnessed other women experience, became a mechanism for self-censorship, leading some women to withdraw from the online space:

> *I've definitely turned down things because I don't want to get abuse. Or I've minced my words or tone-policed a bit … And also, by being off social media, I am probably missing opportunities as well.* (Souad, Academic at a UK university)

> *If I tweet and then people are scornful or sarcastic, then friends and family can see that, and that's an inhibiting factor isn't it?* (Stacey, Senior Police Officer)

> *I've been careful, which has avoided a lot of abuse I could have got. But I've also restricted how much I've engaged online. There are things I wouldn't say because I know I will get attacked.* (Michelle, Journalist based in the UK)

> *I just keep my head down. I'm very clear on that. I'm very careful about what I tweet. There are certain issues I won't touch with a bargepole, even though I have thoughts and opinions Because it's too dangerous. I've been doing this now for eleven years, and from day one it was like, do not engage in anything controversial because it is too fucking dangerous.* (Rose, Academic based in the USA)

There were participants across all four occupational groups who had withdrawn from social media, as a result of the online abuse that they had received:

> *I no longer use Twitter in a professional capacity … because of the online abuse I received in the past.* (Anna, Police Officer)

The evidence provided by Anna highlights an unintended consequence of the police using social media as a mechanism for communicating with the public (Walby & Joshua, 2021). As O'Connor (2017) confirms, by using online platforms as a way of providing information, individual officers may find themselves in the position of being 'risk communicators' (O'Connor, 2017, p. 900), which in turn jeopardises their safety and wellbeing.

> *The way I handled [online abuse] was, I started shutting myself off. When things got loud and messy, and it felt that the landscapes were shifting, I just made my accounts private.* (Nicole, Academic at a UK university)

Many women found themselves considering whether the benefits they gained from engaging in the online space was worth the emotional labour it demanded.

> *There's a couple of MPs I spoke to, [named current Parliamentarian] I think she said when she went on maternity leave, she went off Twitter, and she's never gone back ... and I was just like wow! Because actually you don't have to [use social networks]. I think now that there's more people just making that conscious choice.* (Charmaine, Member of Parliament until December 2019)

> *Twitter, which I was on until a month ago ... discourse there has degraded over time. It's become more vitriolic. Abuse has become more open. I think partly because the platform allows it. On the day I left I had someone offering to punch me in the throat, and Twitter said it wasn't in violation of their rules, that's when I thought I'm not going to be on this platform.* (Linda, UK-based journalist)

> *When I withdraw, there's several reasons for it. When I can't control it ... it's just too much effort ... it becomes a full-time job trying to keep up with your social media presence, and that's not where my interest lies, I just don't have enough hours in the day. Then it's too much noise, I would prefer to be heard in a different way.* (Nicole, Academic at a UK university)

> *I remember saying to friends, it's like being in an abusive relationship and if I saw a friend of mine like that I'd say get out, you're better than this, you don't have to put yourself through this, no one should have this just because they're trying to do their job.* (Phyllis, Member of Parliament until December 2019)

But the decision to withdraw from the online space was not without consequence, both personal and professional.

> *I left Facebook when the birth of my daughter coincided with a documentary I put out on the BBC ... as I had some safety issues around that. The safest thing was to shut down Facebook. Then I had a baby and I wanted to engage with other young mums in my area and it became almost impossible for me to engage in baby programming without having a Facebook account.* (Christie, Academic at a UK university)

> *Many people would be personally affected by some of the things that have been said to me. I did withdraw. I stopped doing things online for a couple of months. I've gone a bit quiet on Twitter and [my followers] say please come back. I don't post huge amounts. I have considered withdrawing completely, but it's expected of me in my job, I think.* (Samantha, Senior Police Officer)

The opposing demands of career obligations and emotional wellbeing meant that occasional breaks from social media were more common than complete withdrawal, giving women the opportunity to prioritise their mental health, whilst still maintaining a presence in the online space.

> *I had a three month pause from Twitter and Instagram, I just had so much more time. You realise that if you don't go onto social media, you feel so much better. Regardless of abuse, I'm very rarely looking at Twitter or Insta right now.* (Charmaine, Member of Parliament until December 2019)

> *I have had colleagues say to me that if they were me, they would have shut down the account by now because you shouldn't put up with this level of abuse. But I've never got to the stage with Twitter where I've thought I'll withdraw completely. But there have been periods of time where I've just gone a bit quieter, where I've just felt that the public noise and angst has risen to a point when I thought I don't actually want to be in the middle of this frenzy. Then I've gone a bit quieter and just retweeted stuff.* (Sarah, Senior Police Officer)

These accounts illustrate how silencing is used against women in public facing occupations, as an integral part of the misogyny that underpins online abuse. Silencing is different from other forms of online abuse, as it often operates in an insidious manner, coercing women to silence themselves or remove themselves from the conversation by leaving the online space. Unlike some of the other elements of online abuse discussed in this chapter, the silencing of women's voices is multi-faceted and can be demonstrated both overtly and implicitly. What is interesting is how women have sought their own coping strategies to deal with this dimension of misogyny, whether by forming alliances with other women or by changing the way that they communicate online.

Mapping Twitter Data to the Seven Elements of Online Abuse

This chapter opened by presenting details of three Twitter storms. Before concluding this chapter, there is a value in returning to this corpus, to illustrate how individual tweets displayed the same seven elements of online abuse. This is provided in Fig. 9.

	EXAMPLE:	RECIPIENT:
Threat	It would rule if you died	(Doyle; 22/02/20 22:57:40)
Emotional harm	Making such a storm in a teacup, I can't help but think that you're a fake	(Brabin; 04:02:20 17:42:26)
Harrassment	You're parliament porn	(Brabin, 05/02/20 00:55:23)
Defamation	You're a journalist. You're all liars. No sympathy.	(Munchetty; 25/04/20 19:01:57)
Silencing	Shut up you sexist bitch. All these women are fucking whores.	(Doyle; 22/2/20 13:15:41)
Belittling	The stupid cow said she hurt her ankle, so she dressed like a stripper. Why should we pay her salary & excessive expenses?	(Brabin; 05/02/20 21:03:20)
Appearance	Your shoes are silly, given it's 6am, that's why people don't respect her.	(Munchetty; 27/4/20 22:40:16)

Fig. 9. Examples of Tweets in Each of the Seven Categories of Online Abuse.

Conclusion

This chapter contains a huge amount of detail about the online abuse directed at women working in public facing occupations and the associations that exist between online abuse and gender-based violence. By viewing online abuse through the seven separate lenses of defamation, emotional harm, harassment, criticism of physical characteristics, belittling, silencing and threat, the true enormity of the situation faced by women working across the public sphere can be appreciated. This study is the first to present empirical data from the four professions of academia, journalism, policing and politics in one place and to use this information to provide a comprehensive understanding of online abuse delivered to women in these professions.

Chapter Six

'They Think You're Fair Game' – Challenges Encountered by Women Serving in Public Facing Occupations

Abstract

This chapter explores two factors that are specific to online activity within public sphere occupations: the expectation that those holding positions within academia, journalism, policing and politics be always accessible online and that occupational seniority can act as an insulator from abuse, not by preventing pernicious communication, but by limiting exposure to it. The chapter then considers the consequences that can result for both the individual and their organisation when they are targeted for online abuse. This chapter identifies the elements specific to public facing occupations that make a sustained onslaught of online abuse particularly problematic. The chapter concludes by discussing the various benefits accrued from maintaining an online presence, highlighting why advising women to simply abandon their professional online activity is neither a realistic nor acceptable solution to online abuse.

Keywords: Online abuse; public sphere; online space; occupational seniority; mutual support; feminism

Introduction

This chapter continues to draw upon empirical data to analyse the factors that are intrinsic to the online experience of working in the public sphere. These factors were identified by interview participants as having had a specific impact on their

Gendered Online Abuse Against Women in Public Life: More Than Just Words, 95–131
doi:10.1108/978-1-83549-724-120251006

use of online technologies and affected the nature and severity of the online abuse that they subsequently received.

Expectation that Women in Public Facing Occupations Be Active Online

Many of the participants in this research expressed the opinion that there was an expectation from the public that they have an active online presence and they will be constantly available. However, this assumption must be viewed with a degree of caution, as those expressing this view were already active users of a range of social media platforms. The demand for the constant availability of those in the public sphere is not always beneficial, especially to the individual. Research by Walby and Joshua (2021) highlights how the Canadian police force use social media platforms as a way of improving their engagement with the community, whilst also seeking to increase their legitimacy. However, as both this study and the work of O'Connor (2017) suggest, the intention of police communication online is typically to provide information, rather than engaging in a public dialogue. However, this assumption by police forces fundamentally misunderstands the nature of social media sites, which operate upon a premise of engendering a greater openness with the public (Wessels, 2010). By adopting a model of one-way communication, the police service as an institution frequently chooses to ignore the public's response to its online activity (O'Connor, 2017). For whilst an organisation may choose to operate its social media communication in a unilateral manner, this is not always equally adhered to by a public that wants to engage in an online dialogue. In the event of a communication mismatch, the responsibility for responding to individual members of the public often falls to individual officers.

Furthermore, as highlighted in the experiences of journalists (e.g. Antunovic, 2019; Searles et al., 2020) and academics (Kapidzic, 2020), the expectation that women in public facing occupations habitually engage in online dialogue reframes the online presence from a purely leisure pursuit into a facet of occupational activity and thus the consequent online abuse into a form of workplace harassment. This supports the work of both Hochschild (2012) and Vera-Gray (2017) in their wider interpretation of the emotional impact of malign workplace activity and supports the discussions in Chapter Two, which defined online abuse as another form of the occupational sexual harassment first identified in the 1970s (Croall, 1995):

> There's pressure as an academic to have an online presence and to be disseminating your work in that way. We have an impact factor in academia, and you have to prove that you are being impactful. As a young academic it is expected that I am on social media and that it is accessible to my students. My social media is part of my work, and we talk about workplace safety, but I don't have health and safety worrying about my online presence, even though I'm constantly encouraged to be putting things online. (Christie, Academic at a UK university)

I've just signed the contracts for my new book, and in my contract, it said I'm obliged to tweet about my books when they come out. The reason I joined social media in the first place, is because my first book was coming out and there was that same expectation in writing that you would be on social media. I really didn't have any interest in joining it. I tried not to use it as a personal platform, just work stuff. (Linda, UK-based journalist)

I need it [social media] for the job that I do. People want you to be open and accessible and visible. So to delete it and not have that presence would have a detrimental impact on my professional life. (Wendy, Local Councillor)

These contributions highlight the commonality of this experience across the public sphere, confirming that women feel a huge pressure to be visible and accessible online despite the potentially negative consequences associated with doing so. Once again, participants positioned the issue of gender at the forefront of their experience. This contribution proved particularly apposite:

I definitely got more online abuse than my male colleagues, but that's legit. Right? That is fair game. I'm in the public eye. (Caroline, Member of Parliament until December 2019)

The phrase 'fair game' was used repeatedly by interviewees when describing their role and the online activity that it generated, and in particular, the expectation of an active online presence, echoing the findings of Veletsianos et al. (2018):

I think people feel that we're fair game. And I think the way the media treat people has really deteriorated … in the run up to the last election, there was quite a lot of unpleasant social media content. We just hid it, but when you actually click the button and realise it is somebody you go running with … I think people do just forget that you're human …(Nicola, Member of Parliament)

People will always say 'you're in politics, grow a thick skin', but I don't accept that at all, because I think everybody, regardless of how thick your skin is, is a human being. And you see the abuse all the other women MPs get, and you think ok, by doing this you're putting yourself in the lions' den for further abuse, that that's part of the job. (Smita, Local Councillor)

You're fair game, I think. I can imagine how difficult this must be for actual public figures. I'm just a journalist, but for politicians and pop stars and such, it must be horrendous. I can't even imagine what they go through all the time, the number of lies that gets spread about them online and they really can't do anything. (Linda, UK-based journalist)

Interviewees frequently minimised their own experiences of online abuse, as illustrated in Linda's contribution. The reasons for doing so remain unclear but may be symptomatic of women downplaying their occupational achievements and career experiences (Lopata, 1993), or a reflection of the institutional failure to take online abuse seriously (Dragotto et al., 2020; Powell & Henry, 2018), with it instead being seen as part of the 'wallpaper of sexism' (Lewis et al., 2018, p. 531) all too frequently associated with working in the public sphere:

> *I've been lucky actually, I don't know why but a lot of my fellow activists have had it a lot worse than I've ever had it ...* (Mary, Academic at a UK university)

> *I do sometimes wonder whether because I am a law enforcement officer, I get slightly less than other people? When I look at politicians' accounts, when I look at accounts from women in media, and when I look at some of the female Police and Crime Commissioners, I definitely don't get as much as they do.* (Sarah, Senior Police Officer)

One participant not only sought to minimise the online abuse she had received during an election campaign, but expressed a sense of guilt for not standing for political office again, partly as a result of her experience:

> *I feel a bit of a coward actually for not wanting to be a candidate again, because I look at people like Jess Phillips or Diane Abbott and I see the strength that they have, and the admiration I have for them, and I feel like I'm letting people down.* (Klaudia, Politician in Scotland)

However, not all participants felt an expectation from either their employer or the wider public that they are active in the online space:

> *Having an online presence is a personal choice. We don't tell officers they have to have an online presence as a senior policewoman. Certainly I don't feel under pressure to have an online presence, and nobody's ever told me to.* (Geetika, Senior Police Officer)

> *Police forces do not force you to have an account, and don't want everyone to have an account. There are Chief Officers who use it as a tool, but certainly in my force nobody is made to do it.* (Karen, Senior Police Officer)

Seniority of Position Provides Insulation from Abuse

By speaking to women holding a variety of positions within the occupations of academia, journalism, policing and politics, it became obvious that whilst having a senior role in an organisation frequently earmarked an individual as a target for increased amounts of online abuse, at the same time, the more senior a person became, the more likely they were to have staff members who would deal with the abuse for them. Until Elon Musk took over Twitter in October 2022 (Rohlinger et al., 2023), women holding senior positions in public facing occupations were frequently granted 'verified' account status. This is the process whereby an individual was independently deemed by Twitter to be judged 'of sufficient public interest in diverse fields, such as journalism [or] politics' (Paul et al., 2018, p. 1). When account verification was first introduced in June 2009 (Cashmore, 2009), Twitter asserted that the process of verification 'lets people know that an account of public interest is authentic. To receive the blue badge, your account must be authentic, notable, and active' (Twitter, 2021, p. 1), with a detailed set of criteria to be met. However, there were concerns that the process was opaque, with decisions surrounding verification made arbitrarily. Nevertheless, securing account verification provided those whose accounts were verified with a 'blue tick' a number of additional controls, which together created an additional level of protection from abuse. For example, it enabled verified users to limit their notifications, meaning that they were unlikely to receive the same number of alerts as a standard user of the platform. This allowed holders of verified accounts to take measures to avoid the mass attacks of online abuse commonly described as 'Twitter storms' and 'pile-ons' (Cover, 2023). However, the advantages of having a verified account relied on both an individual correctly receiving verified status and also relied on those holding verified accounts being aware of the tools available to set the appropriate privacy settings.

Less than one month in to taking ownership of the social media platform, Elon Musk announced his intention to launch a subscription service for Twitter users, denouncing what he described as the 'lords and peasants system for who has or doesn't have a blue checkmark' (Barrie, 2023, p. 2), alluding to the high status that has become attached to the possession of a blue tick since its inception in 2009 (Barsaiyan & Sijoria, 2021). Twitter Blue was introduced in November 2022, with Musk claiming that opening up verified status to anyone willing to pay a monthly fee provides 'power to the people' (Musk, 2022, p. 1), whilst also declaring that that the $8 charge to retain (or indeed acquire) a blue tick was necessary, in order to 'pay the bills somehow' (Cruse, 2022, p. 1), referring to the precarious financial position in which many social media companies find themselves (Bobrowsky, 2022). However, the evidence presented in this research shows that the move to a subscription model is likely to further jeopardise the safety of women in the online space, by removing the content filters that facilitate safer participation on the platform. These tools act as a shield against abusive and threatening contact, as well as providing the ability to connect with women in other public facing roles who are able to offer support. To be clear, the verified account status available to individuals in the public sphere between June 2009 and November 2022 did not stop online abuse, but it did go some way towards providing women the space they needed to maintain an online presence without experiencing the psychological trauma of seeing multiple abusive comments. When the range of different protections on a verified Twitter account were optimised, it meant that whilst the abuse still occurred, its targets did not see it, leaving perpetrators shouting into a virtual void (Watson, 2022).

Differences in the Nature of Online Abuse within Public Sphere Occupations

This research has identified differences in the nature of online abuse *within* the occupations of academia, journalism, policing and politics. For during conversations with women working in these areas, it became apparent that women operating at different levels of a professional hierarchy experienced online abuse in contrasting ways. Perhaps unsurprisingly, when individuals reach a certain level of seniority, they are more likely to have access to a range of protective measures that insulate them from seeing and experiencing the worst excesses of online abuse. These measures would have originally taken the form of the Twitter verification process discussed above but now occur through the management of an individual's social media profile by others.

Sarah, a senior Police Officer, explained how being part of a large organisation offered a buffer from the worst ravages of online abuse:

> *So, I have some layers of… protection's too strong a word because it isn't really protection, but I've got an extra set of eyes looking at it to protect me. I've never reported anything to the police, because to be frank, if it were to reach that sort of level, probably the security team within [the named force] would investigate it for me.*
> (Sarah, Senior Police Officer)

Similarly, when women reach a senior position in politics, they typically see less of their social media even though the actual amount of abusive communication being directed at them increases:

> *When you are in a position of leadership, you have to withdraw from social media to an extent, and in some ways that gives you a lot of freedom. Because I wasn't seeing the abuse, I wasn't aware of it. My staff were having to wade through it all, and it was taking hours.*
> (Charmaine, Member of Parliament until December 2019)

In contrast, it became clear that for politicians, women at a relatively junior level were frequently left to manage their own social media presence, as the few staff members they employed were almost entirely engaged in constituency casework:

> *When I was a junior minister I would still be reading my Twitter mentions, I would see sometimes that people would tag me and also Nick Clegg or David Cameron, and I'd get lots of abuse. But obviously David Cameron and Nick Clegg weren't reading their Twitter mentions. And so I think that some of the people who probably end up bearing the brunt of the impact of such abuse, are either the staff of those whose positions are in leadership, or people who are in senior roles like being an MP, or an academic or journalist who are*

in the public eye, but who are not always operating at a level where they would have staff to manage it for them. Such as backbench MPs or junior ministers. (Charmaine, Member of Parliament until December 2019)

Furthermore, the organisation of the Parliamentary system at Westminster does little to provide universal institutional support to individual members. Instead, the House of Commons has been described as:

659 individual small businesses, working under an ever-increasing load and more complex environment. They now deal with issues and communicate in ways unheard of a few years ago. They require more backup staff, more computer resources, and more allowances to enable them to travel back and forth to Parliament, living away from home for days at a time, while keeping in touch with the problems and issues of their constituents (Besley & Larcinese, 2011, p. 292).

This problem is exacerbated for local authority Councillors, who have no staff support, and who receive only very limited expenses, and are often simultaneously undertaking paid employment.

Holding a position of seniority within the public sphere is also likely to provide women with greater access to the police and other law enforcement agencies if they find themselves on the receiving end of online abuse. For politicians in particular, this appeared to be a broadly positive relationship, encouraging them to report incidents of online abuse or threatening behaviour. In addition, the police often work in co-operation with the Parliamentary security team, to monitor the social media accounts of politicians, as Patricia explained:

I was on a coach down to London for the People's Vote march[1] and the police called me to say they'd picked up this tweet and that they were worried. I hadn't even seen it. So, fair dues to the police for doing a good job there. They handled it really quickly. (Patricia, Member of Parliament until December 2019)

Charmaine illustrated how her staff had worked with the police and parliamentary security to identify a perpetrator of abuse:

I had one case where someone who made a threat towards me had sent multiple unpleasant tweets and emails in the past, and my staff recorded it all on a spreadsheet. So that was more ammunition for the police. So, the police went around and arrested him. Sometimes the police took action, sometimes it was more a kind of tracking

---

[1] 23 March 2019

and using parliamentary security services. I felt like parliament had really upped its game and the police took it really seriously. It felt that they were professional in providing that support, so that was good. (Charmaine, Member of Parliament until December 2019)

Loretta recounted a similarly positive relationship with the police in her constituency:

The [local] police have been amazing, they have taken this seriously from the word go. I know this is very different for my colleagues from all parties. From the point this all started, we have emailed [threats or abuse] to a point of contact, we've emailed with copies and screenshots of anything we've seen. And they've assigned a police officer to look at all of the communications from this person over the last couple of years, and the police have built a much bigger case from the cumulative effect of the posts, and linking them to stronger, more unpleasant language. The police have been really good. (Loretta, Member of Parliament)

However such positive experiences were not universal. Peggy demonstrated how, whilst generally well-meaning, the treatment she received from her local police force often necessitated having to relive the abuse she had encountered, which was traumatising:

When I initially received multiple rape threats [in 2015], I went to the police and back then I think they were less prepared for this sort of digital crime. I think they are better now. But like any victim of a crime, and violence against women and girls crimes seems to be the worst, the onus is on me to do the work. When I initially went to the police, they gave me hundreds of pages of evidence of people saying stuff to me [online], and I was expected to read though it all. I just gave up because it made me feel ill and I didn't want to do it. It's very, very time consuming and I don't have a lot of spare time. And that hasn't changed. To get a conviction against people who are perpetrating online abuse, I have to be caused harm; so the mechanisms that I would use to protect myself, they have to be undone in order for me to take cases to court. I will be caused harm, because I will read it and I will read the things about how they want to kill my children, and it's very harmful to me. And it's harmful to how I behave in the future. And there is a problem with that, it shouldn't be me who has to do it. (Peggy, Member of Parliament)

Peggy's experience reflects wider concerns about the way women are treated by the criminal justice system when they seek to report gender-based violence (Jackson, 2021).

Jane (2017a, p. 88) has been more forthright in sharing her view that criminal justice agencies have 'done little to support women, to bring offenders to account, or to even acknowledge the problem of gendered cyberhate as a problem', an assertion that is supported by the finding that the police in England and Wales rarely enforce legislation relating to online abuse (Salter, 2017).

The explanations presented for this are both diverse and complex and encompass issues of misogyny, power and freedom of speech.

For women employed in public facing occupations outside of the political sphere, and particularly those based in the USA, their interactions with the police when reporting online abuse were far more varied, which is more consistent with the findings of Jane (2017a) and Koziarski and Ree (2020):

> When I had received a threat online, I called the police and they literally said ... 'we have nowhere in our system to record this'. And they said we feel for you, but we have no way to record this information ... good luck to you. They were utterly uninterested. (Sophie, Academic and Journalist, USA)

> I have reported online abuse to law enforcement in the past, although nothing's ever come of it, so I've stopped doing that. (Judith, Journalist based in the USA)

Both Sophie and Judith chose to forego contact with the police when faced with episodes of online abuse instead seeking to block known abusers, or increase security settings on their online accounts. They implemented these solutions themselves, without intervention from criminal justice agencies, which they believed would be futile.

Catalysts for Online Abuse

It is not only the role that they hold that singles out women in public facing occupations for online abuse. The abuse is frequently exacerbated by the news cycle, the political landscape, the nature of the debate and certain key contentious issues, any (or all) of which can coalesce with an individual's perceived position of authority within an organisation to create a toxic combination where abuse appears to flourish. Sometimes abuse may be triggered by a trivial event or throwaway comment. Nevertheless, this study has discovered that there are certain issues that act as a catalyst for abuse. These issues are predominantly those that require people to adopt a binary position. Three issues which were repeatedly mentioned were the issues of Scottish independence, Brexit and gender identity.

Scottish Independence

The referendum on Scottish independence took place on 18 September 2014. In a hard fought, and often tempestuous campaign, Scotland voted by 55.3 per cent to 44.7 per cent to remain part of the UK (Mullen, 2014). The result was not uniform across the country, however, and some areas, including Glasgow and Dundee, voted heavily for independence (Mullen, 2014). Despite a decade passing since the campaign, Scottish politicians continued to identify the referendum as being a catalyst for online abuse, with supporters on both sides of the debate frequently engaging in derogatory communication.

> *I know there are some who want to tell us that the referendum campaign was wonderful, which Salmond[2] himself said was terrific and joyous, I can tell you it wasn't. It was utterly horrible, foul, nasty and abusive and it gave the public permission to be exceptionally bad. I was seeing it online. I responded to a comment which was 'scum out of Scotland' or something, and they just shouted abuse at me …*
> (Sally, Politician in Scotland)

Even politicians from other parts of the UK who expressed support for the 'NO' campaign (those wishing Scotland remain part of the United Kingdom), found themselves the target of abuse:

> *You would know if you posted something about campaigning to remain in the Union, that you would get this onslaught from Scottish Nationalists, or trolls or whoever. Within minutes, you'd get a hundred and something [tweets] based on what you'd said on Twitter.*
> (Loretta, Member of Parliament)

Wendy, a local councillor in Scotland, similarly felt that her position on the Scottish independence issue made her a target for online abuse:

> *The SNP, being the front for independence, we are a very targeted group in terms of online abuse.* (Wendy, Local Councillor)

The Scottish referendum campaign presented what some believe was the first orchestrated campaign of online abuse against women politicians in the UK:

> *I think the independence referendum was the first mass political campaign that generated online abuse, certainly in a UK context. I believe Scotland was the petri dish … for really rabid online abuse. It's not exactly a very proud thing for Scotland to have been first in! I don't know what the Scottish independence referendum would have been like without social media. It's hard to think how it could have been any worse.* (Klaudia, Politician in Scotland)

---

[2]Alex Salmond, who was Leader of the Scottish National Party at the time of the independence referendum of 2014 (Mullen, 2014).

Research in this area (McKay, 2020) confirms that the independence referendum of 2014 saw female politicians receiving a large amount of sexist and homophobic abuse. Set against a backdrop that depicts Scotland as an open and inclusive society that is more egalitarian than other parts of the UK (Nicolson & Korkut, 2022), it could be assumed that the online environment in Scotland is similarly equitable. The reality is very different, with research confirming the perpetuation of a gender gap in online political engagement, both throughout Scotland and the wider world. Men in Scotland are more likely than women to use social media and other online forums to discuss political and current affairs (Quinlan et al., 2015). The reasons for this are complex but are likely to include the enduring presence of sexist viewpoints that believe women in politics are subverting traditional gender norms (Childs, 2008), an ideology that is likely to be magnified in the case of LGBTQ women (Pedersen et al., 2014).

Many contributors felt that the continuing campaign for independence brings together several controversial issues:

I think there were different groups of people who I annoyed by existing. So, there was kind of Brexity, UKIPy people, there were the cybernats. Obviously the Brexity people said how dare I want to remain in the EU, the cybernats said how dare I want to stay in the UK, the Corbynistas said how dare I have been in coalition with the Conservatives! (Charmaine, Member of Parliament until December 2019)

The Scottish independence referendum was one of the first times that binary identity politics was felt so strongly by so many. Brexit is another. The Scottish independence referendum was about the idea of losing your country ... (Klaudia, Politician in Scotland)

In the run up to, and in the aftermath of, the Independence referendum, that's when it [social media debate] was at its most heated. And that's because we push people to extremes, and people become less tolerant of each other. And when there's only two answers to one question, that's compounded. (Julia, Politician in Scotland)

Julia continued, drawing parallels between the Scottish independence referendum, and other binary debates that have taken place in the UK since 2014:

There's no doubt in my mind that political culture's got harsher and less tolerant because we've been obsessed with binary questions. We face complex questions presented as having two easy answers when really, the truth is that you can't resolve these things with a tick box exercise ... (Julia, Politician in Scotland)

Since the evidence discussed here was collected, there have been major changes to the political landscape in Scotland, affecting both the Scottish and Westminster

Parliaments. In February 2023, the resignation of Nicola Sturgeon as First Minister and leader of the Scottish National Party (SNP) elicited widespread surprise (Carrell et al., 2023), which was only surpassed by the subsequent police investigation into alleged financial irregularities within the Scottish National Party (Gecsoyler & Carrell, 2023). Sturgeon's resignation came just weeks after the resignation of New Zealand's Prime Minister, Jacinda Ardern (Muzaffar, 2023), with the departure of two strong women leaders (Diers-Lawson, 2022) in quick succession increasing concern over the demands placed on women politicians (Cowper-Coles, 2020; Harmer, 2017). Pivotal to these concerns is the growth of online abuse.

Brexit

The neologism 'Brexit' was first coined in 2012 when it emerged in reference to debates about the UK withdrawing from the European Union (EU) (Fontaine, 2017). The subsequent referendum produced a national vote in favour of leaving the EU by a margin of 51.9 per cent (Matti & Zhou, 2017) to 48.1 per cent (Mavragani & Tsgarakis, 2019). Like the Scottish independence referendum, the decision to vote 'leave' was not uniformly reflected across the country, with wide geographic and demographic variations in the result (Matti & Zhou, 2017). The rancorous nature of the Brexit referendum campaign, coupled with the tortuous parliamentary negotiations that followed, as the UK government attempted to pass into law the results of the legally non-binding result (Smales, 2017), has led to a large amount of debate and scrutiny. There have been several studies highlighting the rise in online abuse that occurred in the Brexit referendum campaign and its aftermath (e.g. Evolvi, 2019; Gorrell et al., 2020; Ward & McLaughlin, 2020; Watson, 2019). It was unsurprising, therefore, to find that Members of Parliament had found themselves similarly targeted:

> *[Brexit] was vicious. There was an attempt to really make me feel as though I was not welcome here. And that was UKIP, and there's been some really vicious stuff in this area from UKIP. Really vicious stuff against other women.* (Patricia, Member of Parliament until December 2019)

> *I don't think they would have done that [online abuse] to the men. There are male MPs who took the same Brexit position as me, and both ultimately have lost their seats, but they didn't get the abuse. It was just legitimised. The lack of respect and the aggression was horrific.* (Phyllis, Member of Parliament until December 2019)

> *The Brexit referendum definitely polarised people... I am seen as just a Brexiteer. There's nothing more to my personality, according to some people online, than me being a Brexiteer, and that makes me terrible. [In their opinion] I'm scum, I'm a traitor, I'm all sorts of stuff, which I was never really getting before.* (Simone, Member of Parliament)

Despite being the target of online abuse, some were philosophical about the consequences of such a polarised debate, believing it inevitable:

> *In terms of Brexit … I received both abuse and support, both from Remainers and Brexiteers, because there was no way that you're ever going to make everyone happy in the Brexit debate. Broadly speaking, everybody got a level of abuse about Brexit because you couldn't have it otherwise. I campaigned for Remain, I also then voted for the deal because I think it needs to be over, and my constituents voted Leave, and so I was pragmatic in my approach towards Brexit … Everybody got a level of abuse. If I'd had been very pro-Remain, I'd have got loads of abuse from Brexiteers, and vice versa. I mean, some of the more middle-class abuse I got from Remainers was quite entertaining.* (Caroline, Member of Parliament until December 2019)

> *I think particularly after Brexit and the way in which politicians were treated by the media [online abuse increased]. Because it divided the country in two … there weren't many people who were indifferent! And therefore, by their very nature, they were going to be confrontational.* (Nicola, Member of Parliament)

However, what was surprising was that women in other areas of politics, such as Members of the House of Lords, and local authority representatives, were also targeted. Smita confirmed the rise in Islamophobic abuse on social networking sites post-Brexit:

> *Whenever something big happens, like Brexit, or if there's been a big terrorist incident … then I know that I've just got to deal with things online, in a different way. After the abuse I received during Brexit, I discussed it with other BME councillors, and we picked it up with the [council] leader, and she recognised it as a wider issue, and just said, 'look, if anybody feels that they are under attack or they are receiving abuse as a result of Vote Leave, then you've got to report it straight away', and I think she reassured us a little bit that we weren't on our own at that point. And then a lot of the colleagues around the room stood up and said, you know, I voted to leave but there's no way that I would ever endorse that kind of activity. So, that reassured us a little bit.* (Smita, Local Councillor)

Similarly, women across the other three occupations being investigated also found themselves receiving more online abuse both during and after the Brexit referendum.

> *I do think – this may just be a coincidence – my book came out last summer, which was after the Brexit vote, that there is a little bit more confidence among racists to be openly racist now, which they didn't have before.* (Linda, UK-based journalist)

> *We were involved in an investigation into something that was con-
> nected to the referendum. The abuse against me, from both sides
> of this argument, massively increased at that time. Whenever I've
> tweeted about the police's role in providing advice to government on
> the use of the EU powers, I get a lot of comments saying 'oh, she
> must be a Remainer', a complete poo-pooing of any professional
> views I might have.* (Sarah, Senior Police Officer)

Gender Identity

The third catalyst for online abuse is the issue of gender identity. Unlike the other
two events discussed in this chapter, this is a debate that has not been subject to a
public vote. Indeed, some have gone so far as to argue that it is a debate that has
occurred predominantly online (e.g. Colliver, 2021). Nevertheless, despite lacking
an overt and more traditional political platform, the debate around gender identity has gained a notoriety for generating online abuse.

Debate has centred around the awareness of the structural rights (Colliver,
2021) of (mainly) transgender women to access public spaces using their preferred
gender identity and the concerns of others that some single-sex spaces remain
(Aspani, 2018). In Scotland, this debate has coalesced around the discussions that
have arisen as a result of the Gender Recognition Reform (Scotland) Bill (2022)
(Pedersen, 2022). Debate on this issue has been notable in several ways. In addition to being located predominantly online, it has also brought together people
with a number of different intersectional identities and has proven challenging for
many women who have previously found their identities as feminists and champi-
ons of women's rights unchallenged by a dominant hegemony. However, in common with the Scottish independence campaign, and the Brexit referendum, this
issue has once again seen women in public facing occupations become the target
of unpleasant and violent abuse:

> *I just need to put a photograph of a [trans] flag out, and you get the
> abuse coming in. I receive online abuse fairly regularly because some
> of the things I put out on social media are clearly linked to trans
> rights and trans issues. I do find it quite upsetting. Most of what
> I put out is not controversial. But I get abuse back that's political:
> 'what are the police doing ... the police should be out locking up bur-
> glars', and all that kind of thing. That's one thing. Then there's the
> complete anti-trans stuff, which is really hurtful.* (Samantha, Senior
> Police Officer)

Samantha then discussed what had happened when she had tweeted about the
police using preferred pronouns:

> *I knew that it was always going to have a degree of controversy,
> because many people will say, 'what right has anybody got to tell me
> what pronouns I should be using?'. I knew that would be the case.*

I never expected it to get over one million views. I think if I had, I'd have probably spent a bit longer planning it. That said, I don't think I'd have changed anything about what I said. (Samantha, Senior Police Officer)

It was not just in the realm of criminal justice that gender identity was a point of conflict:

The gender identity issue has also led to a massive reaction. I tweeted something asking people to fill in a consultation response, something that's not controversial, just asking people to fill in a government consultation, and then I'll get replies to that, saying that I hate women, or that I am a misogynist. (Wendy, Local Councillor)

When I've been engaging very carefully in a debate around trans issues and whether trans women should be able to compete at the Olympics, on the back of something I tweeted, I had an email from an individual saying, 'we're watching your Twitter account, you tweeted two things from the Daily Mail, how dare you, if you tweet a further thing from the Daily Mail, you'd better watch out'. (Agita, Member of the House of Lords)

I will not engage in any conversation about trans rights, no matter what I think, because it doesn't matter how carefully people phrase what they're thinking. If you do it wrong … you get absolutely hammered. And it genuinely scares me. (Rose, Academic based in the USA)

Lack of Nuance in Debate

What these catalysts for online abuse share is a demand that individuals adopt an immovable position on a given issue. Such an insistence leads to the forming of very binary opinions. Many participants in this study highlighted this lack of nuance in important debates.

The increased polarisation of opinion, as described by participants in this research, echoes the work of Sunstein (2009a) on group polarisation, and Pariser (2012) on filter bubbles, first discussed in Chapter Four. Whilst not directly referencing either theory, participants did describe their concerns over the polarisation of debate. Of most concern, was the perceived lack of nuance in discussions that occur over social media (Harlow et al., 2020):

What's been demonstrated to me is that we've lost the nuance of debate. And I think that's one of the things that social media has exacerbated. (Esther, Member of Parliament)

In reality, lines are fuzzy and humans are awkward, and there will always be someone that you annoy. There will always be an exception to the rule, and [people online] do not want to deal with exceptions. They don't want to deal with nuance and complication and humanity. They want everything to be simple. If we don't manage to get a set of manners on how we interact on social media, and we spend more of our lives in fact on social media, then we lose the ability to debate. (Rose, Academic based in the USA)

One of the problems with our political system is nuance is dead. People are looking for ulterior motives and debate has gone. (Caroline, Member of Parliament until December 2019)

For Esther, a Member of Parliament elected for the first time in 2019, there is a link between the lack of nuance in debate, and both the Scottish Independence and Brexit referenda, which only offered a binary choice to voters on important issues. It has been argued that making decisions in this way traduces political debate and increases polarisation (Reisach, 2021):

I think we like to put people in boxes. We like to know what categories people fit into, before we can attach all our assumptions onto them, and I think there's no doubt that both referendums have been incredibly divisive. (Esther, Member of Parliament)

Speaking to people for this research has revealed support for a possible link between the lack of nuance in debate and a growth in intolerance, as suggested by Sunstein (2009a):

I feel that people are being radicalised and egged on by others [online] in a way that is much more impactful than a random group of friends that meet down the pub. A part of it is because people gravitate towards others that are like them, so the people who are most extreme find others who are extreme. (Charmaine, Member of Parliament until December 2019)

The reason we're in this situation is that we're in such a polarised world now … and social media really amplifies that. If you have a face-to-face conversation, there's much more nuance. [But when] you get on social media, suddenly you have to pick a side, then you have to stick to that side, and people dig their heels in. And you're not allowed to say, 'I don't know', or 'I haven't thought about it'. You have to have an opinion. And that's very dangerous, because if you look at [many] debates, you're not allowed to say 'I just don't know' because social media doesn't give you that space for grey. It's all very black and white. (Michelle, Journalist based in the UK)

Twitter can be very divisive. I think that nature of the beast has changed a lot over the years. It was very different ten years ago.

It was quite gentle; it wasn't the way that it is now. It's really morphed into something else since. I do think the extremist elements online are successfully dominating those platforms more and more, making it more difficult for everyday people with nuanced opinions ... most of us don't hold very extreme opinions ... to exist online. I think we're getting pushed further and further away. (Sally, Politician in Scotland)

Sally is not alone in identifying an increase in the polarisation of political discussion in Scotland. This issue was also highlighted by Bennett et al. (2021) in their identification of the various political cleavages in Scotland, including independence, Brexit and the relationship with the Westminster parliament. It is clear from both the literature and this empirical research that entrenched differences in opinion create silos not only between political parties but also within them, as the continuing fissures in both the SNP and the Labour Party have demonstrated (Julios, 2022).

Linda, a journalist based in the UK, felt that the voices most often heard in online debates were white and male, reflecting research undertaken by Kasana (2014) that reported that the most vocal online political commentators fitted that description:

If you happen to be a woman, or you happen to be a minority, and a minority woman in particular, then it's almost impossible to be heard without receiving abuse. It's really unfair. (Linda, UK-based journalist)

Linda made an important distinction, however, between opinions aired on online platforms and the reality. Her opinion chimes strongly with that of Bruns (2019), who is sceptical about the power attached to filter bubbles and echo chambers:

I think it's a very poor gauge of public opinion. I think the people who are on it [social media] are certain kinds of people. And it's definitely not representative of the population at large. And I think it's becoming more unrepresentative as time goes on, because of the extremist element who are so disproportionately active on it. (Linda, UK-based journalist)

Julia, a politician who has worked on numerous campaigns, agreed with Pariser's (2012) description of online filter bubbles, believing that political discussion that occurs on online platforms is likely to reinforce the views of those contributing:

It delivers on a confirmation bias, where you convince people that agree with you already that you are even more right in your outlook, but what you don't do is persuade people of your cause ... (Julia, Politician in Scotland)

Several contributors felt that the polarisation of debate in itself was a contributory factor in the growth of online abuse:

> *I think Brexit has changed the conversation in terms of what people think they can tweet.* (Agita, Member of the House of Lords)

> *In politics generally, the atmosphere is so toxic. I'm not sure we can divorce social media from everything else in this respect, it's just one of the more intense expressions of the horrible state that the country's in at the moment. The country's in a dark place. It's frightened, it's negative, it's scapegoating everything and everybody, including the European Union. Social media has become a really focused and intense expression of that.* (Patricia, Member of Parliament until December 2019)

> *If you dare to say, 'it's not as clear cut as that' [about any issue], then you're immediately attacked … they'll pile on. And otherwise-rational people tell you you're cruel and heartless. People get very worked up and they grab on to things very tightly and I think that creates an environment where abuse becomes a natural biproduct. As soon as you take this to its logical end, abuse is the end point, and it is almost always abuse of women.* (Rose, Academic based in the USA)

Consequences of Online Abuse

There are many consequences of experiencing online abuse. At an individual level, one of the main consequences is withdrawal from the online space. However, the consequences of online abuse are broader than this, and frequently extend into the occupational and organisational sphere.

Two further consequences of online abuse have been identified in this research: the occupational impact; and the framing of abuse as an attack on the wider organisation that women in public facing occupations represent.

There is a value in analysing the impact of online abuse at a wider level, namely the harm that is inflicted on an individual's occupation. Once again, the four public facing occupations of academia, journalism, policing and politics are scrutinised, drawing upon the experiences of women employed across these areas.

In October 2019, the House of Commons Joint Committee on Human Rights (House of Commons, 2019b) published the report of their inquiry into threats posed to Members of Parliament. Following a detailed investigation, the report concluded that 'MPs are regularly threatened with physical violence and are subject to harassment and intimidation whilst going about their wider public duties. This undermines our democracy and demands action' (House of Commons, 2019b, p. 3). It is a fact that MPs have always faced a threat to their safety. The terrorist murder of David Amess MP in October 2021 and the assassination of Jo Cox in June 2016 (Durie, 2021) are only the latest deaths of politicians. Before these most recent attacks, seven other Parliamentarians had been killed, including the Prime Minister, Spencer Perceval, who was killed in 1812 by a man who blamed the Conservative government for his wrongful imprisonment in Russia and Anthony Berry, who was staying at the Grand Hotel in Brighton when it was bombed by the Provisional IRA in 1984 (Power, 2019). However, the investigation undertaken by the House of Commons Joint Committee on Human Rights (2019b) identified that online platforms present a new source of hazard. The committee declared that:

> The advent of social media means that the whereabouts of MPs, whether at home or at work, are very widely known. Social media is important for MPs to communicate directly with their constituents and account for what they are doing on a regular basis. It can be a tool to foster democracy, to enable people to discuss the issues of the day and to allow people to learn about and assert their rights. But it is also used by people who anonymously threaten MPs and by those who whip up hostility and violence towards MPs. (House of Commons, 2019b, p. 5)

This concurs with research published by Amnesty International (2017) and is echoed in the empirical evidence presented here.

As well as having a significant negative impact on individuals, the online abuse and associated threats detailed in this study has a similarly malign effect on an individual's ability to do their job effectively. This has far-reaching effects on both their professional standing and their ability to serve the public in the way they intend:

> *It [online abuse] has an impact on my job. I find it really hard to do surgeries, I only have one surgery a month. I would love to do more, but to do four surgeries a month on my own … I wouldn't feel comfortable doing that. So, I do one a month, and I do that alone. I know my male colleagues do more. It limits my participation in politics.* (Wendy, Local Councillor)

> *Of course it [online abuse] does impact all the time, that's why we do the job in a totally different way than we did. So, for instance, I never advertise where I'm going to be. I used to do open surgeries all over the constituency: supermarkets, libraries. People would just roll up. Now, we do them all in the office, where we've got huge security. Every person who comes into the office, must provide their name, their address. If anybody's coming, we know who they are, where they live, and if we have any worries, we'll just do the surgery over the phone. It's massively impacted the way we do the job.* (Loretta, Member of Parliament)

It is not only politicians who face curbs on their occupational activity as a consequence of online abuse. As Veletsianos et al. (2018) reveal, women academics are also frequent targets for abuse, which damages their occupational impact. The demands of the Research Excellence Framework (REF) also expose UK academics to online abuse. The pressure to build professional collaborations (Kapidzic, 2020) and perform successfully in the REF leads many academics to increase their online presence, in a bid to evidence public engagement with their research (Barlow & Awan, 2016). But this in turn has led to an increase in the amount of abusive and threatening communication they receive. Writing in advance of the REF in 2014, Alison Phipps urged that 'HEFCE[3] and the higher education sector in general need to understand and acknowledge what they are asking academics to do, offer us better support, and pay particular attention to the problems faced by women in the public eye. It is harder for us to have impact in the first place – and when we do, it comes at a price' (Phipps, 2014, p. 1). Christie confirmed this when recounting her own experience, believing that the safety work (Vera-Gray, 2018) that women are necessitated to engage in is a manifestation of institutional gender bias:

> *It's unfair to say, 'well because you're a woman you need to operate differently and potentially limit career opportunities for yourself because it's unsafe'. That's just entirely unequitable. It's a real point of contention … I'm constantly having to unfortunately argue to do things that are less safe, for the purposes of my career.* (Christie, Academic at a UK university)

In the USA, academics must achieve tenure in order to obtain job security and career progression (Shreffler et al., 2023). One way that a candidate is judged suitable to be awarded tenure is through their level of public engagement (Tierney & Lechuga, 2010), with online platforms increasingly used as a mechanism for securing public engagement in research (Barlow & Awan, 2016). The targeting of women academics for online abuse and threats is having a deleterious effect on this process. Eileen is an academic from the USA; at the time of this research, she was on a secondment to mainland Europe but recounted her experience aiming to secure tenure in the USA:

> *My job is my ability to speak as an expert in this field. So, in the US we have the tenure system for faculty … basically you're in a job and then you have six years to demonstrate that you are an expert in your field, and if at the end of that time they say yes, you've demonstrated that, you get to keep your job. And if you don't, you're fired. And women are denied tenure at a much higher rate than men. And so, if something is affecting your ability to be an expert and speak out as an expert, and if you're dealing with harassment all the time, instead of writing papers, it just continues to widen that gap. And so online*

---

[3]Now the Office for Students and UKRI

abuse is not about thoughts and feelings. It's about how it affects my *job, and that affects my pay cheque, that's the bottom line. Online* *abuse has a real consequence to it.* (Eileen, Academic at a European university)

The early investigative work undertaken by journalists to document the existence of online abuse (Cranston, 2015), means that there is a larger amount of evidence of the online abuse received by women journalists than many other professions. In one of the first pieces of quantitative research to be undertaken into online abuse, Gardiner et al. (2016) analysed the comments that were made in response to articles published on the Guardian newspaper's website. Their study found that:

whilst the majority of our regular opinion writers are white men, we found that those who experienced the highest levels of abuse and dismissive trolling were not. The ten regular writers who got the most abuse were eight women (four white and four non-white) and two Black men. Two of the women and one of the men were gay. And of the eight women in the 'top 10', one was Muslim and one Jewish (Gardiner et al., 2016, p. 1).

As well as highlighting the gendered nature of online abuse, Gardiner et al. (2016) confirm the negative impact that intersectional identities have on those engaging online. More recent research has concurred with this view, emphasising that being the target of online abuse can have a negative impact for both the journalist and their publication (Searles et al., 2020).

Three journalists spoken to during this study recounted the impact that online abuse had had on their ability to work effectively:

There is one kind of online abuse that is becoming more common, *which is … taking offline action. So, they're calling your employer.* *I've heard stories about abusers calling the Department of Family* *and Children's Services, trying to have somebody's kids taken away.* (Sophie, Academic and Journalist, USA)

If and when I move on from [current employer], it will be really nice *not to do this every day.* (Michelle, Journalist based in the UK)

I've had people tweet at and call my previous employers saying that *I should be fired for my political views.* (Judith, Journalist based in the USA)

In comparison to the other three occupations being investigated in this research, there is little research into the experiences of police officers in relation to the occupational impact of receiving online abuse (Lee, 2020). This was borne out by the data in this study, which confirmed that police officers are less likely to receive online abuse that makes a direct threat:

> *What is interesting, and I can only conclude that it must be because I am a law enforcement professional ... perhaps they conclude that I can do more about an overt threat than an average member of the public.* (Sarah, Senior Police Officer)

This further strengthens the finding that police officers are more likely to be targeted for abuse that questions their integrity or ability or criticises their appearance, voice or age, rather than making direct threats.

Online Abuse as an Organisational Attack

By exploring the online experiences of different occupations, it is possible to reframe episodes of online abuse into organisational rather than a personal attacks:

> *I and other women I know, have given up real opportunities in our work, such as speaking engagements, because of threats and bomb threats to our organisations* (Ann, Academic and Journalist, USA)

> *I don't see [perpetrators] as dangerous. I think they're abusive, and I think they are trying to discourage you from doing the kind of reporting you do. Ultimately they're trying to discourage you from covering the topic that is criticising them.* (Linda, UK-based journalist)

For some contributors, realising that the online abuse they received had an organisational target, rather than being intended for them as individuals, made it easier to deal with:

> *When you look at the profiles of some of the people that dish out the abuse, they are anti-establishment, anti-everything. I look at them and think, I wouldn't want to meet you, I wouldn't want to have anything to do with you.* (Samantha, Senior Police Officer)

> *Some accounts ... every time you tweet something, immediately respond with some sort of insult, based on a real or perceived view they have of your organisation, or what it might stand for.* (Sarah, Senior Police Officer)

Impacts Specific to Women in Public Facing Occupations

Online abuse directed at women in public facing occupations can impact at multiple levels. Many of these impacts are specific to the public sphere due to the nature of the role and the public exposure that it often brings. This is especially the case in two key areas: the impact on women's participation in certain occupations and the wider impact on democracy.

On 4 July 2024, the greatest ever number of women MPs – 263 – were elected to the House of Commons (40 per cent of the total). Following this General Election, 46 per cent of Labour MPs are women, 24 per cent of Conservative MPs are women, and 44 per cent of Liberal Democrat MPs are women (Cracknell & Baker, 2024, p. 8). 90 non-white MPs were elected in 2024, 50 of whom are women (Helm, 2024). This makes the 2024 Parliament the most ethnically diverse in history, with 25 more non-white MPs than were elected in 2019. The majority of these are Labour Party representatives ($n = 66$) (Katwala & Rutter, 2024).

The 2024 General Election also saw 132 Members of Parliament stand down (Cracknell & Baker, 2024), a figure significantly higher than the 77 MPs who retired in 2019 (Belam et al., 2019). 33 of those standing down were women (Priddy, 2024). However, unlike in the run-up to the General Elections of 2019 and 2017, there was not a significant amount of media coverage citing online abuse as an underlying cause of these resignations. Whilst *some* women MPs did reference their experiences of online abuse as a factor in their decision making, with Mhairi Black, Dehenna Davidson and Joanna Cherry each mentioning the online abuse that they had received as a factor in their decision to leave the House of Commons (Drysdale, 2023; Ivers, 2023), there was less discussion of the issue of the online abuse of politicians in the 2024 General Election, than there was in other campaigns. It seems that this lack of coverage belied the reality on the ground. Jess Phillips, an MP who has spoken openly in the past about the online abuse she has received (e.g. Galpin, 2022; Ginsberg, 2019; Phillips, 2017), was heckled whilst making her acceptance speech following the most recent election. The reception she received prompted her to describe in visceral detail the morphing of digital threats into tangible physical dangers, claiming that 'this election has been the worst campaign I have ever been involved in' (Haynes, 2024, p. 1). In the days following the General Election, the Electoral Commission announced that they were launching an investigation into the treatment of parliamentary candidates, in response to reports of an increase in the harassment of those standing in the General Election, which 'did put people off campaigning, did put people off hustings' (Ouaguira, 2024, p. 1). Speaking shortly after polling day, the Chief Executive of the Electoral Commission, Vijay Rangarajan, said 'We also saw, in addition, a tremendous amount of online abuse of MPs, of candidates in general, and some of those were really quite disturbing - manipulated videos, misogynistic videos in particular' (*ibid.*). By summer 2025, the Electoral Commission report is yet to be published.

The General Election of December 2019 also saw what was then a record number of resignations ($n = 77$) (Belam et al., 2019). Just as in 2024, the reasons for the departure of so many MPs in 2019 were varied and undoubtedly affected by internal disputes occurring at the time in both of the two main parties. However, upon announcing their decision not to stand again, several women cited the online abuse they had received as a reason (Watson, 2019). For example, the former MP for South Cambridgeshire, Heidi Allen, told her constituents in an open letter printed in the local newspaper that:

> I am exhausted by the invasion into my privacy and the nastiness and intimidation that has become commonplace. Nobody in

any job should have to put with threats, aggressive emails, being shouted at in the street, sworn at on social media, nor have to install panic alarms at home. Of course public scrutiny is to be expected, but lines are all too regularly crossed, and the effect is utterly dehumanising. In my very first election leaflet, I remember writing 'I will always be a person first and a politician second' – I want to stay that way. So, I have reluctantly come to the decision that I will not re-stand when the next general election comes (Pengelly, 2019, p. 1).

This sentiment was shared by a number of politicians spoken to in this study:

My feeling when I lost was at first shock, and then the next day relief. It was just relief that I didn't have to put up with it anymore. That it was worth paying the price of losing my job, losing my career, and everything, because it meant the end of social media abuse. That's how much it weighed on me. I remember saying to friends, it's like being in an abusive relationship and if I saw a friend of mine like that I'd say get out, you're better than this, you don't have to put yourself through this, no one should have this just because they're trying to do their job. (Phyllis, Member of Parliament until December 2019)

When Brexit was at its height and divisions were strongest amongst political parties, I did hear a few of my colleagues say I wonder whether this is worth it, my family are upset. (Lauren, Member of Parliament until December 2019)

All of my children, at some point over the last two or three years have said to me, is this really worth it Mam? Do you really want to stand again? All have thought, perhaps you should just not do this anymore, which is quite a thing coming from the type of family that we are. There's quite a lot of people in politics at the minute, who have not been able to cope with it. It's had an impact on their health. (Loretta, Member of Parliament)

As well as affecting their own decisions to stand for public office, several politicians expressed concern about the possible impact online abuse could have on women choosing a political career:

I'm forever encouraging women to get involved, but I know one hundred percent there are young women that look at the replies that I get on Twitter and look at how I deal with things on Twitter, and they say to me, 'oh, I couldn't deal with that, I couldn't do that, I couldn't do what you do'. I know it's putting women off. (Wendy, Local Councillor)

I felt hypocritical, because [when I was an MP] I would go into schools on a Friday and encourage people to get involved in politics, going 'it's great, hopefully you guys will be MPs one day', and in my heart I was thinking I wouldn't touch it with a barge pole. (Phyllis, Member of Parliament until December 2019)

Two women (who had previously sought public office) revealed that their experiences of receiving explicit and violent online abuse had prompted them to seek alternative careers:

About fifty per cent of the reason why I'm not standing is because I am not putting myself up for public scrutiny in the way that Diane Abbott is, or Dawn Butler is, having no support or ownership from their own party. (Souad, Academic at a UK university)

One of the things that puts me off getting back into politics in a serious way is the compromise you have to make in terms of the persona and the realness ... I think that the two aspects of the abuse, the abuse that you get and the level of accountability that you are held to unreasonably, frankly drives anyone normal away from politics, and then you end up just having very ideologically driven sociopaths being the only people who are willing to get into that space, and if they fill the vacuum, it just makes matters worse. (Klaudia, Politician in Scotland)

Klaudia's view is echoed in research by McKay (2020), which confirms that the Scottish independence campaign led women politicians to receive a large amount of sexist and homophobic abuse. The reasons for this are complex, underpinned by cleavages in political opinion, social class and national identity (Bennett, 2021; Nicolson & Korkut, 2022). In addition, the enduring presence of sexist viewpoints which assert that women in politics are subverting traditional gender norms (Childs, 2008) remains a potent tenet (Julios, 2022). In addition, instances of misogynistic, sexist and racist abuse are frequently minimised (Scott et al., 2020) and branded as 'banter' (Scott et al., 2019, p. 122), creating an online environment that is hazardous to navigate.

It is not solely in the occupation of politics that there are problems of recruitment and retention. There is growing evidence that women from other public facing occupations are also leaving the workplace. Kavanagh and Brown (2020) highlight the deleterious impact that online abuse has on women academics, substantially harming their professional progress (Citron & Norton, 2011):

We have different tolerance levels. The thing that got me really involved in doing this [interview] was the number of women that I knew that were stopping their public engagements. (Eileen, Academic at a European university)

Similarly, whilst the number of women serving at a senior level within the police service has increased over the last decade, only a third of senior officers are women (Allen & Zayed, 2024). Evidence obtained for this study suggests that one of the many factors that may be acting as a disincentive to more women applying for promotion within the police service is the hostility that they may encounter online:

> *I do know a lot of women who have talked to me about not wanting to get into really senior positions because of online abuse. They just think that intrusion is too great.* (Imogen, Senior Police Officer)

If women serving in public facing occupations leave these professions, or choose instead to follow a career in the private sector, multiple negative consequences will result. These were succinctly summarised by Julia:

> *The idea that people might choose not to participate in democratic activities because of their fear of abuse, in a digital or a physical sense, I find really disturbing … I fear about the future of politics, because what you'll end up with is more very confident, privately educated, 50-year-old, white, middle-class men. We all pay a price.* (Julia, Politician in Scotland)

The organisational and structural ramifications associated with a decline in the number of women in public facing occupations, as predicted by Julia, could include a roll back in efforts to counter sexual harassment in the workplace (Jane, 2018), a widening of the gender pay gap (Kavanagh & Brown, 2020) and a policy vacuum at the heart of government. Ultimately, when online abuse forces women out of public life (in whatever form), the outcome is a further silencing of women's voices, this time at a level that jeopardises women's power and representation across society (Ginsberg, 2019).

In addition to these potential structural impacts that could be precipitated by the online abuse of women in public facing occupations, there is an even greater structural threat posed by pejorative communication – namely, a threat to democracy itself. Whilst such a claim may appear exaggerated, evidence gathered during this research has concurred with the findings of Gorrell et al. (2020), Krook (2020) and Majó-Vázquez et al. (2021) that the targeting of one section of the population for abuse, threat and violent invective in this way is of profound concern.

The potential threat to democracy posed by online abuse was most clearly articulated in this research by politicians, who recounted their experiences during the numerous Parliamentary debates following the publication of the European Union (Withdrawal) Bill. The Bill was first presented to MPs in July 2017 (Walker, 2021) with the passing of the European Union (Withdrawal Agreement) Act 2020 finally becoming law, having received Royal Assent, on 23 January (Walker, 2021). The tortuous legislative process, which included the resignation of Theresa May as Prime Minister and the 'snap' General Election of December 2019

(Prosser, 2021), was accompanied by numerous protests and demonstrations outside the Palace of Westminster (Elbaum, 2019), which frequently left MPs feeling at risk for their safety:

> *In that period outside of Parliament when we had all those demonstrators, it got very difficult at one point to walk down the street without people shouting after me and being told I was a traitor. This was from the Brexit side particularly. I knew it was going to be really hard and that's exactly how it turned out. There was an awful attempt to shout me down, I was having abuse thrown at me, online and in person.* (Patricia, Member of Parliament until December 2019)

Patricia proceeded to express her frustration with the advice that was given to Parliamentarians not to engage in certain activities:

> *When all the people were demonstrating outside, the Parliamentary authorities would say things like 'don't go over to interviews unaccompanied'. But that is what being an MP is all about. The media were camped out on College Green, and we were being asked to go out there and do stuff, and that's what MPs do.* (Patricia, Member of Parliament until December 2019)

Lauren also referenced the same demonstrations, emphasising the risk to the safety of those working within the Parliamentary estate:

> *It was especially hard when the Brexit debates were on, people were outside the Palace [of Westminster], chanting and goodness knows what else. Things got heated if there were protests, so I'd always make sure that my staff contacted me on the WhatsApp to make sure they got home safely.* (Lauren, Member of Parliament until December 2019)

It is important to note that it was not just in Westminster that MPs were being threatened:

> *Just before the run up to the General Election, with the 'Surrender Bill'* [4] *bollocks that Boris Johnson and his allies were advocating, there was a massive piece of graffiti appeared up in my constituency that called me a Nazi ... Now given how well documented my [Jewish] faith has ended up being, there are definitely interesting connotations to all of that. That completely freaked me out*

---

[4]Prime Minister Boris Johnson used the phrase 'Surrender Bill' in the autumn of 2019 to describe the European Union (Withdrawal) (No. 2) Act 2019, which the Conservative government opposed (Mason, 2019).

because I'd not had that kind of stuff in the constituency before. (Caroline, Member of Parliament until December 2019)

Some actions towards MPs were investigated by the police and remained the subject of criminal proceedings:

> *There are a couple of people at the moment who are on a charge. They have been charged with criminal offences from the Brexit angle because of an attack they made on me on social media. They threatened me with a weapon.* (Patricia, Member of Parliament until December 2019)

In its investigation into the abuse of MPs and the associated threat to democracy, the House of Commons Joint Committee on Human Rights (2019b) emphasised the danger of such threats:

> MPs should be able to get on with their work and with the job for which they were elected, vote without looking over their shoulder and freely engage with their constituents and the wider public. No MP should face a barrage of abuse for doing their work as a holder of public office. It is in no one's interest, if to stay safe, MPs retreat and become far more remote for constituents (House of Commons, 2019b, p. 23).

This assertion was substantiated by Phyllis, an MP until December 2019, who spoke about the impact that online abuse had on her ability to properly fulfil her responsibilities as a constituency MP:

> *You can't be a very good MP if you're protecting yourself. It's not just about the physical thing of being out there, it's a psychological thing. You can't be a very good MP if you're defensive and you think people are against you and everyone's out to get you and you feel threatened. You've got to go out there smiling and shaking hands and saying hello to everybody and wandering around being pleased to see them.* (Phyllis, Member of Parliament until December 2019)

Peggy highlighted how attacks made on online platforms can cross over into the offline space, becoming a genuinely physical threat:

> *A man attacked my office, because of what he thought I had said about people who voted Brexit. He was charged, and he was convicted of causing public disorder. I have since met with him and talked to him, which is good because it meant that I got to find out why he felt that way about me. And the reason that he felt that way about me was because of things he'd read about me by these people who troll me online. He said to me, 'I read that you said that people*

who voted Brexit were stupid'. So, I showed him a video of me at the People's Vote march where I'm stood on the stage in front of all the Remain campaigners and I start my speech by saying I never ever want to hear anybody saying that the people who voted Brexit are stupid. (Peggy, Member of Parliament)

Within the confines of the House of Commons chamber itself, the fear of the threat to personal safety had a huge impact on the behaviour of some politicians, who made decisions that ultimately risked jeopardising the democratic process:

Once we got into the votes against Article 50, or the votes against the Withdrawal Bill, any of those votes, there was a lot of stuff [online abuse] that looked like it was coming from the constituency, to give you the psychological frighteners, to criticise and undermine and get you to vote in a different way. I was worried about people's psychological resilience during large votes, so when we had a big vote on the Prime Minister's deal on Brexit, colleagues would go out and brief the media that they were going to vote with the Tories and then over the course of the day there would be a Twitter pile on, and then by the time it came to voting, there'd be twelve tonnes of anguish and then they'd vote with the Opposition. I'm worried that people's [MPs] minds were changed by social media. I'm worried about the fact that they can be swayed politically by it. I think that's bad for democracy. (Beth, Member of Parliament until December 2019)

I've sat in rooms with colleagues who have said that they voted, that they felt frightened about the way that they might vote and have changed the way that they were going to vote in Parliament, based on online abuse. It was women who were saying it. (Peggy, Member of Parliament)

There was one time where I had voted in a particular way and I was going to put something out on Twitter about it, but it was quite late at night, and I just thought, I really don't need this now, so I didn't say anything. (Lauren, Member of Parliament until December 2019)

Peggy highlighted that it was not just on debates around Brexit that politicians' votes were swayed by the impact of online abuse. The validity of other votes, including those on military action, and time limits on abortion, was also jeopardised:

In matters of war, I remember there was a significant amount of abuse sent to the women who were considering voting for the bombing in Syria, and I certainly suffered this. There was a huge amount of images sent to me of decapitated bodies and stuff, but those pictures were not in any way associated with allied forces. They were

> *not even in that country. You get quite a lot of that in the abortion debate as well, sending you graphic images of dead foetuses and things. And that can change… it won't change the way a person thinks, but it makes people [MPs] think I'm just going to abstain from this.* (Peggy, Member of Parliament)

Whilst it is politicians who are predominantly affected by the threat to democracy posed by online abuse, potential disruption to the democratic process as a consequence of online abuse is also felt by women in other public facing occupations. In the USA, the register of electors in many States is a public document, available for anyone to access (Bennett, 2016). Whilst some voters may request that their home address remain confidential, this is frequently only permissible if the individual can prove that they have previously been a victim of domestic violence (Roberts, 2024). Online abuse, targeting or other victimisation is not included as a reason for exclusion from the registers, leaving many women fearful of being targeted:

> *I have a friend who eventually just took herself off of the voting rolls because she was so anxious … and that's bad, right? Not being able to vote, as a citizen. But even if you spent a lot of time and money, which many of us do, removing our private information from the Web, in the United States at least, your address is public information if you vote. Also, something that I've been talking to legislators about, there needs to be a way for people's public information, their residential and private information not to be public facing, as a function of their being able to exercise their right to vote.* (Ann, Academic and Journalist, USA)

> *If you have very basic information about someone, and you know where to look you can find their information in the voter rolls; or if you're willing to lie you can buy a tranche of voter rolls very cheaply, that's likely to have your person in it. It's very easy, through the voting rolls, to find somebody's real address. I know people who don't vote because of this, who literally have been disenfranchised … because they decided that the risk calculus goes a different way for them.* (Sophie, Academic and Journalist, USA)

It is clear from the empirical evidence presented here that women across the public sphere are deeply concerned that online abuse is negatively impacting on the articulation of democratic freedoms in many countries:

> *These trolls are stopping us from exercising democracy in this country. That is the message I want to get out there. These people are stopping us exercising democracy. It is serious stuff that they're doing.* (Jill, Member of Parliament)

Negative online activity gives space and oxygen to the types of views and commentary or communities that polite good manners would have prevented previously, and it has an impact on how people are seen in the public eye, which is broader than them just not wanting to be in it. It is actually undermining. You're seeing people being taken down [online], and shamed, and that has a fundamental impact. It is not helpful for our democracy and for the way in which women are perceived in society. (Charmaine, Member of Parliament until December 2019)

The pollution of the digital space … which was once termed a great democratic space is anti-democratic. That's the sorrow of it. That we've allowed the information space to become so polluted that it's eating its own baby. (Helen, Academic based in the USA)

A number of the politicians who contributed to this study have now left the UK Parliament. Whether they had chosen to not stand again, or were beaten by an opponent, many found that once they had left the public sphere their online interactions both decreased and became less abusive:

Before the election, I said if I lost, the one thing I would do would be to throw my phone in the sea and not have any social media. And of course, I've set up my own Facebook account now, but actually it's nice to enjoy it as a normal person and member of the public. (Phyllis, Member of Parliament until December 2019)

I remember after the election when I lost my seat feeling I don't want to go onto Twitter because of the gloating, which I was sure would happen because the abuse was quite bad when I was a minister. And when I finally did go on a few days later I was like, woah, this is quite lovely, because it was like a tap had turned off. As soon as I lost my seat, the abuse stopped. (Charmaine, Member of Parliament until December 2019)

It all stopped once I was no longer in the public eye. I like the lack of pressure, I'm mostly quiet. I don't care. For me, not being in the public eye so much now, is good. It's a tool I can have, like when I want to go onto Twitter, I can choose how I want to use it. So I get in less bother! (Julia, Politician in Scotland)

The experiences of these three women upon leaving the political arena confirms the exhaustive nature of emotional labour (Hochschild, 2012), and the toll it takes on women across the public sphere.

However, despite the multifarious malign effects experienced and recounted by the women in this book, there remain huge benefits to individuals serving in public facing occupations as a result of having and maintaining an online presence. The data presented here have highlighted three key benefits of online interaction as a facet of work in public facing occupations, namely its value as a communication tool, the importance of having and maintaining a voice in the online space and the opportunities provided for mutual support, especially from other women also working in public facing occupations.

The benefits offered by the multiplicity of online platforms as tools to communicate with the wider public are potentially innumerable, but at the most basic level, include the opportunity to interact directly with constituents and other members of the public, beyond the confines of traditional media (Coleman, 2005), and the scope to gain a snapshot of public opinion in a much quicker way than would have been possible before the advent of the internet (Soontjens, 2021).

Despite their personal experiences, the vast majority of participants remained able to capitalise upon the use of online platforms as a means of communication:

> *I get an awful lot of casework come through Facebook. A constituent can contact me via Twitter, via Instagram, via any of those means, I think it's useful being that open and transparent, and giving people as many possible ways to get in touch with you as they can.* (Simone, Member of Parliament)

> *The social media accounts you have during the campaign you always maintain, so people are instantly able to contact you once you're elected. You walk in on a Monday and look at a laptop and the email is already up and running. People's expectations of contact and response are different to what they were twenty years ago.* (Esther, Member of Parliament)

> *It was a tool for me to communicate with my constituents. Sharing your insights with people and noting future predictions or observations that are slightly left field can be very validating, and that's one of the things where I think a different gender or different race perspective can come in and allow parity of being heard. So, that's why I think online platforms are important. Everyone's equal.* (Lauren, Member of Parliament until December 2019)

Even those who have now left frontline politics still appreciated the benefits of online interaction:

> *For me, even though I'm not in the public eye so much now, [social media] is still in some ways good. It's a tool I can have, like when I want to go onto Twitter and have a conversation, I can choose how I want to use it.* (Charmaine, Member of Parliament until December 2019)

The communication benefits were the most apparent for politicians, but women in other public facing occupations also harnessed the benefits accrued from having an online presence. Nevertheless, the threat posed by online abuse remained:

> *I wrote an article that was shared a hundred-thousand times or more. It actually does mean that people are interested in talking, and there was lots of positive stuff that happened, and I had lots of journalists and writers and historians got in touch, and that was really interesting. It created a community.* (Emma, Academic at a UK university)

> *You have to balance the benefit of tweeting out and informing people as to what it is that we are up to as an organisation, against being the subject of ridicule and abuse.* (Stacey, Senior Police Officer)

Academics including Crawford (2009), Jackson and Banaszczyk (2016) and Harp et al. (2018) have written in detail about the role that social media platforms have in giving women a voice, and many of the women contributing to this study support this viewpoint:

> *It's really important. It gives me a channel to the outside world, that I wouldn't otherwise have. Because we're a small party, and our political system and our media's quite hostile in a way to small parties. It is really important for me to have a way of putting my perspective out there* (Maya, Politician in England)

> *People have the right to information. National media has not shown themselves to be terribly adept at always promoting what is correct.* (Nicola, Member of Parliament)

In addition, several women spoke of the importance of maintaining their own Twitter account, as a means of having an 'authentic' voice, over and above the corporate channels of their organisation that were frequently run by internal PR teams:

> *I wanted to make sure that [my organisation] had its own voice separate to mine. [The organisation] can't say things that I can say, and vice versa, and I wanted to make sure that was clear.* (Souad, Academic at a UK university)

> *I have had over time, particularly from communications professionals, people suggest that they run my Twitter account. But then I think you do lose [my] voice, and over time it just becomes a corporate account which I think is less interesting.* (Sarah, Senior Police Officer)

> *I felt that it was important to maintain an authentic first-person presence on Twitter, because that was the most effective way of using it.*

> *People wanted to believe it was you and they were engaging with you,*
> *and that I was responding to things.* (Julia, Politician in Scotland)

However, as the online space has become more crowded, some felt that their ability to make their voice heard effectively had waned, and they found themselves moving away from social media:

> *Being in the public sphere I'm actually really introverted, and I think*
> *I just naturally gravitate away from places where there's noise, where*
> *I have to fight to be heard.* (Nicole, Academic at a UK university)

Balancing the desire to maintain 'authenticity', fight through the accumulated 'noise' within the online space and preserve personal safety highlights once again how exhausting working in the public sphere can be. It also has echoes of emotional labour (Hochschild, 2012), with much of this effort going largely unnoticed.

There is also clear evidence in the literature (e.g. Dragiewicz & Burgess, 2016; Huntemann, 2015; Salter, 2013) that women have sought out and formed a variety of informal networks to counter the personal and professional impact of online abuse. Over time, and as awareness of the issue has increased, these networks have become more occupation-specific, and it is now possible to access the support of academics (Hodson et al., 2018), journalists (Gardiner, 2018), police officers (Tomyn et al., 2015) and politicians (Al-Rawi et al., 2021) when faced with an onslaught of abuse as a result of activity in the public sphere. Furthermore, organisations such as Women's Aid, long tasked with supporting victims of gender-based violence in the physical space have also launched online versions of their services (Women's Aid, 2023), whilst other purely online campaigning groups have also been instigated, to both amplify the existence of abuse, and seek to mobilise a movement against such nefarious activity. A good example of this is the #EverydaySexism project, founded by Laura Bates in 2013, where women from around the world submit examples of the sexism they have experienced, in both the online and physical space (Bates, 2016). The campaigning organisation, Glitch, launched in 2017, focusses specifically on tackling the impact of online abuse in the public sphere, particularly for women of colour in the UK (Sobande, 2020). Glitch has had some notable successes, such as the 'Draw the Line' campaign in association with BT Sport (Glitch, 2021). However, this campaign focusses on combatting issues of racist abuse in sports, and whilst a worthy cause, is not specifically concentrated on addressing the underlying misogyny intrinsic to much of the abuse discussed in this research. For the women spoken to during this study, the importance of informal networks remained crucial, and far outweighed their use of more formal support mechanisms, echoing the findings of Hodson et al. (2018):

> *Our [senior] women officers group recognises the need to support*
> *one another, but that's not because we feel in any way isolated from*
> *our male colleagues. When I talk to colleagues who've suffered it*

[online abuse] and come out the other side, they say there's some-thing hugely affirming about how many supportive messages they get, how much action is taken that they don't have to ask for, so that you don't feel alone when it's going on, and that's really affirming. (Imogen, Senior Police Officer)

I think sometimes what has helped is talking to other female politi-cians about it, to say, 'oh well, it's not just me'. I watch out for other people as well, so when I've seen other people getting online abuse I kind of check in with them to see how they are. I've become much more aware of it. (Agita, Member of the House of Lords)

I get emails, because people know I work on this issue, saying things like 'oh I've a colleague who's going through this sudden deluge out of the blue, how do I help them?' ... Or 'I know a woman whose part-ner is stalking them online' ... it's become part of our job to triage other people – nobody's paying us for this, it is yet another tranche of women's work ... (Sophie, Academic and Journalist, USA)

Sometimes, this support had a protective purpose, especially during a Twitter storm or similar form of online attack, and can help turn the narrative from a negative to a positive:

When I see individuals receiving some sort of negativity, I always chip in with a positive comment, and you can see other people doing that as well. So, you can see that there's a lot more people trying to throw in more positive stuff, when there are individuals that have to be negative about everything. (Smita, Local Councillor)

I run my own social media accounts unless I'm being deluged by an online attack, at which point I have a few friends who will take it over for me temporarily, so that I can know what's coming in without having to drink directly from the feed. My roommate at the time of my first experience of online abuse was the first person to do it, and she just said, 'I will monitor [it], I will tell you what's going on'. (Sophie, Academic and Journalist, USA)

The informal networks forged online are even more vital for women of colour:

I have been online for twenty-five years, fully knowing that this is not a friendly space, this is not a safe space, but it's the only way I can contact my community of fellow women of colour who are political activists or activists ... We know this. And that means the commu-nity was also very quick at sharing information about how to protect ourselves and what to do. We share techniques and strategies; we speak up for each other. It's a constant process of solidarity that's

> *in place. We know we see the world differently. We are able to say*
> *uh-uh, we don't believe that.* (Emma, Academic at a UK university)

A number of women shared their own experiences, which confirmed how crucial informal support networks are for women experiencing online abuse in the
course of their work:

> *It is important too for women who were victimised ... when you join*
> *with other women it does help, you feel a little bit more empowered.*
> *We can be emboldened and able to take the forefront on some of*
> *these issues as long as we're not fearful of actual physical bodily*
> *harm.* (Tiprat, Academic based in the USA)

> *Women of colour have always come with that attitude [of distrust*
> *in the platform] online, as well as elsewhere, because frankly we*
> *know we can't trust the cops, we can't trust the institutions, we can't*
> *trust our employers. The only way it works is if we protect ourselves.*
> (Emma, Academic at a UK university)

> *In this day and age, when our leaders are really intent on leading by*
> *fear and division, connection is one of the most radical things we*
> *can be building with each other.* (Sophie, Academic and Journalist,
> USA)

However, whilst informal networks are valuable, there was also the call for
more formal support, financed by the technology platforms:

> *Somebody needs to be doing this work and the companies aren't*
> *doing it, at least not in any effective way and so we're all picking it*
> *up and no one even notices it's getting done ...* (Sophie, Academic
> and Journalist, USA)

> *We need to translate existing mechanisms of law into the online*
> *realm. And even though it doesn't necessarily help you in real time,*
> *there's some comfort in knowing you're part of trying to campaign*
> *for this stuff to improve. We're trying to do the heavy lifting to get*
> *those who wield power and have responsibility for these platforms, as*
> *well as the legal system, to catch up with the twenty first century and*
> *put protections in place that'll make things better for women now,*
> *and our daughters and their daughters and the generations that are*
> *coming after.* (Maya, Politician in England)

> *We're now seeing start-ups that are trying to find solutions to online*
> *abuse and harassment, all led by women. What we're seeing from*
> *younger women is a feeling of... 'I'm not putting up with this and*

you shouldn't either'. Younger women really want things to be better.
(Rose, Academic based in the USA)

However, whilst the empirical evidence presented here demonstrates the value of informal support systems and grassroots campaigning around the issue of online abuse, it is important to recognise that the opportunity to utilise support is not equally shared (Salter, 2013).

Conclusion

This chapter considers the facets of a career in public service that appear to initiate and exacerbate online abuse. The chapter has also identified three issues that appeared to provoke online abuse: the Scottish independence referendum of 2014, the referendum on membership of the European Union, which took place in June 2016, and the debate around gender identity. Whilst very different issues, all three of these topics are potentially binary in nature, forcing people to favour a particular 'side', a position that appears to be exacerbated by the nature of discussion on social networking sites (SNS), where there is a clear lack of nuance. The latter sections of the chapter outline the consequences of online abuse, at an individual, organisational and democratic level. The final section considers the role that online platforms play in providing a mechanism for mutual support for women in public facing occupations, and how these support systems, both formal and informal, can be particularly valuable for women who are members of minoritised communities.

Chapter Seven

Analysing the Policy Landscape on Gender-based Violence and Online Abuse in England and Wales

Abstract

This chapter provides an overview of the policy landscape on gender-based violence and online abuse, assessing the numerous developments that have been proposed in this area. The sporadic nature of policymaking is illustrated, with a discussion of the consequences of the lack of a comprehensive or structural approach to addressing online abuse. This chapter considers the emerging impact of the Online Safety Act which became law in October 2023, comparing the policy and legislative regime in the UK with other countries, highlighting the bifurcation in approach, with some places likely to prove better locations for women to work in public facing occupations than others.

Keywords: Public policy; criminal justice system; Online Safety Act (2023); regulation; legislation; feminism; campaigning

Introduction

Numerous proposals, initiatives, and legislation on gender-based violence have emerged over the last decade. Analysis of developments in this area reveals a variety of policy choices, all of which profess to tackle varying forms of gendered abuse. Such calls for action have been introduced piecemeal, often emerging in response to public pressure (e.g. Mantilla, 2015; Penney, 2020; Zakrzewski, 2020), or as Walby et al. (2014, p. 188) have vividly described (with reference to Jimmy Saville and Dominic Kahn), as a response 'to the violence that emerges into public view in the form of "scandals", when some famous man is accused of perpetrating gendered violence'.

Nevertheless, what has often been lacking is a comprehensive approach to addressing the gendered violence committed online. At the same time, growing concerns about the safety of women and girls in the physical space, particularly following the murders of Sarah Everard and Sabina Nessa in London in 2021 (Stöckl & Quigg, 2021), and the increase in domestic homicide during the multiple Covid-19 lockdowns (Rochford et al., 2021) have led to calls for a wider public discussion about the impact of male violence in society (e.g. DeCook & Kelly, 2023; Dungay, 2021; Grant, 2021; Zempi & Smith, 2021). This chapter presents an analysis of the policy landscape in England and Wales as it relates to online abuse and gender-based violence.

A Brief History of the Legislation on Gender-based Violence

In 1395, Margaret Neffield from York appeared in front of the ecclesiastical court to testify that her husband had caused her significant physical harm, including numerous broken bones. Despite hearing evidence supporting Neffield's claim from several independent witnesses, the court ruled that there were inadequate grounds to grant her a judicial separation and ordered her to return to her husband (Dwyer, 1995). This is the first recorded case of gender-based violence in England and Wales, emphasising the historical and enduring hierarchy by which men possess and control women (Dobash & Dobash, 1980), a patriarchal legacy which endures to the present day. Legislation prohibiting gender-based violence has been entered into statute since the 19th century when the abolition of the right of chastisement in 1829 outlawed a man's right to use physical force against his spouse – a privilege that can be traced back to the Roman era (Dobash & Dobash, 1980). However, despite this change in the law, the status of women in relation to men remained subordinate, arguably until the second wave of feminist activism emerged in the 1970s (Maguire & Ponting, 1988), with very little progress made in upholding the rights of women, or even acknowledging the scale of gender-based violence between the end of the first world war and the final third of the 20th century (Mooney, 2000). In the 1970s, feminist activists campaigned explicitly for the criminalisation of gender-based violence (Hester, 2006), with the pioneering work of Dobash and Dobash (1980) revealing the hitherto 'hidden' crime of domestic abuse (Walklate, 1995). However, despite the passing of the Domestic Violence and Marital Proceedings Act (1976), which provided the first intervention by the criminal law into acts of domestic abuse (Williams & Walklate, 2020), and the Domestic Proceedings and Magistrates' Court Act (1978), which extended the powers available to magistrates to enable them to grant personal protection orders that excluded an abusive spouse from the matrimonial home, providing there was evidence that harm would be caused to residents if the individual remained in the property (Graham Hall, 1978), there is copious evidence that gender-based violence remained an issue of little importance in criminal justice policy for much of the 20th century (Walby et al., 2014). Furthermore, it is important to remember that like much of the law in this area at the time, this legislation only applied to married, heterosexual couples.

This lackadaisical attitude is exemplified by the comments of the then Commissioner of the Metropolitan Police, Sir Kenneth Newman, who in 1984 expressed that he wanted to shed the police's responsibility for gender-based violence: describing it as 'rubbish' work that was not a police matter (Radford & Stanko, 1991). For until the end of the 20th century, the legislation proscribing gender-based violence within relationships applied solely to physical assault, as rape within marriage was not criminalised in England and Wales until 1991 (1989 in Scotland) (D'Cruze, 2011), even though sexual and physical assault in interpersonal relationships commonly occurs simultaneously (West, 2004). Until the law changed in 1991, rape remained a man's marital right and a woman's marital duty (Renzetti, 2013).

In April 2021, after successfully navigating a legislative path that was fraught with obstacles (Bennett et al., 2019; Solace Women's Aid and the Justice Studio, 2021), the Domestic Abuse Act became law (Home Office, 2021), and in doing so, provided a legal definition for the offence of domestic abuse (Stephens et al., 2021). This legislation contained a number of important legislative changes, including recognition of emotional and economic abuse, and the frequent occurrence of both within coercive control (Hulley, 2021). Other policies contained in the Act include the addition of non-fatal strangulation as a specific offence (Ministry of Justice, 2022) and the confirmation of the existing criminal law that places important restrictions on the 'sex games gone wrong' defence when such activity leads to femicide (Yardley, 2021b), as well as a legal obligation upon local authorities to provide accommodation for domestic abuse victims and their children (Holt & Lewis, 2021). The legislation also brings the provisions on coercive control contained in the Serious Crime Act (2015) into this wider ordinance on domestic abuse. However, whilst the then Conservative government described this new law as providing 'landmark protection' (Home Office, 2021, p. 1) to victims of domestic abuse, the legislation has also been criticised, with 'the removal of "violence" as a key rubric [suggesting] a "watering down" or obfuscation of the serious and gendered nature of domestic violence and abuse' (Aldridge, 2021, p. 1824). There are concerns that this latest piece of legislation is incongruous with the efforts being made to strengthen policies protecting women and girls from gendered violence (Aldridge, 2021) and perpetuates the undermeasuring of the crime (Walby et al., 2014). Furthermore, despite evidence of a link between online abuse and gender-based violence (Lewis et al., 2017; Southworth et al., 2007), there is no mention of either technology-facilitated sexual violence (Henry & Powell, 2015) or technology-facilitated coercive control (Dragiewicz et al., 2018) (or any form of online abuse) within the Domestic Abuse Act (2021).

Further development of policy around gendered violence was announced by the then Home Secretary, Suella Braverman in 2023. This statement included a pledge to add the most dangerous domestic abuse offenders to the Violent and Sex Offender Register, including violence against women and girls within the

Strategic Policing Requirement and piloting new Domestic Abuse Protection Notices and Orders (Braverman, 2023). It remains unclear how many of these aims were enacted before the election of the Labour government in July 2024 (Lloyd, 2024).

Legislation on coercive control was first introduced in 2015 when Section 76 of the Serious Crime Act (2015) made it a discrete offence (Wiener, 2017). The most recent guidance on coercive control, issued by the Crown Prosecution Service in April 2023 (CPS, 2023), provides a list of actions that can indicate the presence of coercive and controlling behaviours in intimate or family relationships. The introduction of this law in England and Wales in 2015 evidences a recognition in law of the wider scale of gender-based violence offences. This extends the narrow definition of gender-based violence first enshrined in statute (Stark, 2009) to include sexual, psychological and economic abuse (Heise et al., 1999).

Whilst the passing of the offence of coercive control was a watershed moment, with the UK[1] becoming one of the first countries in the world to pass legislation on coercive control (Nugent, 2019), prosecutions of coercive control offences remain low, partly due to a difficulty (or possible reluctance) from the police to gather necessary evidence (Lewis et al., 2018; Wiener, 2017). This, along with a recurrent failure to secure convictions for rape and other sexual offences (Brown, 2011; Daly, 2021), has echoes of the police's lackadaisical response to physical gendered violence evidenced in the 1970s and 1980s (Radford & Stanko, 1991).

Statutory Responses to Cybercrime and Online Abuse

There is widespread recognition that there was an increase in the number of cases of domestic violence during the period of the Coronavirus pandemic (Sasidharan & Dhillon, 2021). At the same time, there was an analogous increase in the number of cybercrime offences being reported to the police since the multiple Covid-19 lockdowns of 2020 and 2021 (Buil-Gil et al., 2021). This increase in reporting has put a strain on police resources (De Kimpe et al., 2020) whilst also causing problems for a service organised on local boundaries confronted with offending that can be perpetrated by or enacted upon people based in different locales (Koziarski & Ree, 2020). Furthermore, many police officers remain unfamiliar with the specificity of online offending (Wall, 2007) and may fail to appreciate its seriousness and complexity. When combined, these issues serve to exacerbate an underlying public concern that the internet is unsafe (Wall, 2008). This may contribute to a decline in police legitimacy, as people lose trust in the ability of the police to prosecute cybercrime offences successfully (Koziarski & Ree, 2020). Evidence from the literature combines to suggest that both the Crown Prosecution Service and law enforcement remain at a disadvantage when attempting to confront online abuse and other forms of cybercrime. This is largely due to a lag in responsiveness in policy formulation and implementation (Jane, 2017a), which

---

[1]Scotland passed similar legislation in 2018, which also covers former partners (Burman and Brooks-Hay, 2018)

leaves organisations constantly on the 'back foot' in the face of constantly evolving technology.

For this reason, the criminal justice system in England and Wales, in common with criminal justice systems elsewhere, has frequently appeared unable to respond to the threat posed by online abuse (Barker & Jurasz, 2018). Nevertheless, an increased awareness of the phenomenon has led to a greater analysis of existing legal sanctions surrounding this behaviour. In October 2016, the Crown Prosecution Service issued guidelines regarding the prosecution of cases involving social networking sites (CPS, 2016), highlighting that some 15 existing pieces of legislation can be used to prosecute individuals accused of sending online abuse, including the Offences Against the Person Act 1861, the Protection from Harassment Act 1997, the Malicious Communications Act 1988, and the Serious Crime Act 2015 (CPS, 2016). The multiplicity of this legislation mirrors the application of legislation in relation to gender-based violence, where, unlike countries such as Cyprus and Sweden (Walby et al., 2014), the UK (until 2021) has tended to apply general law rather than introducing discrete legislation. This may perpetuate the perception that online abuse is not a significant issue, and as with gender-based violence, it frequently remains a 'hidden' crime (Radford & Harne, 2008). Despite the absence of online abuse from the Domestic Abuse Act (2021), there is clear evidence of technology being used in offences of coercive control, whether in the installation of tracking devices on victims' mobile phones or enabling remote access to the home computer (Wiener, 2017); using surveillance devices such as Air Tags or Ring doorbells (PenzeyMoog & Slakoff, 2021) or by removing victims' access to the technology that facilitates relationships with others, such as text messaging and access to social networking sites (Fernet et al., 2019). All such activity is mentioned within the Crown Prosecution Service's guidance on the offences that constitute coercive control (CPS, 2023).

Jane (2017a, p. 88) has argued that criminal justice agencies have 'done little to support women, to bring offenders to account, or to even acknowledge the problem of gendered cyberhate as a problem' an assertion that is arguably strengthened by the finding that the police in England and Wales have rarely enforced legislation in relation to online abuse (Salter, 2017). It was hoped that this situation would improve once the Online Safety Act was passed into law in October 2023.

The Online Safety Act (2023)

The growth in online abuse across multiple countries has led to a growing demand for regulation of social networking sites and other online platforms. Campaigners have long called for the introduction of robust regulatory frameworks to limit the dissemination of hate speech and threats of gender-based violence articulated via the internet (e.g. Citron, 2014; Suzor et al., 2019; Taddeo & Floridi, 2016; Waterson, 2018). In the UK context, this was emphasised in the White Paper on online harms, published in 2019, which stated that:

> [...] we should not ignore the very real harms which people face online every day. In the wrong hands the internet can be used to

spread terrorist and other illegal or harmful content, undermine civil discourse, and abuse or bully other people. Online harms are widespread and can have serious consequences. ...We cannot allow these harmful behaviours and content to undermine the significant benefits that the digital revolution can offer. ... This White Paper therefore puts forward ambitious plans for a new system of accountability and oversight for tech companies, moving far beyond self-regulation. A new regulatory framework for online safety will make clear companies' responsibilities to keep UK users, particularly children, safer online with the most robust action to counter illegal content and activity (House of Commons, 2019a, p. 3).

This view was reinforced by the House of Lords Select Committee on Democracy and Digital Technologies (2020, p. 6), which declared that 'there is a need for Government leadership and regulatory capacity to match the scale and pace of challenges and opportunities that the online world presents'. Whilst the Committee felt that the government's White Paper 'presents a significant first step towards this goal' (*ibid.*), they also stressed that 'it needs to happen; it needs to happen fast; and the necessary draft legislation must be laid before Parliament for scrutiny without delay' (*ibid.*). Despite the urgency placed on the necessity for primary legislation, it took six years for the Online Safety Bill to become law. In the time that the draft bill was making its way through Parliament, it was heavily diluted (Elgot, 2022), with a total of four Prime Ministers and seven Culture Secretaries removing different aspects of the original legislation since the White Paper was published in 2017. The Online Safety Act eventually passed into law in October 2023. However, the Act is now predominantly focussed on protecting children from digital harms, with the original plans to protect adults, such as the proposal to impose criminal sanctions on senior executives whose platforms enabled misogynistic abuse, disappearing completely. The current Online Safety Act only addresses existing illegal harms and makes minimal mention of violence against women (Glitch, 2023). Indeed, it appears that the UK has gone from seeking to be the 'safest place in the world to be online' (DCMS, 2017, p. 1), to being overtaken in this aim by numerous other countries. Furthermore, no political parties had policies to tackle the online abuse of adults in their manifestos for the 2024 General Election. In contrast, the Digital Services Act, which was passed by the European Parliament in July 2022 (Mazúr & Gramblicková, 2023), brought comprehensive regulation of digital platforms into law across all EU Member States on 1 January 2024. The Digital Services Act seeks to provide a 'uniform level of protection throughout the Union' (Turillazzi et al., 2023, p. 86), involving the regulation of content and strict rules for social media companies to follow, underpinned by a system of fines.

Participants in this research felt that regulation of social media platforms was a vital step in making the online space a safer environment for women:

> *I think more regulation is required. If social media is going to be used for responsible reasons, then they do need to exercise more*

control over the platform, because it's not a free platform, it is owned
by a company that should have more regulated responsibilities for
how that platform is used, because they're profit-making companies.
So, like any other profit-making company, they have responsibility
for the safety of the people using it. (Geetika, Senior Police Officer)

It is not only in the EU that regulatory and legislative activity of social networking sites is occurring. In 2019, the Kenyan government appointed a Data
Protection Commissioner to enforce data governance regulations (Houghton,
2023). According to Amnesty International, this legislation, which includes strict
rules on the activities of social media companies, places Kenya ahead of both
Europe and the USA in terms of data governance (Houghton, 2023). In 2021,
the Australian Online Safety Act introduced a number of safeguards designed to
improve online safety (Gizzo et al., 2022). In contrast to the UK's Online Safety
Act, this legislation contains specific provisions outlawing technology-facilitated
gendered violence against adult women (Gizzo et al., 2022). Meanwhile, in New
Zealand, in 2023, the then Labour government undertook a public consultation
to review existing laws around media platforms in order to provide safer online
services – which included specific reference to the plan to outlaw misogynistic hate
speech that occurs online (New Zealand Department of Internal Affairs, 2023).
However, following a concerted campaign by two freedom of speech campaign
groups, which saw 18,978 of the 20,281 submissions received via pro-forma tem-
plates originating from the 'Voices For Freedom' and 'Free Speech Union' websites (New Zealand Department of Internal Affairs, 2024), along with the election
of a new right wing coalition following the General Election in October 2023
(Corlett, 2023), plans for any legislative change were 'quietly dropped' (Donnell &
Peacock, 2024, p. 1).

As evidenced by the public consultation in New Zealand, regulation of the
online space remains highly contested. Many concerns are based around issues of
freedom of speech, particularly in the USA (Mantilla, 2015). Furthermore, there
is a concern that the introduction of regulation could lead to greater surveillance
from both corporate and state bodies (Duffy & Chan, 2019). This has led to a
wider discussion about the potentially malign consequences of online engagement on individuals' privacy (Marwick & Hargittai, 2018), personal information,
and wider freedoms (Trottier, 2015). In addition to these ideological concerns is
the practical challenge of how global platforms that are owned by private corporations can be effectively regulated and policed by individual nation states (Yar &
Steinmetz, 2019). This dilemma has arguably led to a fragmented regulatory
response (Phillips, 2009). Whilst libertarians insist that the internet should remain
a bastion of freedom (Wessels, 2010), the reality is more complicated. There is an
argument that suggests that the way that online platforms operate is in itself in
opposition to freedom of speech (Poland, 2016). This opinion posits that, rather
than viewing online platforms as a medium designed to extend freedom on the
internet, social media companies can instead be viewed as a central point of control, acting as 'intermediaries [that are] providing citizens with access to the digital
public sphere' (DeNardis & Hackl, 2015, p. 761). Furthermore, the predominance
of wealthy white men leading social media companies (Suzor et al., 2019), their

location and focus on a North American audience (*ibid.*) means that only some voices are heard. It is men that continue to hold the power in the online space, as evidenced by who owns and manages the big tech platforms, namely, rich white men (Salter, 2017). The online space, therefore, replicates and reinforces existing inequalities, ensuring that it is the same voices that remain prominent – those of white men. This observation was further emphasised by Emma:

> *To me there's no difference between online and real life, I mean, all our cities, all our villages, all our roads, all our public spaces are meant to exclude women. Any space we occupy is despite the best efforts and despite the design. It's not because they were made for us.*
> (Emma, Academic at a UK university)

The takeover of Twitter by Elon Musk in October 2022 (Rohlinger et al., 2023) led to a significant reduction in the use of content moderation and the suspension of abusive accounts on the platform. The most notable of these changes was the lifting of the 'ban' on President Trump, which was imposed following the riots in the US Capitol in January 2021 (Arbel, 2021). Musk reinstated Trump's Twitter account on 20 November 2022 (Karell & Sachs, 2023), following a poll on Twitter which allegedly saw 52 per cent of the 15 million participants vote in favour of rescinding the ban (Hendricks & Schill, 2024). One development that has been observed since the beginning of Musk's tenure is the rise of – or what some would argue (e.g. Brown, 2022) is a return to – the use of the platform by political extremists seeking to promote a radical populist agenda (Barrie, 2023). Given Musk's own declaration that he is a 'free speech absolutist' (Witalisz, 2023, p. 5) and his commitment to remove existing restrictions previously placed upon Twitter's most controversial users (Witalisz, 2023), this should not be a surprise.

The disseminating of false information via Twitter was a topic of concern well before Musk's $44 billion purchase of the platform (Jia & Xu, 2022).

This is evidenced by analysis of the accounts suspended by Twitter for infringing their terms and conditions in three national elections that were held in France, Germany and the UK in 2017 (Majó-Vázquez et al., 2021), which showed that it was only accounts articulating opinions drawn from the most extreme ends of the political spectrum that were sanctioned and that action was overwhelmingly focussed on accounts that were believed to be spreading misinformation, rather than personally abusive or violent tweets (Majó-Vázquez et al., 2021). The same study revealed that decisions regarding the suspension of social media accounts were predominantly made 'unilaterally by private, for-profit companies with little accountability, oversight, or transparency' (Majó-Vázquez et al., 2021, p. 13). This confirms that technology is not value neutral (Murray, 2000) and that it instead magnifies issues of everyday life, absorbing and amplifying the beliefs and experiences of those responsible for its design (Boyd, 2015).

The endurance of libertarian theories within computer-mediated communication first discussed in Chapter Two means that the regulation of online platforms is highly contested. Many concerns are based around issues of freedom of speech, particularly in the USA, related to the First Amendment of the US Constitution (Mantilla, 2015). As also demonstrated in the recent public consultation on online regulation carried out in New Zealand (New Zealand Department of Internal Affairs, 2024), many freedom of speech advocates feel that any attempt at controlling the content displayed on social media platforms would undermine freedom of expression (Citron, 2014). Furthermore, as both the influence and scope of computer-mediated communication increase, there is a concern that the introduction of regulation could lead to greater surveillance from either (or both) corporate and state bodies (Duffy & Chan, 2019). This has led to a wider discussion about the potentially malign consequences of online engagement on individuals' privacy (Marwick & Hargittai, 2018), personal information, and wider freedoms (Trottier, 2015). In addition to ideological concerns is the practical challenge of how global platforms that are accessed worldwide and owned by private corporations can be effectively regulated by individual nation states (Yar & Steinmetz, 2019). This dilemma has arguably led to a fragmented or non-existent regulatory response (Phillips, 2009), which has only escalated as new pieces of legislation have been introduced. Whilst there is widespread support for regulation of social media platforms to protect women from technology-facilitated gendered violence at the grassroots in many countries, there remains no universal worldwide regulatory regime. Consequently, developments in different countries are leading to a bifurcation in approach, with some places better locations for women to work in public facing occupations than others.

Campaigning Against Gender-based Violence

Alongside an increase in legislative activity, the past 25 years has seen a growing awareness from the third sector of the danger posed by gender-based violence (Matczak et al., 2011). In 1993, the UN General Assembly passed the Declaration on the Elimination of Violence against Women, with the aim of advancing international policies and legislation to eradicate gender-based violence (UN, 1993); whilst in 1996, the World Health Organisation declared gendered violence a major public health issue (Krug et al., 2002). The policy advances made by these two organisations were followed in quick succession by organisations such as the World Bank, the European Union, and Amnesty International (Joachim, 2007), reflecting the growth in awareness of gender-based violence as an issue, and building on the work done by the feminist campaigners of the 1970s and 1980s. Within this mix, organisations working in local communities, including Refuge, Rape Crisis and Women's Aid remain of fundamental importance in advancing the policy agenda (Matczak et al., 2011). However, despite the increased legislation on this crime since Margaret Neffield's unsuccessful attempt to gain a legal separation from her husband on the grounds of his violence in the 14th century (Dwyer, 1995), it is estimated that in 2022, some 89,000 women worldwide were intentionally killed (UNODC, 2023), the highest number for over 20 years. 54 per cent or 48,800 of these women were killed by a partner or family member (UNODC, 2023). This means that, on average, more than 133 women or girls were killed every day by someone in their own family, a number that is increasing annually (UNODC, 2023, p. 5). The Femicide Index (2023), collated annually by feminist campaigners (Rogers, 2021), recorded 100 women killed by men across the UK between 1 January and 31 December 2023. The latest statistics gathered from the Crime Survey for England and Wales report that in 2023, some 1.4 million women experienced domestic abuse (Jones, 2023); a figure is likely to be higher in reality because gender-based violence remains a predominantly 'hidden' crime (Radford & Harne, 2008).

Policy Response to Misogyny

Several investigations have been undertaken in the UK around hate crime and online abuse (e.g. Amnesty International, 2017; Home Affairs Select Committee, 2017; House of Commons, 2019b; House of Lords Select Committee on Democracy and Digital Technologies, 2020). Many of these investigations have considered (both directly and indirectly) the role played by misogyny, and as awareness of gendered online abuse has grown, the calls for misogyny to be categorised as a hate crime have increased, all of which have been rejected. The latest pronouncement on the issue came in 2021 when the Law Commission announced that 'sex or gender should not be added as a protected characteristic for the purposes of aggravated offences and enhanced sentencing' (Law Commission, 2021, p. 208). Law Commissioners felt that there was a lack of consensus in the best way to apply hate crime legislation to acts of violence against women and girls, and a concern that making misogyny a hate crime was not the most effective way of dealing with crimes of this nature, recommending instead that the government consider introducing a specific offence to tackle public sexual harassment, which it felt would be more effective.

In the General Election of 2024, all opposition parties declared that if elected, they would change legislation to categorise misogyny as a hate crime (Law Commission, 2021; McKiernan, 2024). The Labour Party manifesto for the election stated that 'Violence and abuse against women and girls does not come from nowhere. Misogyny is one root cause, and therefore Labour will ensure schools address misogyny and teach young people about healthy relationships and consent. We will ensure police forces have the powers they need to track and tackle the problem' (The Labour Party, 2024, p. 68). However, the King's Speech given to Parliament on 17 July 2024 made no mention of misogyny (HM Government, 2024).

Whilst there remains no law in this area, a successful pilot treating misogyny as a hate crime was carried out by Nottinghamshire police in 2016. This pilot has since been adopted by several police forces across England and Wales (Mullany & Trickett, 2018).

The Policy Landscape

The relative paucity of academic research into online abuse in the years since Web 2.0 has undoubtedly delayed the development of policy in this area (Barlow & Awan, 2016). This in turn contributed to the languid introduction of legislation in this area (Hardaker & McGlashan, 2016), a finding demonstrated yet again by the absence of online abuse from the most recent legislation on domestic abuse in England and Wales. Legislation as evidenced in the form of Acts of Parliament is important, as it provides key definitions of offences that can then be operationalised by criminal justice agencies, whilst in the longer term also changing social norms, and ultimately containing the potential to 'transform online subcultures of misogyny to those of equality' (Citron, 2009, p. 404). However, as Citron (2009) confirms, the failure of legislative bodies, criminal justice agencies and social policy institutions to take decisive action in this area sends a message to those engaged in online abuse that such behaviour will not be investigated robustly, whilst simultaneously signalling to women that their experiences of abuse will not be taken seriously. In this way, online abuse both perpetuates the inadequate treatment of gendered violence witnessed in the physical space and allows technology to act as an amplifier for many forms of misogynistic abuse.

The responsibility for the inertia in tackling online abuse is shared between governments, law enforcement agencies and private technology firms (Jane, 2016) and requires action at three levels – the personal, the organisational and at a societal or cultural level (Hodson et al., 2018). Hodson et al.'s (2018) framework is a useful mechanism for summarising the multiplicity of policy recommendations found in the literature, whilst also confirming that the failure to tackle online abuse has occurred at every level (Jane, 2017a).

Individualised Responses to Online Abuse

It is impossible to make policy recommendations that can be universally enacted at a personal level. Nonetheless, given the finding that the vast majority of those receiving online abuse rarely involve law enforcement agencies (Jane, 2017b), the measures taken by women at an individual level to tackle online abuse deserves recognition. The individual strategies adopted by women may include seeking informal advice support from family members (Hodson et al., 2018), or from a wider feminist 'sisterhood', created to directly challenge online abuse (Antunovic, 2019). However, whilst personally valuable, it appears that many women have chosen to respond to receiving online abuse in this way *because* of the paucity of the legislative, occupational or criminal justice sector response (Jane, 2017b). Tackling online abuse at a personal level, without recording or reporting it, results in the extent of online abuse being perpetually under recorded (Backe et al., 2018) and contributes to the often-hidden nature of the offence (Campbell, 2017), and its links with victim blaming (Lewis et al., 2017).

Organisational and Governmental Responses to Online Abuse

It is at an organisational level that the greatest action is required, from both the public and private sectors. Ideally, this would be enacted globally, with the development of an international consensus (Dragiewicz et al., 2018) although the political and practical hurdles associated with implementing such a strategy are likely to prove insurmountable. Nevertheless, academic research designed to contribute to the development of necessary actions should be undertaken in an interdisciplinary fashion, to optimise the various strands of scholarship that are already in place (Backe et al., 2018).

The literature suggests that in many countries, the laws available to tackle online abuse are inadequate (Henry & Powell, 2015). However, as illustrated in England and Wales, even where there is legislation in place that facilitates the prosecution of online abuse (e.g. CPS, 2018), the number of prosecutions remains low whilst abuse rises (Salter, 2017). Scholarship in this area suggests that the policing of online abuse needs to be improved. There needs to be greater collective pressure applied to police forces to tackle the issue (Bliss, 2019), along with an improved awareness from individual police officers of the scale and consequences of online abuse. Fundamental to this is better training for police officers (Lewis et al., 2018), whose lack of technical competence (Edström, 2016) and understanding of the pervasiveness and operation of social networking sites has been offered as a reason for a lack of action in addressing criminal activity (Eckert, 2018). Nevertheless, it is important to recognise that if every case of online abuse were to be reported to the police, then the criminal justice system would be completely overwhelmed (Barlow & Awan, 2016). This raises further resourcing dilemmas, particularly in the UK, where the social policy landscape has been under-funded for many years, as a result of the austerity agenda pursued by successive Conservative governments (Brown & Silvestri, 2020; Lewis et al., 2018). The election of a Labour government in July 2024 cannot guarantee that this situation will change, as there remains an overwhelming demand upon depleted government finances from wide swathes of the public sector (Emmerson et al., 2024).

Technology companies also have a responsibility to enact robust and responsive reporting mechanisms (Barlow & Awan, 2016), as at present provision is both patchy and sporadic. Given the huge advances made in computer-mediated communication, and the large number of tasks that are now undertaken online, it seems unlikely that the explanations for a fragmentary response to online abuse are solely technical. Instead it is proposed that this is an issue of the prioritisation of resources (Meserve, 2014). Meserve (2014) is one of many commentators to ponder how, with such technical experts in their employ, there must be more options to halt online abuse available to technology conglomerates than the existing 'report button'.

However, even when action is taken at a corporate level, the effects are not always significant. As Jane (2017a) has highlighted, when Facebook banned anonymous accounts in 2015, in an attempt to curb online abuse, it made very little difference. The amount of online abuse that was perpetrated via the platform did not reduce, and it appeared that those engaging in abuse continued to do so, even when their identity was in full view. This suggests that the potential for identification did not serve as a deterrent, possibly because the likelihood of subsequent criminal sanction was scant.

Furthermore, when online platforms do act to remove and delete abusive posts, this can have the unintended consequence of destroying the very evidence needed for a criminal prosecution, placing the onus on individual women to capture and store their own abuse via screenshots if they wish to pursue the matter via the criminal justice system (Burgess et al., 2017).

Promoting Societal and Cultural Change

Achieving societal and cultural change is very difficult, as it requires challenging ingrained attitudes, beliefs and biases. However, if policy change were to be enacted at the first two levels, then this may hasten the necessary cultural shift. The type of change that is required at a societal level could be encouraged if a 'woman defined understanding' (McGlynn et al., 2017, p. 38) were adopted to categorise the types of abuse that is defined as threatening and potentially violent (McGlynn et al., 2017). This would provide a much clearer understanding of both the nature and consequences of online abuse. Having more women lead technology companies (Carson, 2018) would also promote a cultural change moving forwards.

Conclusion

This chapter outlines the key legislative and policy changes (as applied to England and Wales) in the areas of online abuse, gender-based violence and misogyny. In doing so, a range of policy changes, acting at different levels, have been discussed, which could make offer improvements in key areas. These ideas are further developed in Chapter Eight.

Chapter Eight

'Dude, it's not OK': Recommendations for Tackling Abuse

Abstract

This chapter presents a series of policy recommendations proposed to tackle online abuse. These recommendations have been organised into a series of actions at an individual, organisational, legislative and structural level, reflecting a synergy with the levels at which the impacts of online abuse occur. These recommendations come with clear policy suggestions, locating the work squarely in both a criminal justice and social policy framework.

Keywords: Social policy; criminal justice system; structural change; legislation; regulation; censorship; freedom of speech

Introduction

This chapter presents the recommendations proposed by the participants in this research to tackle online abuse. These recommendations have been organised into a series of actions at an individual, organisational, legislative and structural level, which reflects a synergy with the levels at which the impacts of online abuse occur.

In line with the epistemology underpinning this book, the identification of gender as a driver of online abuse is central to the recommendations outlined in this chapter. These recommendations draw upon the principles of phenomenological research (Aagaard, 2017), with a clear orientation to the importance of lived experience (Fendt et al., 2014). By placing an emphasis on the primacy of the voices of women participants, it reaffirms the importance of intersectionality across the levels upon which recommendations are based. Souad was one

Gendered Online Abuse Against Women in Public Life: More Than Just Words, 147–174
doi:10.1108/978-1-83549-724-120251008

contributor who highlighted the need for the voices of women of colour to be central to any discussion about improvements to be made to online platforms:

> *Black Lives Matter, Black Twitter, Feminist Twitter are huge communities, yet they are constantly being marginalised or forgotten about when it comes to product changes, or new things that you can do on the platform. They're not thinking about how it might impact those communities or giving them greater agency.* (Souad, Academic at a UK university)

Supporting Women Working in Public Facing Occupations

From their induction into employment, women working in public facing occupations should be given the skills that they need to both contend with and call out online abuse, both for themselves and their co-workers:

> *We need better digital literacy. We need to help people. For instance, if we ask students to make digital content, we should be also teaching digital logistics and digital safety. I think we need to expand that to the workplace as well.* (Christie, Academic at a UK university)

> *We need good digital security habits, the same way you lock the doors in your house when you go to sleep, you need to be aware of what the risks are of using social media. Studies have shown that women are less aware of what the technological risks are. They're less aware of what the back doors are, what the privacy issues are, and I think that's just a matter of confident fluency with technology more broadly.* (Ann, Academic and Journalist, USA)

This opening tranche of recommendations is not designed to circumvent the need for the organisational or structural change that follows. However, there is a need for a practical array of digital responses that individuals can adopt in recognition of the fact that women serving in public facing occupations who are experiencing frequent episodes of online abuse do not have the luxury of waiting for structural change to materialise. Several participants shared the acts of digital self-care that they had implemented, both for themselves and their colleagues:

> *Understanding what kind of content goes best where is actually useful. That's what I do to limit my exposure to abuse. For instance, I express my most controversial opinions on Facebook because I know only my friends and family can see it.* (Mary, Academic at a UK university)

> *I don't have my personal account linked into my work accounts. So I've got a Twitter account, I've got an Instagram account which*

> *is with friends, but I don't share those two things. I keep my personal life off the internet.* (Jacqueline, Academic at a UK university)

Jacqueline identified how this bifurcation of her online presence could be defined as another example of safety work undertaken by women (Vera-Gray, 2018):

> *The best part of the safety work that women are doing, we are doing automatically. I've made a conscious decision to not talk about my son online, I didn't talk about him when I was on maternity leave. I guess that is in part about abuse and it is just the knowledge I guess that trolls or people that want to make you feel bad are willing to try anything they can that might give you that fear of something happening to you in the actual real world. So I kept those details offline.* (Jacqueline, Academic at a UK university)

Michelle undertakes very similar safety work in relation to her family, as she explained:

> *I'm careful about what I put online. For example, I don't mention that I have children on Twitter at all, and on Facebook I don't mention their ages or genders. I think if you read my Facebook, where I'm very careful with my friends, you can see that I'm a parent, but you can't see more than that.* (Michelle, Journalist based in the UK)

In politics, in 2018 the National Democratic Institute (NDI) launched an online safety tool, which is designed to help women running for office:

> *NDI have developed a safety planning tool, it's called Think #10, which says that if you're a woman going into politics, there are ten things you need to focus on in order to enhance your safety and security. And one of them is your digital footprint. So if the safety planning tool says you're at moderate risk, you should maybe change your password once a month. If the safety planning tool says you're at elevated risk, change your password twice a month. If you're at a severe risk, then change your password every day, or, maybe have two or three different machines. So, it's the same ten things, but depending on your own assessment of your risk level, you may have to do them differently.* (Helen, Academic based in the USA)

Several politicians described how they had been assisted – and had in turn assisted others – with measures similar to those implemented on a more formal level by the NDI:

> *It's much better to ruthlessly block and ruthlessly hide or delete tweets and Facebook posts that are negative, to clean up your feed.*

You don't want these people in your life. You just don't need to see that [abusive content], but I think that kind of digital hygiene, a lot of politicians find really hard. I was showing a colleague of mine how to block, and this woman said I never block anyone ... But you have to. (Beth, Member of Parliament until December 2019)

I turned off notifications so that my phone didn't light up every time somebody said something mean about me on the internet. I was astonished when I would talk to colleagues in Parliament about it, because so many of them hadn't taken that basic step to protect themselves. And I would show them how to do it and it would provide immediate relief. (Julia, Politician in Scotland)

We need to make people aware of the options available to them when it comes to reporting accounts. Making them aware of cases where those reports have been successful as well, because I know a lot of my colleagues have received abuse, and I've said, oh, well report it to Twitter, report it to Facebook or whatever, and a lot of them have said, what's the point, nothing ever happens. And then I'll say to them, well I managed to get this account removed and this one removed, and this. And I've found that they're a bit more willing to hit that report button. So, part of it is making people aware that those options are there. (Simone, Member of Parliament)

Women were asked whether their own experiences would make them reconsider their decision to serve in the public sphere. The vast majority strongly asserted that it would not, and that instead, young women should continue to be encouraged to enter public facing occupations, to ensure that women's voices continue to be heard in these spaces:

I want my Goddaughters to see me asking the Prime Minister questions, and that being a wonderful thing ... and they can say to the world there is no glass ceiling they can't break. I want that. I don't want them to think that they've been bullied online since they were kids and why would they put themselves through that again. (Caroline, Member of Parliament until December 2019)

You need to ignore the bastards. You've got to crack on. Each generation has had its own complainers of doom, and reasons why women shouldn't get involved. (Beth, Member of Parliament until December 2019)

I recommend young women to get stuck into politics. But I do so in the hope that having more women participating will help to change the systemic nature of the abuse that we face. (Wendy, Local Councillor)

Nevertheless, it was felt that women must be aware of the online environment that they are entering:

> *I try to say to young women starting out 'this is hard and real and it's unfair'. I really like to validate that upfront: it's so unfair. And yet here we are and so here are some tips, right? Because I think if we skip that it's unfair part it can wind up being victim blamey. Here's the world we live in, we can't change it, so here are the things YOU have to do … because we don't want to lose our voices and everything they want to contribute and so, here are some things we know about how to manage this horrible situation we're in.* (Sophie, Academic and Journalist, USA)

> *I will never stop encouraging young women to get involved in politics. But I would say it with the caveat that this space isn't great, and it does need to change, but hopefully if we get more women participating it will change.* (Wendy, Local Councillor)

> *Young women should build healthy self-care habits around their digital presence. They should think about what they're saying and how it may affect them … and build healthy habits like stepping away when things get too much.* (Mary, Academic at a UK university)

For some, however, their experiences of online abuse had made them wary of encouraging others to enter the same profession:

> *I'm always encouraging women to get involved, but I know one hundred per cent that there are young women who look at the replies that I get on Twitter, and they say to me, 'I couldn't deal with that, I couldn't do what you do'. So, I know it's putting women off. I've got loads of evidence from women saying, I'd hate to be a politician.* (Wendy, Local Councillor)

> *When we've looked at the factors which deter people from standing for elected office or being involved in public life, the single biggest factor that turns women off is how they're treated online … there's so much talent and potential there who might now choose to do something different other than stand for elected office. They'll probably go on and do amazing things in much quieter, private spheres …* (Julia, Politician in Scotland)

Organisational Responsibilities: Action Necessary from Employers

The recommendation that employers provide greater support to staff members facing online abuse is potentially complicated, as it requires action from organisations that are themselves likely to attract public attention as a result of the changes that they implement in this area. Nevertheless, it is clear that women working in the public sphere require protection from online abuse to be provided by their employers, an aspect that is frequently lacking.

Sejal Parmar (2016), in a study of women journalists, demonstrated how those holding leadership positions within the industry were often unaware of the scale and content of the online abuse that their employees received. Women frequently report having to source support from their own informal networks, as there is little formal support available from their employers (Lees Munoz, 2016). This is echoed in the work of Martin and Murrell (2020), which found that the occupational culture within newsrooms was one that demanded that journalists simply 'grow a thicker skin' (Martin & Murrell, 2020, p. 100) in order to manage online abuse. The findings of such research illustrate the need for greater awareness of the issue from leaders and decision makers within the public sphere, along with better training from HR departments for staff. The conclusions of previous studies are similarly reflected by participants in this research:

> *When I think about my job, I feel like a lot of the men just don't even know [about the online abuse I receive]. The chair of my department or the head of the unit, or the people on the tenure committee. Giving those people a solid training in the barriers that women face when they want to exude expertise, particularly in controversial fields.* (Eileen, Academic at a European university)

> *It's about awareness, I guess, which I didn't have when I started my PhD. I didn't have an awareness that this [online abuse] was something that could possibly happen. So, I think it's about being aware that this is something that can possibly happen, and maybe try and have a safety plan in advance, for the actions I would take.* (Jacqueline, Academic at a UK university)

Yet again, it is intersectional women who are most likely to be at the forefront of any abuse, and therefore, consideration of their needs must be paramount when it comes to raising awareness:

> *There are all of the intersections that are quite persistent, if you're a person of colour, if you're a religious or sexual minority, it's amplified. You're double, triple jeopardy. So if you're a Black, Muslim women, all bets are off in terms of what your institution might do to stand behind you … if you want women to succeed in your organisation, in your political party, in your newsroom, then you need to be aware that the standards generally used to access what risk is, or what threat is, are standards of essentially the least vulnerable in the organisation, usually able-bodied men, usually white, who don't have experience of being harassed on the street, or sent rape*

threats, it is just not within their world view. (Ann, Academic and Journalist, USA)

Souad highlighted that political parties were often failing to provide adequate training or support for women candidates, with their (typically) male leaders failing to recognise online abuse as a widespread issue:

> *We know that employers, who will predominantly be made up of white men, won't have a clue how to protect their colleagues, specifically the women, around online sexual harassment now. Political parties are still not taking responsibility for having to make candidates safe.* (Souad, Academic at a UK university)

Souad is not alone in her criticism of political parties:

> *Louise Ellman[1] had Neo-Nazi material sent to her, and the party said that that wasn't racist. It was downloaded from a Neo-Nazi American website. I literally had to print off copies of it and put it on every desk at the PLP[2] meeting, for that person to be suspended, and for the Chairman and Jeremy Corbyn to comment. That's how bad it was.* (Caroline, Member of Parliament until December 2019)

> *Political parties need to do much more to protect women, and platforms need to do much more to dial it down.* (Peggy, Member of Parliament)

Ultimately, in order for policies on training and support to be successfully implemented within an organisation, there has to be endorsement from the senior leadership of that organisation for doing so, as Eileen summed up:

> *We need to teach the people in charge that are making personnel and job decisions, and we need to teach the men around us.* (Eileen, Academic at a European university)

Central to providing an effective organisational response to address online abuse is the need for employers to provide support and a sense of collective responsibility to their employees when individuals are faced with unpleasant, threatening, or violent online invective. This support can take many forms, but the assistance most identified as useful by contributors in this study involved the recording and reporting of abuse by institutions, which would in turn make it easier to seek further action from online platforms and law enforcement.

---

[1] Member of Parliament for Liverpool Riverside 1997–2019.
[2] Parliamentary Labour Party.

Sometimes, support can be as simple as ensuring that all online contact goes via an institutional email account:

> *If something comes through your institutional email address, you've got the university there to support you, and you can keep records of all of this.* (Jacqueline, Academic at a UK university)

A number of contributors provided their own examples of effective organisational support implemented for employees at risk of online abuse. It is gratifying to see such systems in place and proves that there is no reason why this cannot become commonplace:

> *Hope Not Hate train staff in how to be careful. And then their research team report for them to Twitter directly. They work hard to keep people safe, keep activists safe online, making sure that whatever they're doing online, they're not exposing themselves, because they need those people to be in that space.* (Michelle, Journalist based in the UK)

> *When I did some work for the BBC, I got proper support for the first time ever, because it was deemed to be a high-risk project. That was the first time that I've ever experienced that, and there needs to be more of it. The BBC have a very good standard of aftercare ... and they were really worried for me. They had a digital forensic person who was in charge of helping me to protect myself and change my social media practises in order to do that.* (Christie, Academic at a UK university)

However, others provided examples of a lack of support, where women had been left to tackle online abuse without any organisational assistance. One notable case that was mentioned, which has also been the subject of analysis by Thielman (2020) and Waisbord (2024), was the experience of Felicia Sonmez, a journalist in the USA:

> *There was a case here... in the Washington Post, after Kobe Bryant died, the Washington Post reporter Felicia Sonmez, she tweeted an article, she didn't even write it, she tweeted a Daily Beast article... and her publisher sent her an email saying, you're dishonouring the institution by doing this. And then they put her on leave and told her if she felt unsafe maybe she should consider going to a hotel, and in the meantime tens of thousands of people are harassing her online and that just stood in very stark relief to a case the year before where a male political writer was being harassed, and the newspaper paid for him to go to a hotel for three days, and also paid for security for him for three days. And for some reason, because this is a woman*

*commenting on sexual violence, this wasn't considered worthy of their
institutional support. And that was a complete and abject failure.*
(Ann, Academic and Journalist, USA)

In addition to the support provided to individuals, the NDI also works with
political parties and campaigning organisations in a number of countries:

*The NDI are currently working in Zimbabwe and Malawi, to
develop support for women activists who are by their nature and their
issue, in danger. Part of that will develop civic activist online support, to assist women who are operating in the online space. Because
those countries are very hostile to women in the LGBTQ movement.*
(Helen, Academic based in the USA)

Souad emphasised how it is vital to speak to women in public facing occupations about their experiences of abuse in order to put additional safeguards and
support systems in place:

*We have to listen to find out how we can support them both as
employers and brands, as civil society, as legislation we have to
do something about the exodus of people leaving the online space.*
(Souad, Academic at a UK university)

Universities are in a distinct position, as they have an obligation to provide
support to both their staff and their students:

*If as an academic you're sending out young women after gradua-
tion into the world, and you haven't talked about the sexism that
they will face and they already face, you haven't done your job.
That's the reality of it. If we're pretending that women aren't going
to go out into the world and they haven't already been faced with
sexism, we're lying to them. So I keep telling my students exactly
that. The world is not structured for you. We need to figure out
how to change it, but until then you have to learn to survive in
this world and have the resilience to do so.* (Emma, Academic at a
UK university)

Whilst it is vital to involve women in shaping the organisational support that
is provided by employers, it is equally important that this task does not become
yet another hidden responsibility that women must carry out during the course
of their employment:

*I do hesitate [to suggest things] though because we don't need more
work. It's not my job to stand up for harassers and educate the men.*
(Eileen, Academic at a European university)

If online abuse is to be dealt with effectively, it needs to be properly recognised as an occupational task and appropriately recompensed:

> *We need to be properly paid. So many people ask us to do things for free, and people just don't get it. We need more people talking about money when it comes to this work.* (Souad, Academic at a UK university)

Structural and Societal Change

Despite the many improvements that organisations should be making to tackle online abuse, it cannot occur in a vacuum. Organisational change will only prove successful if implemented alongside a comprehensive programme of structural change:

> *I think it's really unfair to put the onus for this on individual women. Online harassment training and seminars etcetera, are all well and good, but I really think energy is better spent trying to create societal change. So many of the issues that I work on, whether it's disinformation or extremism or online abuse, it always comes back to, well what do we do for the individual? And the best thing we can do for the individual is push for systemic change.* (Judith, Journalist based in the USA)

> *I keep telling my students 'the world is not structured for you. We need to figure out how to change it, but until then you have to learn to survive in this world and have the resilience to do it'. But we can't stop there because frankly just telling them that puts them more at risk than anything else. What we also need to do is to say, ok, we're also working to change the laws, we're strengthening our structures, we're changing our institutions, but also, we're teaching girls to fight back. Because I'm sorry, saying well gee, you deserve to wear a short skirt and go out at night is not enough, until we change all the other things. And frankly that change is going to take a long time. So, you know what, teach the girls to not only say yes, this is my right, I have the right to be safe, I have a right to be free, but I'm also going to be able to fight if necessary.* (Emma, Academic at a UK university)

Blumell (2018) asserts that the presence of benevolent sexism, of which paternalism is a key element, can jeopardise the occupational progress of women journalists. Ann agreed:

> *For journalists in particular, freedom of expression is centrally important and the way that companies like Facebook have approached this problem [online abuse] when it pertains to women is quite infantilising, because they actually categorise women and children, like we're*

all on the Titanic and in a lifeboat. It's fucking stupid. And so, at the same time as I was advocating very aggressively for women's safety, I equally aggressively was advocating for their vehement expression, artistic expression, political expression. (Ann, Academic and Journalist, USA)

This identifies a need for a renewed campaign of feminist activism in the workplace, this time oriented at the online space. The empirical evidence presented here emphasises the need to raise awareness of, and to change attitudes towards, misogynistic online abuse, once again echoing the struggles against sexual harassment led by second wave feminists in the 1970s (Vera-Gray & Kelly, 2020).

In a specific recommendation that straddles both the organisational and structural realms within the Labour Party, Caroline suggested that activists found to have engaged in online abuse should have their Labour Party membership rescinded:

People can say whatever they want to say, but that doesn't mean they are allowed to be members of mainstream civic organisations. If they are vile and racist, they don't get to be in the Labour Party. So, they can say it, they just don't get to be in my world. Which I don't think is unreasonable, in terms of freedom of speech in the UK. (Caroline, Member of Parliament until December 2019)

This proposal shares some similarities with the pledge made by former Prime Minister, Boris Johnson, who stated in the House of Commons on 14 July 2021 that any England football supporter who had been found to engage in the online abuse of players following the European football championships would be banned from football grounds throughout the country: 'Today we are taking practical steps to ensure that the football banning order regime is changed, so that if a person is guilty of racist online abuse of footballers, they will not be going to the match – no ifs, no buts, no exemptions and no excuses' (Hansard, 2021, Col. 362). However, despite a significant amount of media coverage at the time, this pledge was not implemented by the Johnson government or taken forward in any subsequent legislation, and the issue of online abuse has remained a hallmark of many subsequent sporting contests (e.g. Burch et al., 2024; Harrison & Huslage, 2023; Sinclair, 2024).

In a similar fusing of structural and organisational reform, the school curriculum needs to be modified to include proactive teaching on online abuse prevention, as part of an existing programme of IT and internet safety:

We have an opportunity through reform of the curriculum, to teach [children] from a very young age, what is appropriate and inappropriate behaviour online. And how to deal with abuse, and also teaching people, boys especially, that misbehaviour is not acceptable and has consequences. And then we need to find ways to make it have consequences. And this means introducing closed social media

*communities into schools and having them properly moderated. We
need to model the good behaviour and demonstrate the consequences
of bad behaviour. The challenge is that schools have no resources, and
the majority of teachers lack the correct understanding. So we need
to get into teacher training, and we need to get into the curriculum
and that needs to happen at all levels. We need to be teaching lectur-
ers how to support their students. We need to be teaching students at
university. We need to have some kind of educational platform for all
ages, where you show what online abuse is, why it's unacceptable, and
this is what you do if you see this happening to other people, this is
what you do if this happens to you, this is where you get support, this
is where you get help, this is where you get counselling. That's what
we need. If we're looking at cultural change, then it's up to us to find
ways to educate younger people so that we start to see that trickle
through.* (Rose, Academic based in the USA)

This recommendation demonstrates how the structural and organisational change required to address this issue is interdisciplinary in nature and requires a social policy response in order to effect viable change:

*One of the things that Google's doing that's really interesting is
online citizenship courses. They're going into schools to teach children how to be a good citizen online. Unsurprisingly they went into
one of my schools, maybe… to prove to me that they were actually doing something … they're now training the trainers and they're
training teachers to do it.* (Caroline, Member of Parliament until
December 2019)

Despite the introduction of the Online Safety Act in October 2023, there remains a need for further legislative change, the implementation of robust regulatory frameworks, and changes in policing to effectively tackle the online abuse of adult women.

All participants identified a need for the greater regulation of online platforms:

*Regulation is very important. Regulation ensures that we keep
[social media] companies accountable, and accountability and
transparency are the cornerstones of any healthy, democratic society.*
(Jacqueline, Academic at a UK university)

*The online space shouldn't be lawless anymore. We need to figure
out some rules and regulations about this. Women shouldn't have to
change their behaviour. We've all moved online, let's make it a better
place to live.* (Christie, Academic at a UK university)

*Long term, we need legislative change. We need a framework that
looks at online harms, and the definition of it, and making sure it's*

intersectional. We need tech companies to look at moderation and invest in it properly. We need tech companies to be designing platforms with safety by design as its core principle, rather than profit. (Souad, Academic at a UK university)

Some felt that state regulation of online platforms was necessary because social media companies could not be trusted to implement the various improvements required without a legal obligation to do so:

They feed off dissent. They feed off rage. That's how they make money. They can't even be trusted to keep their house in order, so I don't think they are anywhere near to knowing how to address gender-based violence properly. I don't trust them to act on it, because they don't. They make money from not very ethical ways. So, they're not driven to find a solution. It would have to come from policy level. (Nicole, Academic at a UK university)

We need to hold the social media companies to account. Government legislation on social media companies is long overdue. Because they're not going to self-correct, because they've got no incentive to do that. We can't wait for the US because they're never going to catch up quick enough with us … (Michelle, Journalist based in the UK)

I think more regulation is required. If social media is going to be used for responsible reasons, and that's why it was designed, then they do need to exercise more control over the platform, because it's not a free platform, it is owned by a company that I think should have more regulated responsibilities for how that platform is used. Like any other profit-making company, they have responsibility for the safety of the people using it. (Geetika, Senior Police Officer)

Despite the largely favourable response to the possibility of greater regulation of online platforms as a mechanism to tackle online abuse, Rose sounded a note of caution:

The regulation question is really interesting, because on the one hand regulation does force companies to take actions that they might otherwise not have bothered to take. On the other, our lawmakers are not particularly savvy, and the law-making process is not responsive. I can see the benefits that regulation would have, but the tech lobby is well funded, and our law makers are not as digitally literate as I would like, and we would potentially be at risk of bad law. (Rose, Academic based in the USA)

Samantha was concerned that in England and Wales, the introduction of legislation covering online platforms may place additional pressures on already stretched local police forces:

> *Social media companies are making a lot of money. It's not in their interests to have loads of regulation. We struggle as the police to get much information from them [when we need it for detecting crime], it's certainly not volunteered very easily. So it just depends on how that greater regulation will manifest itself. It certainly wouldn't be great if it all falls to the police to try and enforce things.* (Samantha, Senior Police Officer)

Tiprat provided a reminder that it is likely to prove impossible to introduce a regulatory regime to be adopted by governments worldwide due to the multiplicity of different laws and regulatory frameworks (Chenou, 2014):

> *Threats of violence should be taken very seriously. Right now they're not. I think that social media companies don't take the idea of violence against women seriously. I think that they need to do more to have more women involved, to be aware of this as a problem. I don't know how much they can do. There's a lot of problems in the United States because website forums, any kind of online forums, there's a rule in our Communications Act that says that they're not responsible for content.* (Tiprat, Academic based in the USA)

Tiprat also highlighted the need for further action from both legislators and technology companies:

> *Legal changes need to happen, both in terms of the laws that are there, as well as in the training of law enforcement. Tech companies need to be doing more, I think they're trying but again, consciousness is really important. I feel like the internet really needs to be governed a lot more. We really need some kind of legal structure that is applicable to the internet, and it needs teeth, so that people who do violate laws are prosecuted and made examples of.* (Tiprat, Academic based in the USA)

Emma presented a paradigm for the future regulation of online platforms, whilst also highlighting several of the issues that are currently viewed as problematic in their operational methods:

> *Tech should be regulated, not only for tax purposes but actually for business processes. I find it really fascinating that we have spent the last decade demonising banks, and the evil bankers. The reality is that the banking sector is more regulated than most parts of our*

economy. And tech is almost as powerful, if not more powerful in terms of reach, political power, social power, as banking and yet it is the least regulated. And we somehow pretend that we can kind of continue this way.

We need taxation, that's the first thing. We need serious regulations about the way social media companies are structured. Look at firms like Facebook, Zuckerberg pretty much has all rights to all decisions made. This is a publicly traded company across the world which has huge impacts. This is a publishing platform in addition to all the other things. Just because we haven't figured out where to fit it in terms of our business ideas, and that's not to do with business, that's to do with politicians, does not mean that we cannot regulate it. (Emma, Academic at a UK university)

Judith presented a possible blueprint for the development of social media companies that she believed would do more to tackle online abuse at a strategic level:

Tech companies need to better protect the vast majority of their users, over that of the privileged few. Tech companies have been so worried about censorship ... but usually that censorship they're talking about is a very small group of extremely vocal and extremely online white men. Most social media users are women and people of colour, and the tech platforms need to centre their policies around the vast majority of their users being able to be online free from harm. (Judith, Journalist based in the USA)

Sarah, a senior police officer, highlighted three areas where change is needed:

Regulation, law change and responsibility on social media companies to provide intelligence to law enforcement about repeat offenders, would be three really worthwhile changes. (Sarah, Senior Police Officer)

Helen believed that it was of vital importance for different policy actors to work together in formulating regulatory and legislative responses to online abuse:

There's a need for three key actors. The main representatives in the political sphere, so you've got to have women in parliament. But you also need an autonomous civil society that is supportive. And thirdly, you need what I call the femocrats, the Commission on Equality or similar organisations. You have to have that public sector civil service element available to you. You need the three-legged stool, in order to progress. (Helen, Academic based in the USA)

Helen's proposition emphasises yet again the importance of having women in the spaces where decisions are made, for the issue of online abuse to be properly and effectively recognised, something that was also emphasised by Julia:

> *Tackling online abuse requires a strategic effort across every aspect of public policy. We already know that women are walking away from standing for elected office, so we have to double down on the idea of quotas and positive action because you can't be what you can't see. We've also got to dramatically change the political culture, and, in part, that's got to be about having fewer binary debates.*
> (Julia, Politician in Scotland)

Reporting Online Abuse

Sarah highlighted the current position of police forces in England and Wales in relation to dealing with incidents of online abuse:

> *They're very focused on what they would describe as high-end social media activity. But I think there is a role for them to take that regulation broader into anything that would be an on-street offence. So, if people were to target an individual repeatedly and make offensive comments on any of the protected characteristics on the street, then that's an aggravated public order offence. But when it happens online, people think the same rules don't apply. To investigate it properly, there has to be a responsibility on social media companies to identify account holders to law enforcement. That would enable police forces to issue harassment warnings. Police forces don't investigate online abuse to the degree they probably should, because it's not really flagged as high-level offending. There's also a secondary responsibility to ensure a legal framework is in place for police forces. Currently, in order to identify who an account belongs to, you have to be able to say it's a serious offence, which in legal definition is an offence that attracts over three years in prison, but few actually meet that bar.* (Sarah, Senior Police Officer)

Geetika was concerned that achieving cooperation between police forces and online platforms may prove problematic, providing an example of the existing relationships with social media companies and wider technology organisations as evidence:

> *When there is a stalking and harassment case over social media, we have to go through the usual channels to try and obtain that information from places like Google and Twitter and some of them are not based in this country, their laws are not the same as ours, so, some of*

those investigations can get very complicated to access that material. (Geetika, Senior Police Officer)

This can impede police investigations:

When it comes down to very particular details of the platforms, or places, or people that are using the accounts that Twitter or Facebook might hold, they have to provide that information to us, as opposed to us being able to extract it out of the system, and it becomes almost impossible to investigate. (Geetika, Senior Police Officer)

Sherrie was able to compare the activities of the police in England and Wales with the actions of the Police Service of Northern Ireland (PSNI):

In Northern Ireland we have the strictest domestic abuse, harassment and stalker legislation. The police need to act, they need to reflect the changed environment in which people are failed. We should have assurances from the police that they will take it seriously and investigate. In my own case, [the perpetrator] got a custodial sentence, albeit suspended. I thought the judge was pretty good at that. I think there is a developing recognition of the harm that this type of abuse can do. The perpetrators should feel shame on their community for having done what they did. (Sherrie, Member of the Northern Ireland Legislative Assembly)

Jacqueline and Tiprat, whilst located in different countries, shared similar experiences when attempting to report online abuse to the police:

They trivialised it and said it's not a problem, it's not as serious as other forms of sexual violence like rape, they did all of the stuff that I'd spoken about in terms of sexual harassment in offline public spaces, which is the discourse around it, and did the exact same things in terms of the online abuse, that's how they chose to discredit it. (Jacqueline, Academic at a UK university)

Every woman I know, who's tried to report to the police has found that it was a complete fiasco, and the police didn't understand, they told her to turn off her computer, and that's ridiculous, because if people are coming after you, turning off your computer's not going to stop them. Law enforcement should do more, because if law enforcement took these threats more seriously, I think that would have a chilling effect on men doing these things, if there were some more men arrested and put in jail for these kinds of things, and I think that's happened a little bit more in the United Kingdom. (Tiprat, Academic based in the USA)

Two contributors offered information about work being done in the USA to increase the knowledge of criminal justice practitioners overseeing cases involving online abuse:

> *I would say the last frontier has been judges, because judges have been very hesitant around technology. So, we've put together a judicial code. The training is to remind judges that cases involving social media are no different to what they've been trained their entire career: to assess credibility. It's more just to get them comfortable with different platforms, how they work, what they do, and how you owe it to the people coming before you that you understand how these platforms work. Otherwise you're out of touch and you're not a good judge.* (Sue, Academic based in the USA)

> *I am working with legislators to establish a swatting database[3], where police are trained in these tactics, and where you can register yourself as a potential target.* (Ann, Academic and Journalist, USA)

The reporting of online abuse to social media platforms was a key topic for participants. At its most basic, women expressed concern about their ability to report incidents of abusive or dangerous communication and often felt that no action was taken to identify or appropriately penalise the perpetrators. This supports work by Hodson et al. (2018), and Regehr and Ringrose (2018), which has identified a widespread dissatisfaction with the outcomes of reporting incidents of online abuse to *all* social media platforms:

> *I do actually believe in free speech. If someone wants to call me a fucking cunt, they can. But that doesn't mean it should be allowed to stay there or remain for ever. Social media companies should have strong systems to act very quickly to ensure that things are pulled down when reported.* (Maria, Member of the House of Lords)

> *Social media companies should have a set of principles, that I should be able consult, if I suffer abuse. An easy contactable line of complaint or an issued formula that investigates it. I also think that people who do abuse others, shouldn't be allowed to be anonymous.* (Sherrie, Member of the Northern Ireland Legislative Assembly)

> *There's a lot of people hiding behind mirrors, feeling able to hurl abuse, knowing that they will never be identified. I think people on Twitter get away with so much, because they're anonymised. People*

---

[3]The act of 'falsely reporting people to the police so that SWAT teams descend on their homes' (Lukianoff, 2015, p. 48).

are just completely anonymous, so you could be talking to somebody in America about something in [name of city], and it's not relevant to them, but they just happen to be racist, and they just want to comment on what you've got to say. I think the anonymisation of individuals should be banned, because it becomes impossible for the police or anybody else to do anything about it. (Smita, Local Councillor)

Smita further emphasised how she felt that there was a difference in the way she was treated when reporting offences to Facebook, as opposed to Twitter. Her experience had led her to conclude that the technical measures available to users, in the form of a single button on the site, made reporting online abuse to Facebook a simpler process:

Facebook is probably easier to report things and I do it quite often, perhaps if I see things that I think are offensive, report the individual and then you get a report back from the administrator to say yes, it is or no it's not ... but even then, I think they need to improve things. (Smita, Local Councillor)

Many participants were disturbed by the continued availability of anonymous accounts on Twitter. Evidence presented here echoes the work of Tromble and Koole (2020), which found that the vast majority of tweets from anonymous accounts sent to politicians in the UK, the USA and the Netherlands were negative and abusive and often contained racist and/or sexist epithets. Consequently, they concurred with the work of Ooi et al. (2021), believing that prohibiting anonymous accounts on the platform would be a relatively simple measure for social media organisations to implement, and one which would ameliorate the most extreme forms of online abuse:

The difficulty with identity, and people not having to prove their identity when they register an account on social media, is that these people [engaging in online abuse] could be anybody. It could be your next-door neighbour, it could be somebody physically close to you, and that's when the risks come. You don't actually know who these people are. It's the responsibility of those running social media to take a more proactive approach to protecting people. (Geetika, Senior Police Officer)

Karen explained how her own force was unable to trace several of the perpetrators who had subjected her to online abuse due to them having anonymous Twitter accounts:

We have been unable to trace some of the accounts [responsible for online abuse] because some of these accounts are difficult for us to trace, and the threats to me are not life and death and therefore Twitter won't reveal where they come from. (Karen, Senior Police Officer)

Samantha expressed a degree of frustration with the continued presence of anonymous online accounts, feeling that the impact on policing was particularly detrimental:

> *On social media people can be anonymous. It really annoys me that the people who tend to be abusive are anonymous and you don't know who they are. And that gives people something to hide behind, because they think they can say and do anything they want to. It annoys me for lots of reasons. You see somebody [online] who purports to be a police officer, but takes every opportunity to be negative about policing.* (Samantha, Senior Police Officer)

Nevertheless, the decision to prohibit anonymity in online platforms risks silencing the voices of members of the most marginalised communities, who may rely upon the benefits afforded by anonymity to fully express their identity or beliefs (Hardaker & McGlashan, 2016; Lingel, 2021). Similarly, victims of online abuse may adopt anonymity or a pseudonym in order to engage online without risking their personal safety (Campbell, 2017).

This emphasises the need to involve a more diverse group of stakeholders in designing the responses to online abuse in order to reflect its multiplicity of users:

> *We're trying to get those who wield power and have responsibility for these platforms, as well as the legal system, to catch up with the twenty first century and put protections in place that'll make things better for women now and the generations coming after. There is a whole swathe of legislative reform that needs to happen because the laws that we have – that may well have been written a couple of hundred years ago – aren't equipped to deal with the twenty first century digital age. Those laws need to be updated and the involvement of women and minority groups who are disproportionately on the receiving end of abuse, have to be a part of that process. They have to be a part of the process that's designing digital citizenship programming and education, the elements needed to help determine how it is rolled out, they need to be part of whatever task force set up to examine how our legislative structures and processes and natural laws need to evolve to mitigate this stuff.* (Maya, Politician in England)

Twitter has long been criticised for allowing users to remain anonymous, should they so wish (Sterner & Felmlee, 2017). However, whilst Facebook has a 'real name policy' whereby users of the site are expected to provide their genuine first and last names, this can easily be circumvented (Barlow & Awan, 2016), and false identities and nicknames are frequently adopted (Dragiewicz et al., 2018).

There was a degree of scepticism regarding the social media companies' attitude to online abuse, and their willingness to position themselves as part of the solution, an issue also raised by Majó-Vázquez et al. (2021):

> *Twitter creates a system that makes it easier for people to abuse anonymously and without repercussions or without taking accountability for what they say.* (Julia, Politician in Scotland)

There was a strong feeling that, ultimately, the solution to online abuse must come from the platforms themselves, as they have the technological expertise needed to create effective barriers to the delivery of abuse. Many expressed frustration about their engagement to date:

> *The platform creators must have the antidote. Nobody else can work at the scale that they can. The issue is that their business model is based on making money out of hate. They are only now just saying 'we need help, we didn't realise it was so bad'. It's just crap. Just rubbish. Activists have been at this for a decade already, and they have been knocking on those doors and they have gone to San Francisco, and they have had those conversations and they've been literally swatted away and abused and discredited. But now their business model is being hit by the bad publicity, as actually women are a very big market. That is now causing them to take it much more seriously, and to try and engage with civil society.* (Helen, Academic based in the USA)

> *Why are the systems not there to protect us? We need to be shining a spotlight on the fact that this is not acceptable. Facebook are not doing a good enough job. I think there should be a Facebook moderator that pops up saying, 'are you sure you want to post this?' or something like, 'would you like it if someone said this about you?' Something really like whoa, to make your stop in your tracks.* (Jill, Member of Parliament)

The complexity of the current situation and of any possible structural, legislative or regulatory solutions is manifest. The situation is perhaps best summed up by Caroline, a politician who lost her seat in the House of Commons in December 2019. Caroline received a barrage of misogynistic and anti-Semitic abuse from a variety of online actors both during and after her time in the Westminster Parliament:

> *So, there will be more research about online hate and women, and it's incredibly important that there is … I'm interested in what recommendations you make, because it has to be more than just acknowledging that there is a problem. Because I don't know what*

> *the answers are to it, and I've lived through it.* (Caroline, Member of Parliament until December 2019)

The presence of misogyny in all elements of online abuse has been a thread weaved throughout this book:

> *Online abuse is like all the forms of violence against women. It's all about control. It's all about reminding you about your position, in terms of the patriarchy. Don't step out of line, don't get too cocky, don't get too vocal, don't have too many followers, don't look like that, don't dress like that. It's a constant reminder of upholding patriarchal norms. And it's another tool that patriarchy can use.* (Souad, Academic at a UK university)

> *Men get to the point where they think it's ok to send indecent images of yourself to women online because actually that's all they deserve. So, I think that's the impact of misogyny at an individual level.* (Sarah, Senior Police Officer)

> *The political landscape certainly encourages online abuse, and in the last five years it's gotten worse. But the abuse of people of colour and women online is a much more deeply rooted political issue. Politics reflects misogyny and racism as a society, rather than the other way around.* (Judith, Journalist based in the USA)

Interestingly, some contributors felt that the presence of misogyny in the online space had raised awareness of the phenomenon, leading it to be more widely discussed:

> *I'm actually quite heartened that misogyny is playing out in a digital space because we can prove it finally. It's not just something done in the quiet of a private space.* (Sue, Academic based in the USA)

> *If somebody is targeting women due to a hatred of women specifically, then yes, I think people feel vulnerable and exposed by that, because it's difficult to know when that's going to extend into the physical space, isn't it?* (Geetika, Senior Police Officer)

Participants made connections between online abuse and the treatment of domestic violence and sexual violence in the 1970s and 1980s, as identified by Dobash and Dobash (1980) and Wise and Stanley (1987):

> *It's like we've gone back to the 1960s in terms of gender discourses in the digital space.* (Christie, Academic at a UK university)

I think online abuse has got worse. But hasn't it always been the case? Men abuse women. Women just have to take it and suck it up? I do wonder where it's going to end, and what all the battles we fought were for. It just seems that men are hardwired to abuse women. What I do know is that not one of the men who send this abuse would be able to do my job, not one. (Agnes, Member of Parliament)

It does feel that we are targeted by young, empowered men who are really abusive to women of a certain generation who fought for women's rights. (Sally, Politician in Scotland)

Consequently, there was a feeling that there is a need for a similar awareness campaign around the issue of online abuse, on a par with that of second wave feminism that took place over 50 years ago:

I feel like this is a problem on a par with raising awareness about rape and domestic violence ... it requires a huge societal change and it's very hard to envision how we're going to get there, but I do think consciousness raising about it is really important. (Jacqueline, Academic at a UK university)

Similarly, just as in the literature (e.g. Henry & Powell, 2015; Jane, 2017a; Suzor et al., 2019), the link between gender-based violence and online abuse was also clear to participants:

I see it all as one, in the sense that in a patriarchal society women's agency, women's independence, women's authentic voice is punished, in the home through domestic violence, in the workplace. In terms of gender-based violence, it is women being out in public or attacked through rape, it's the taking of autonomy to leave your home and do what you want to do. (Jacqueline, Academic at a UK university)

We don't see this as a new phenomenon, it's just the newest iteration of an old phenomenon, all those things that continue to undermine and weaken women's protection in the physical space from violence and domestic partner violence, intimate partner violence, street violence, all those things are at play in the digital world. (Helen, Academic based in the USA)

Online abuse is a constant reminder of just how acceptable violence towards women and gender non-conforming people is. When I see the abuse in my inbox or online, it reminds me constantly of the level of threat that it's still societally ok to lob at women. (Judith, Journalist based in the USA)

Having articulated a link between online abuse, misogyny and gender-based violence, contributors further illustrated the structural impact of online abuse. This is important to consider in order to then be able to devise recommendations.

> *It's really hard to hold the technology companies solely responsible. Do they have a role? Absolutely. But I want us to be talking to men, that this behaviour is out of bounds and it's on all of us to intervene in that behaviour wherever they do it.* (Sue, Academic based in the USA)

> *So, if the bar is lowered on how you refer to women on social media, it just feels like the bar's being lowered all the time in other areas. In terms of some of the stuff I'm looking at around trafficked women and rape, it's terrifying, because it's like women are worthless … that they have no value, so they can just be raped and abused and just calling them a fucking cunt online is ok.* (Agita, Member of the House of Lords)

> *Online abuse is another example of this sense where women are not allowed to occupy certain positions in the social sphere and are punished through violence, through silencing, through threats of violence. Like racism, like any kind of prejudice, threats of violence and then actual occasional violence, keep people from voicing their opinions. They keep people from being more autonomous and being more authentic.* (Tiprat, Academic based in the USA)

In many ways, addressing online abuse at a structural level presents the most complicated policy challenge. However, it is clear from the evidence presented here that it is only by addressing the issue of online abuse at a structural level that real progress will be made. It has repeatedly been shown that policy recommendations which fail to address the underlying structural inequality that precipitates gender-based violence are unlikely to succeed, as they place the onus on the individual to resolve an intractable problem, without providing the necessary mechanisms to do so (Atkinson & Standing, 2019).

> *I think energy is best spent trying to create societal change. Whether it's disinformation or extremism or online abuse, it always comes back to, what can we do for the individual? And the best thing we can do for the individual is push for systemic change.* (Judith, Journalist based in the USA)

Research by Atkinson and Standing (2019) has shown that feminist and intersectional voices have traditionally been excluded from change making at this level, meaning that recommendations that come directly from women, and which are underpinned by a feminist ethos are even more apposite.

Contributors to this research overwhelmingly felt that challenging and changing misogynistic abusive behaviour, whether in the physical or the online space, lay at the heart of tackling this issue from a structural perspective. This supports the work of Edström (2016), who spoke of the need to expose and challenge the behaviour of violent actors online in order to make it unacceptable.

Sue, an Academic based in the USA, termed this the 'Dude, it's not OK' proposition:

> *At a macro level, we need to be arming young men to see it and name it. I want us to give men more tools to be able to say, when there's a rape joke made at a bar, 'dude, not funny'. We've got to intervene and say this is out of bounds, this is unacceptable behaviour. I want more men on Twitter to be interrupting and reporting rape threats the minute they see them, and then challenging the person saying it, saying 'dude, not ok'.* (Sue, Academic based in the USA)

Given the widespread acknowledgement in the literature that the dominant voices online are typically male and white (e.g. Williams et al., 2019), Sue asserted that there is a need for men to use their accumulated power in the online space, in an appropriate way:

> *Men have power, and they need to be flexing it and we need to give them tools on how to do it appropriately, because coming at one inappropriate comment with a flaming minimalization of calling somebody an idiot and stupid is fun, and it feels good, but it's ultimately about saying this behaviour is out of bounds, we need to not confront it with behaviour that's also out of bounds, which is demeaning and belittling.* (Sue, Academic based in the USA)

Sue went on to explain how this approach was more common in other countries:

> *They've done more work in the Scandinavian culture to encourage bystander intervention and engagement and more gender equity. I would love to get some of that and pepper it around the US. I understand the challenges, but I really feel that we need to do more as a society to hold people accountable for their behaviours.* (Sue, Academic based in the USA)

This recommendation was widely supported:

> *Men need to do something about it too. It can't just be women speaking up for women. It's much easier, it's always much easier to intervene on someone else's behalf, than to intervene on your own behalf. So I hope that what we're seeing with the Black Lives Matter movement gaining support from people who aren't Black, that they will now intervene in a way they wouldn't have before. We've*

> *got to expect more from fellow citizens, whether that's online or not, to intervene, to protect.* (Caroline, Member of Parliament until December 2019)

Kerry agreed but emphasised that the responsibility lies with all users of social media platforms to campaign against online abuse and to acknowledge it publicly when it occurs:

> *I don't think things will change unless we see … what the Suffragettes did, what political women did, what women in academia are still doing. You need to know who's your ally … that other people are coming on board to support you. Even if you don't know these people, they should come and support you.* (Kerry, Local Councillor)

Such an approach has been analysed by Wong et al. (2021), who have investigated the effect of bystander intervention in abusive Facebook posts. They discovered that reporting abuse, defending and supporting the victim were the most common interventions and that reporting was far more likely to occur if the reporting of abusive or harmful posts was both simple and anonymous. This confirms the need for online platforms to streamline their reporting mechanisms and to publicise the ease with which reporting can be done.

In addition to practical change emanating from social media companies, Julia highlighted the need for a wider cultural reorientation in the language that politicians use in the public sphere. Political communication needs to become more temperate in order to avoid adding to an already febrile atmosphere which works to silence a genuine multiplicity of voices and opinions:

> *You need to go back and look at how you share power. How do you have more deliberative processes for people to feel like they have agency in decisions that are made about their lives? How do you get politicians themselves to behave better? The language that they use almost creates the environment where people can be bolder in their own choice of words… you've almost got to reteach the politicians the art of persuasion. How they need to behave differently if they want more people to buy into their beliefs. This has been coming for a long time, it's just been expediated by events such as the economic crash, the referendums, and an explosion in productive technology like social media, all of these things have created the climate that we're in so there's not one easy fix.* (Julia, Politician in Scotland)

Conclusion

This chapter provides a range of recommendations that together could be utilised to address the online abuse of women working in public facing occupations.

A strength of these recommendations is that they come from those who have lived experience of online abuse.

These proposals fall into four categories: the actions that women can take as individuals, the support and activity that should be provided by employing organisations, the regulatory and legislative responses that are likely to be effective and finally, the pervasive structural change to gender relations in society that would make misogynistic online abuse unacceptable in mainstream discourse.

At a structural level, it was felt that further equalising the position of women and men throughout society would have the most enduring impact on overcoming online abuse. An integral part of this systemic change is making men more aware of the sheer scale and nature of the abusive content that women in public facing occupations are required to navigate on a daily basis. Such knowledge would assist in embedding the expectation that everyone, especially men, should challenge individual instances of online abuse that they witness in order to further create a climate where such attacks become socially unacceptable. There also needs to be a reorientation of public discourse, to encourage a greater nuance in public debate, which would remove the need for participants in political discussions to repeatedly adopt uncompromising positions.

At a legislative level, there was overwhelming support for greater regulation of online platforms, as outlined in the Online Safety Act (2023). However, the move away from a regulatory regime which could have supported all those who are active in the online space, to legislation which predominantly focusses on children, is a huge missed opportunity and does very little to address many of the issues and experiences discussed here. Similarly, there has been very little training and resourcing of police forces to enable the proper implementation of the new legislation. Finally, it is disappointing to note that there seems little appetite from the Labour government elected in July 2024 to amend the Online Safety Act (2023). This leaves a noticeable gap in the expectation that social media companies should be compelled to take a greater responsibility for the acts of violence, aggression and intimidation that take place on their platforms or an obligation on them to provide innovative solutions to overcoming such activity, using technical means where appropriate.

At an organisational level, participants in this research articulated the view that public sphere employers, whether universities, media organisations, criminal justice agencies or political parties, should provide a greater level of training and support for their employees. Women should feel that they have a guarantee of protection from their employer when faced with abuse during the course of their employment. This should include employers taking on the responsibility for reporting online abuse to the social media companies, or law enforcement, where required. This change to occupational culture should come from the top, with organisational leaders and senior managers aware of the pernicious consequences of online abuse upon all staff, whatever their role or level of seniority. Members of public facing occupations who engage in online abuse should have their membership of the organisation scrutinised, with the possibility of removal, if appropriate.

At an individual level, both women and men should be provided with training in digital literacy, strongly underpinned by the principle that engaging in online abuse is never acceptable. This training should continue through into the continuous professional development schemes that all public sphere employees undertake in order to ensure that women are able to maintain up-to-date skills in reporting and protecting themselves from being targeted online whilst also providing men with the tools they need to act as effective allies against abuse.

Chapter Nine

Conclusion – Assessing the Impact of Online Abuse on Gender-based Violence

Abstract

This chapter summarises the content and consequences of the online abuse of women serving in the public sphere. The chapter revisits the seven elements of online abuse in order to further demonstrate how online abuse directed at women is misogynistic and frequently includes violent threats and dismisses women's contributions to online discussions. The chapter emphasises how online abuse varies by occupation, with police officers most likely to receive abuse that denigrates their ability or appearance, politicians and journalists more likely to receive violent threats and academics receiving abuse of all types. The chapter also outlines how the consequences of abuse are felt at an individual, organisational and structural level, having a malign impact on women's contributions to public life in multiple ways, before revisiting the policy recommendations at the same three levels.

Keywords: Online abuse; public sphere; misogyny; threat; structural change; policy; Online Safety Act (2023)

Introduction

The aim of the empirical research underpinning this book was to investigate the relationship between the online abuse experienced by women employed in public facing occupations and gender-based violence. It was born out of a coalescence of personal concern and academic curiosity arising from the recognition that online abuse is increasingly part of the role for women serving in public

Gendered Online Abuse Against Women in Public Life: More Than Just Words, 175–181
doi:10.1108/978-1-83549-724-120251009

facing occupations. An increasing literature base, coupled with the powerful testimonies presented throughout this volume, confirms that online abuse is highly gendered; often questions women's competence, integrity or appearance and is imbued with threats of violence. The clear conclusion of this work is that the malign impact of technology on women employed in the public sphere must be addressed in order to ensure that the benefits of the new ways of working that have materialised as a consequence of technological advancement can be experienced equally.

The empirical data presented here were collected as part of the successful completion of a PhD degree at the University of York, UK. The research proposal was subjected to detailed scrutiny by the Department of Social Policy and Social Work Ethics Committee, with ethical approval granted before data collection commenced. The subsequent empirical evidence was subjected to robust analytical scrutiny, underpinned by the Braun and Clarke (2006) model of thematic analysis.

This scrutiny has revealed that rather than simply having an impact on gender-based violence, online abuse is *in itself* another manifestation of the gender-based violence first officially recorded back in the 14th century (Dwyer, 1995). Similarly, much of this abuse is underpinned by misogyny and a wider gendered structural inequality that has persisted for centuries. Nevertheless, as well as evidencing striking similarities with gender-based violence that occurs in the physical space, this research also identifies a number of important differences.

It is clear that the online abuse directed at women serving in public sphere occupations is frequently triggered by a topical event or news item and is exacerbated by the increasingly binary nature of political events. Events such as referendums and General Elections and armed conflicts of the sort witnessed in Syria, Ukraine and Gaza (to name but three) frequently act as catalysts for increases in the online abuse that women face even if they themselves have never spoken publicly about any of these topics. The visible articulation of gendered violence in the form of online abuse towards public sphere representatives is new, as it is not shrouded in the secrecy that is commonly found in the gender-based violence that more typically occurs within intimate and familial relationships.

This study has identified two aspects of online abuse that have particular relevance to those working in the public sphere: one negative and one positive, illustrating how having an online presence whilst employed in a public sphere occupation can be both constructive and disadvantageous to women's careers, often at the same time. The first challenge emanates from the expectation that those working in academia, journalism, policing or politics be readily available online and secondly that their seniority may act as an insulator from abuse, not by preventing such communication, but providing ways in which exposure to it can be limited.

This research has also confirmed that engaging in online activity can harness significant benefits, both at an individual and at an organisational level. Communicating with others active in the online space is not only a useful mechanism for the advancement of policies and ideas, but it also enables women to create mutually supportive communities that act as a palliative when abuse occurs.

Cataloguing Women's Experiences of Online Abuse

This research marks the first time that empirical data about online abuse have been gathered from across the public sphere whilst also bringing together the experiences of women based across the UK, the USA and mainland Europe. Combining the experiences of women across professions and locales enables a rich understanding of the challenges faced. Similarly, it has also enabled the mapping of different behavioural elements frequently found in online abuse onto the theories of gender-based violence that were devised to account for violence that occurs in the physical space. This theoretical process confirms that the harms perpetrated online are but another manifestation of the personal and structural misogyny that women have faced for centuries.

By identifying *how* women in the public sphere are targeted online, seven elements of online abuse have been identified. These factors manifest the complex power relationships that occur online. These seven elements are defamation, emotional harm, harassment, silencing, belittling, threat and criticism of appearance. Each of these elements (both individually and combined) was evident in the abusive communication analysed in this study.

Adopting these seven thematic lenses has determined that the online abuse received by women frequently differs according to occupation. Police officers are far more likely to be targeted for abuse that questions their integrity or ability, or which criticises their appearance, voice or age. In contrast, women politicians and journalists are more likely to receive violent or sexualised threats whilst women in academia appear to receive both types of abuse – for reasons that are unclear. It is possible that those who direct online abuse at police officers are more cautious about breaking the law and so engage in abuse that is more subtle whilst not having such concerns when targeting women academics. It may also be a result of the 'anti-woke' perceptions that now underpin much public discourse (Johnson, 2024) and which seem to generate the most extreme responses.

Features of the Public Sphere

This research has also identified that there is an increasing expectation that women working in the public sphere be constantly available online. This expectation increases the unpaid emotional labour (Hochschild, 2012) and safety work (Vera-Gray, 2018) undertaken by women and any staff members they may have. An interesting finding to emerge from this analysis is that seniority of position frequently acts as an insulator against the worst excesses of online abuse. This is because once individuals reach a certain level within an organisational hierarchy, they are less likely to manage their own online accounts, either because the responsibility for the routine operation of these accounts has been delegated to a member of staff or because the various automated safeguards provided by social media platforms means that abuse that occurs is not seen by the individual for whom it is intended. Whilst this may provide a welcome respite for some, it often leaves junior staff members vulnerable to the malign effects of the abuse whilst simultaneously doing nothing to protect those whose positions are not deemed senior enough to benefit from the protection offered by automated tools.

A thread running through this research is the finding that women who hold multiple intersectional identities, whether due to race, class, sexuality or disability, frequently find themselves more heavily targeted for online abuse, reflecting enduring inequalities in the physical space. It is disappointing to confirm that these multiple discriminations perpetuate within newer communication forms.

The Effects of Online Abuse

This research has also discussed how the effects of receiving online abuse are experienced at an individual, organisational and structural level. For the individual, it is clear that receiving online abuse causes huge emotional harm. The empirical evidence concurs with existing literature, to confirm the malign effect of online abuse on an individual's wellbeing. Contributions detailed here also demonstrate the wider impact of emotional harm on others, whether family members, friends or staff, or a combination of all three. This type of emotional harm is pernicious and enduring and illustrates how detriment can occur across multiple levels.

Ultimately, online abuse may cause an individual to withdraw completely from digital interaction, as they choose to exit from the online space. Such action is taken as both an overt occupational choice and an emotional necessity.

However, the effect of online abuse is not only experienced at an individual level, with the consequences frequently extending out to affect the organisational sphere. Online abuse that is directed at women in the course of their employment has the potential to negatively affect an individual's ability to serve the public in the way that they intend. A further consequence of malign online communication is that women may choose to withdraw entirely from the public sphere. This was evidenced in the General Elections of both July 2024 and December 2019 when a large number of Parliamentarians left the House of Commons, frequently citing online abuse as a reason (Watson, 2025). Whilst an individual deciding to pursue an alternative form of employment is not unusual, the motivations for doing so in this situation have a potentially wider impact. Withdrawal from the public sphere risks jeopardising the advancement of women at both an organisational and a structural level, as women lose their voice in the places where power is held and decisions are made, illustrating the act of silencing that is an element of misogyny. When viewed as a whole, the silencing of women has an even greater consequence, as it may also prevent women from forming the occupational and social networks that are essential to both tackling online abuse and facilitating occupational advancement.

This research has also evidenced how online abuse can have a deleterious impact upon women's engagement in the wider public sphere, potentially jeopardising the progress that women have made towards equality across all four of the occupations being analysed in this study. The organisational and structural ramifications associated with a decline in the number of women holding senior positions in the fields of academia, journalism, policing and politics could include a reversal in efforts to counter sexual harassment in the workplace (Jane, 2018), a widening of the gender pay gap (Kavanagh & Brown, 2020) and a policy vacuum at the heart of government.

Moreover, this research has revealed that democracy itself is jeopardised by online abuse, as women may alter the way they vote in parliamentary debates as a consequence.

However, it has been emphasised throughout this book that online interaction is rarely wholly negative. Despite the malign effects described here, there remain huge benefits to individuals serving in public facing occupations as a result of having and maintaining an online presence (Khan et al., 2014; Marwick & Hargittai, 2018). Three key benefits include the value of online interaction as a communication tool, the importance of having and maintaining a voice in the online space and the mutual support that is gained from other women working in the public sphere, particularly during episodes of online abuse.

Problems Reporting Online Abuse

This research has also identified important differences in the reporting mechanisms available on the different social media platforms, which complicate the reporting process. Furthermore, there appeared to be little homogeneity of experience in this regard, with participants' satisfaction with online platforms varying considerably. This has made women sceptical about reporting abuse although holding a position of seniority within the public sphere does appear to provide greater access to law enforcement agencies when abuse occurs. Whilst of benefit to the individual, this highlights inequity in the criminal justice system, with 'ordinary' women unable to benefit from such ease of access. However, despite potentially having greater access to official reporting mechanisms, the attitude of police when investigating cases of online abuse involving high-profile women still often resulted in revictimisation, with the onus on the individual to evidence instances of threatening, violent or sexualised abuse. This mirrors attitudes towards victims of domestic violence and sexual harassment that were held in the 1970s and 1980s.

Where women did choose to report instances of online abuse, this often arose out of a wider concern for the safety of their staff, co-workers or family members, who were often perceived as the 'collateral damage' of online abuse, increasing the emotional harm and stress on an individual, and blurring the line between occupational and personal identity.

Finally, when women held more junior positions within a profession, or were without staff to call upon for technical assistance, there was often a lack of knowledge about how to report online abuse, and who to best make any report to, whether police or social media platforms. This emphasises the need for greater digital literacy, ensuring all women know how to report online abuse and to feel confident in doing so.

The latter chapters of the book have brought together the recommendations for addressing online abuse proposed by research participants. They have been framed as policy proposals, which are designed to work at a structural, legislative, organisational and individual level. It is suggested that government (as operationalised through Ofcom) and public facing occupations, in their role as employers, work with the multiplicity of social media companies to create an interdisciplinarity of approach, to dovetail with the interdisciplinary range of investigative techniques and potential solutions to the problem of online abuse. Stepping outside academic and policy boundaries in this way increases the potential to harness the plurality of policy solutions and technical approaches to resolve a problem that occurs beyond traditional disciplinary parameters.

Just as technology develops in a never ending cycle, so it is with the associated research in this area. One such opportunity for future research identified by this study is the further exploration of the nature of abuse directed at women in different occupations within the public sphere to further unpack the differences in abuse received by academics, journalists, police officers and politicians. In particular, there is a paucity of research considering the online experiences of women police officers when compared to the other occupational groups discussed here, and it would be a worthwhile exercise to attempt to address this gap in a further study. Since this research commenced, a number of events have occurred that have called into question the occupational culture of policing, principally in relation to the Metropolitan Police Service. The abduction, rape and murder of Sarah Everard by a serving police officer, and the subsequent police response to a vigil held in her honour (Wistrich, 2022); along with the conviction of two serving police officers for illegally distributing images of the bodies of Bibaa Henry and Nicole Smallman to a WhatsApp group (Jones & Wilson, 2021) are two cases that have attracted significant public outrage. In February 2022, a report by the Independent Office for Police Conduct (IOPC, 2022) into the dissemination of misogynistic online abuse (including rape jokes) via WhatsApp by police officers serving at Charing Cross Police Station was published (Dodd, 2022). The subsequent charging of two men with multiple counts of sending 'grossly offensive messages on a public communications network contrary to Section 127 of the Communications Act 2003' (IOPC, 2022, p. 1) whilst the public concern about gender-based violence was already high (Wistrich, 2022) ultimately led to the resignation of the Commissioner of the Metropolitan Police, Dame Cressida Dick. In 2023, the Casey Report into the conduct of the Metropolitan Police identified the presence of a negative police culture operating in the force (Turner, 2024), describing the Metropolitan Police as 'institutionally racist, misogynistic and homophobic' (Casey, 2023, p. 7).

In addition to the scope for further work, there are also a number of potential limitations associated with this research. Firstly, there is a disparity in the numbers of participants represented from each occupational group, with more politicians recruited than other occupational categories. It is possible, therefore, that the impacts of online abuse on this group have influenced the wider findings of the study although the triangulation of semi-structured interviews with Twitter data and a comprehensive literature review has been undertaken to negate the presence of any unintended bias. The small sample size found in some of the occupations investigated here is an inevitable consequence of choosing to focus on 'elite' participants (Gray & Jones, 2016). Furthermore, the reliance on snowball sampling, whilst an effective way of gaining access to research populations, will also negatively impact upon generalisability. Despite this obvious and acknowledged limitation, the relatively small total number of women in senior roles in some of the occupations under consideration (e.g. policing) means that the sample size, when viewed as a proportion of the total population, is not as insignificant as may first appear.

This imbalance in participant recruitment is also a result of the limited availability of women across the public sphere, which ultimately dictated the scheduling of interviews.

Similarly, the data gathered from Twitter via the API provide a novel and informative qualitative analysis of increases in social media traffic. However, these data provide a snapshot of one period of time, on one social media platform and, therefore, cannot be relied upon to provide a definitive or comprehensive account (Majó-Vázquez et al., 2021) of the online experiences of all women employed in the public sphere.

Conclusion

This book analyses the presence of the misogynistic online abuse that routinely occurs in the working routines of women employed across a range of public facing occupations. This research has demonstrated that such abuse is not simply a factor within gender-based violence, but it is gender-based violence. The evidence recounted here has often proved challenging to chronicle, as its content and consequence have frequently been distressing. However, Peggy, a politician who continues to sit in the Westminster parliament, reminds us why it is imperative that these experiences are recorded:

> *We don't fight this by hiding from it. I'm much more scared of a world where online abuse stops people coming forward than I am scared of a world where people come forward and might suffer it. I'm willing to give my life to that. I'm much more frightened to sit down than I am to stand up.* (Peggy, Member of Parliament)

Appendix: Pseudonymised List of Participants

Table 3. Pseudonym and Occupation of Each Interview Participant.

Pseudonym Applied	Occupational Sector
Eileen	Academia
Sue	Academia
Carol	Academia
Jacqueline	Academia
Mary	Academia
Tiprat	Academia
Christie	Academia
Souad	Academia
Ann	Academia
Rose	Academia
Ranjit	Academia
Helen	Academia
Emma	Academia
Nicole	Academia
Linda	Journalism
Sophie	Journalism
Michelle	Journalism
Judith	Journalism
Anna	Policing
Samantha	Policing
Sarah	Policing
Geetika	Policing
Imogen	Policing
Karen	Policing
Stacey	Policing
Smita	Politics

(*Continued*)

Table 3.   (*Continued*)

Pseudonym Applied	Occupational Sector
Patricia	Politics
Phyllis	Politics
Klaudia	Politics
Simone	Politics
Sherrie	Politics
Constanta	Politics
Loretta	Politics
Sally	Politics
Peggy	Politics
Charmaine	Politics
Kerry	Politics
Julia	Politics
Beth	Politics
Maya	Politics
Maria	Politics
Agnes	Politics
Wendy	Politics
Caroline	Politics
Svetlana	Politics
Nicola	Politics
Agita	Politics
Lauren	Politics
Jill	Politics
Esther	Politics

References

Aagaard, J. (2017). Introducing post phenomenological research: A brief and selective sketch of phenomenological research methods. *International Journal of Qualitative Studies in Education, 30*(6), 519–533.

Aaltio, I., Kyrö, P., & Sundin, E. (2008). *Women entrepreneurship and social capital: A dialogue and construction.* Copenhagen University Press.

Abbate, J. (2000). *Inventing the internet.* The MIT Press.

Ackerly, B. A. (2001). Feminist theory: Liberal. In N. J. Smelser & P. B. Baltes (Eds.), *International encyclopaedia of the social & behavioral sciences.* Pergamon.

Ahmed, S., & Madrid-Morales, D. (2021). Is it still a man's world? Social media news use and gender inequality in online political engagement. *Information, Communication and Society, 24*(3), 381–399.

Akande, O. N., Badmus, T. A., Akindele, A. T., & Arulogun, O. T. (2020). Dataset to support the adoption of social media and emerging technologies for students' continuous engagement. *Data in Brief, 31,* 1–7.

Aldridge, J. (2021). "Not an Either/or Situation": The minimization of violence against women in United Kingdom "domestic abuse" policy. *Violence Against Women, 27*(11), 1823–1839.

Allen, G., & Zayed, Y. (2024). *Police service strength.* House of Commons Library.

Al-Rawi, A., Chun, W. H. K., & Amer, S. (2021). Vocal, visible and vulnerable: Female politicians at the intersection of Islamophobia, sexism and liberal multiculturalism. *Feminist Media Studies, 22*(8), 1918–1935. https://doi.org/10.1080/14680777.2021.1922487

Amnesty International UK. (2017). *Social media can be a dangerous place for UK women.* Retrieved July 28, 2020, from https://www.amnesty.org.uk/files/Resources/OVAW%20poll%20report.pdf

Angelotti, E. M. (2013). Twibel law: What defamation and its remedies look like in the age of Twitter. *Journal of High Technology Law, 13*(2), 431–507.

Antunovic, D. (2019). "We wouldn't say it to their faces": Online harassment, women sports journalists, and feminism. *Feminist Media Studies, 19*(3), 428–442.

Arbel, T. (2021, January 8). Twitter bans Trump, citing risk of violent incitement. *AP News.* Retrieved July 18, 2024, from https://apnews.com/article/election-2020-donald-trump-media-michael-flynn-social-media-f41b11060d7703e3a3136ddb5eefa055

Aspani, R. (2018). Are women's spaces transgender spaces? Single sex domestic violence shelters, transgender inclusion, and the equal protection clause notes. *California Law Review, 106*(5), 1657–1754.

Atkinson, K., & Standing, K. E. (2019). Changing the culture? A feminist academic activist critique. *Violence Against Women, 25*(11), 1331–1351.

Backe, E. L., Lilleston, P., & McCleary-Sills, J. (2018). Networked individuals, gendered violence: A literature review of cyberviolence. *Violence and Gender, 5*(3), 135–146.

Bailey, J., & Burkell, J. (2021). Tech-facilitated violence: Thinking structurally and intersectionally. *Journal of Gender-Based Violence, 5*(3), 531–542.

Báles, R. F., Strodtbeck, F. L., Mills, T. M., & Roseborough, M. E. (1951). Channels of communication in small groups. *American Sociological Review, 16*(4), 461–468.

Balkin, J. M. (2004). Digital speech and democratic culture: A theory of freedom of expression for the information society. *New York University Law Review, 79*(1), 1–58.

Banet-Weiser, S. (2018). *Empowered: Popular feminism and popular misogyny*. Duke University Press Books.

Barker, C., & Jane, E. A. (2016). *Cultural studies: Theory and practice* (5th edn.). Sage.

Barker, K., & Jurasz, O. (2018). *Online violence against women: The limits and possibilities of law*. Open University Law School. Retrieved June 1, 2020, from http://oro.open. ac.uk/53637/1/OVAW%20-%20The%20Limits%20%26%20Possibilities%20of% 20Law%20%282018%29.pdf

Barlow, C., & Awan, I. (2016). "You need to be sorted out with a knife": The attempted online silencing of women and people of Muslim faith within academia. *Social Media and Society*, *2*(4), 1–11.

Barlow, J. P. (1996). *A declaration of the independence of cyberspace*. Retrieved May 8, 2024, from https://scholarship.law.duke.edu/cgi/viewcontent.cgi?article=1337&cont ext=dltr

Barratt, S. A. (2018). Reinforcing sexism and misogyny: Social media, symbolic violence and the construction of femininity-as-fail. *Journal of International Women's Studies*, *19*(3), 16–31.

Barrie, C. (2023), Did the Musk takeover boost contentious actors on Twitter?. *Harvard Kennedy School Misinformation Review*, *4*(4), 1–19.

Barsaiyan, S., & Sijoria, C. (2021). Twitter blue tick – A study of its impact on society. *Indian Journal of Marketing*, *51*(11), 38–52.

Bates, L. (2016). *Everyday sexism: The project that inspired a worldwide movement*. Simon and Schuster.

Beard, M. (2015). The public voice of women. *Women's History Review*, *24*(5), 809–818.

Beard, M. (2017). *Women and power: A manifesto*. Profile Books.

Beckman, L. J. (2014). Training in feminist research methodology: Doing research on the margins. *Women and Therapy*, *37*(1–2), 164–177.

Beer, D. (2019). *The data gaze*. Sage.

Belam, M., Walker, P., & Levitt, D. (2019). Which MPs are standing down at the 2019 general election? *The Guardian*. Retrieved June 22, 2021, from http://www.theguardian. com/politics/2019/oct/31/which-mps-are-standing-down-at-the-2019-general-election

Bell, B. (2021). *Erin Pizzey: The woman who looked beyond the bruises*. Retrieved November 24, 2021, from https://www.bbc.co.uk/news/uk-england-london-59064064

Beltramini, E. (2020). Against technocratic authoritarianism. A short intellectual history of the cypherpunk movement. *Internet Histories*, 1–19.

Bengtsson Meuller, E. (2024). The misogynist incel in the news: Analysing representations of gender-based violence in Britain. *British Journal of Politics and International Relations*, 13691481231224275.

Bennett, C. (2016). Voter databases, micro-targeting, and data protection law: Can political parties' campaign in Europe as they do in North America? *International Data Privacy Law*, *6*(4), 261–275.

Bennett, S., Moon, D. S., Pearce, N., & Whiting, S. (2021). Labouring under a delusion? Scotland's national questions and the crisis of the Scottish Labour Party. *Territory, Politics, Governance*, *9*(5), 656–674.

Bennett, T., Wibberley, G., & Jones, C. (2019). The legal, moral and business implications of domestic abuse and its impact in the workplace. *Indiana Law Journal*, *48*(1), 137–142.

Berg, B. L., & Budnick, K. J. (1986). Defeminization of women in law enforcement: A new twist in the traditional police personality. *Journal of Police Science and Administration*, *14*(4), 314–319.

Bernstein, M. S., Monroy-Hernández, A., Harry, D., André, P., Panovich, K., & Vargas, G. (2011, July 17–21). *4chan and/b/: An analysis of anonymity and ephemerality in a large online community*. Conference paper at the Association for the Advancement of Artificial Intelligence fifth international conference on weblogs and social media. Barcelona, Catalonia, Spain.

Besley, T., & Larcinese, V. (2011). Working or shirking? Expenses and attendance in the UK Parliament. *Public Choice, 146*(3), 291–317.

Binns, A. (2017). Fair game? Journalists' experiences of online abuse. *Journal of Applied Journalism and Media Studies, 6*(2), 183–206.

Bishop, J. (2014). 'U R bias love:' Using 'bleasure' and 'motif' as forensic linguistic means to annotate twitter and newsblog comments for the purpose of multimedia forensics. Proceedings of the International Conferences on ICT, Society and Human Beings 2014, Web Based Communities and Social Media 2014, e-Commerce 2014, Information Systems Post-Implementation and Change Management 2014 and e-Health 2014 – Part of the Multi Conference on Computer Science and Information Systems, MCCSIS 2014: 115–122.

Blank, G., & Reisdorf, B. C. (2012). The participatory web. *Information, Communication and Society, 15*(4), 537–554.

Bliss, L. (2019). Little Mix member Jesy Nelson confronts the harsh realities of online abuse – And she's not alone. *The Conversation.* Retrieved November 25, 2019, from https://theconversation.com/little-mix-member-jesy-nelson-confronts-the-harsh-realities-of-online-abuse-and-shes-not-alone-123555

Blundell, J. (2008). *Lady thatcher: A portrait.* Algora Publishing.

Blumell, L. E. (2018). Bro, foe, or ally? Measuring ambivalent sexism in political online reporters, *Feminist Media Studies,* 1–17.

Bobrowsky, M. (2022, February 3). Facebook Feels $10 Billion Sting From Apple's Privacy Push; Meta COO Sheryl Sandberg says adjusting to the iPhone maker's app-tracking changes will take time. *Wall Street Journal.*

Bohall, G., Bautista, M. J., & Musson, S. (2016). Intimate partner violence and the Duluth model: An examination of the model and recommendations for future research and practice. *Journal of Family Violence, 31*(8), 1029–1033.

Bohman, J. (2004). Expanding dialogue: The internet, the public sphere and prospects for transnational democracy. In N. Crossley & J. M. Roberts (Eds.), *After Habermas: New perspectives on the public sphere.* Blackwell.

Boseley, S. (2017). Mary Beard abused on Twitter over Roman Britain's ethnic diversity. *The Guardian.* Retrieved July 28, 2020, from https://www.theguardian.com/uk-news/2017/aug/06/mary-beard-twitter-abuse-roman-britain-ethnic-diversity#:~:text=Mary%20Beard%20has%20said%20she,a%20wave%20of%20online%20abuse

Boyd, D. (2015, October 20). *What world are we building? Everett C Parker Lecture.* Washington, DC. Retrieved July 17, 2020, from http://www.danah.org/papers/talks/2015/ParkerLecture.html

Braun, V., & Clarke, V. (2006). Using thematic analysis in psychology. *Qualitative Research in Psychology, 3*(2), 77–101.

Braverman, S. (2023). *Statement on tackling violence against women and girls.* No. UIN HCWS564, House of Commons. Retrieved July 19, 2024, from https://questions-statements.parliament.uk/written-statements/detail/2023-02-20/hcws564

Brennan, I., & Myhill, A. (2022) Coercive control: Patterns in crimes, arrests and outcomes for a new domestic abuse offence. *The British Journal of Criminology, 62*(2), 468–483.

Bridgen, L. (2011). Emotional labour and the pursuit of the personal brand: Public relations practitioners' use of social media. *Journal of Media Practice, 12*(1), 61–76.

Brooks, A. (2019). *Women, politics and the public sphere.* Policy Press.

Brown, J. (2011). We mind and we care but have things changed? Assessment of progress in the reporting, investigating and prosecution of allegations of rape. *Journal of Sexual Aggression, 17*(3), 263–272.

Brown, T. (2022). *Twitter-Watch: Tracking the far right on Twitter.* Github.

Brown, J., & Silvestri, M. (2020). A police service in transformation: Implications for women police officers. *Police Practice & Research: An International Journal, 21*(5), 459–475.

Brown, J., Fleming, J., Silvestri, M., Linton, K., & Gouseti, I. (2019). Implications of police occupational culture in discriminatory experiences of senior women in police forces in England and Wales. *Policing and Society*, *29*(2), 121–136.

Brown, J. M. (1998). Aspects of discriminatory treatment of women police officers serving in forces in England and Wales. *The British Journal of Criminology*, *38*(2), 265–282.

Brown, J. M. & Walklate, S. L. (2011) (Eds.), *Handbook on sexual violence*. Taylor & Francis Group.

Bruns, A. (2019). Filter bubble. *Internet Policy Review*, *8*(4), 1–14.

Buchanan, I. (2024). *Women in politics and public life*. House of Commons Library.

Buil-Gil, D., Zeng, Y., & Kemp, S. (2021). Offline crime bounces back to pre-COVID levels, cyber stays high: Interrupted time-series analysis in Northern Ireland. *Crime Science*, *10*(1), 26–42.

Burch, L. M., Hayday, E. J., Geurin, A. N., Smith, A. C. T., & Hushon, B. (2024). Discriminatory virtual maltreatment and online abuse in digital sporting spaces: An examination of the experiences of six Olympic athletes. *The International Journal of Sport and Society, Common Ground Research Networks*, *15*(3), 69–90.

Burgess, M. C., Byars, F., Sadeghi-Azar, L., & Dill-Shackleford, K. E. (2017). Online misogyny targeting feminist activism: Anita Sarkeesian and Gamergate. In P. Sturmey (Ed.) *The Wiley handbook of violence and aggression*. Wiley.

Burman, M., & Brooks-Hay, O. (2018). Aligning policy and law? The creation of a domestic abuse offence incorporating coercive control. *Criminology & Criminal Justice*, *18*, 67–84.

Cabinet Office. (2023). *Statistical bulletin – Civil Service Statistics: 2023*. Retrieved May 13, 2024, from https://www.gov.uk/government/statistics/civil-service-statistics-2023/statistical-bulletin-civil-service-statistics-2023

Camp, R. A. (2018). Pursuing accountability for perpetrators of intimate partner violence: The peril (and utility?) of shame. *Boston University Law Review*. Boston University. School of Law: 1677–1736.

Campbell, E. (2017). "Apparently being a self-obsessed ct is now academically lauded": Experiencing Twitter trolling of auto ethnographers. *Forum of Qualitative Social Research*, *18*(3), 1–19.

Carrell, S., Stacey, K., & Brooks, L. (2023, February 15). SNP in turmoil after Nicola Sturgeon resigns as first minister. *The Guardian*. Retrieved July 15, 2024, from https://www.theguardian.com/uk-news/2023/feb/15/nicola-sturgeon-expected-to-resign-as-first-minister-of-scotland

Carson, A. (2018). *How is social media benefiting or harming feminism? A systematic literature review and qualitative analysis*. Royal Roads University.

Carver, T., & Chambers, S. A. (2011). *Carole Pateman: Democracy, feminism, welfare*. Routledge.

Casey, L. (2023). *An independent review into the standards of behaviour and internal culture of the Metropolitan Police Service*. Retrieved May 8, 2024, from https://www.met.police.uk/police-forces/metropolitan-police/areas/about-us/about-the-met/bcr/baroness-casey-review/

Cashmore, P. (2009, June 12). *Twitter launches verified accounts*. Mashable. Retrieved June 28, 2024, from https://mashable.com/archive/twitter-verified-accounts-2

Castells, M. (2009). *Communication power*. Oxford University Press.

Chapman, J. (2014). Violence against women in democratic India: Let's talk misogyny. *Social Scientist*, *42*(9/10), 49–61.

Chenou, J. (2014). From cyber-libertarianism to neoliberalism: Internet exceptionalism, multi-stakeholderism, and the institutionalisation of internet governance in the 1990s. *Globalizations*, *11*(2), 205–223.

Childs, S. (2008). *Women and British party politics: Descriptive, substantive and symbolic representation*. Routledge.

Christopherson, K. M. (2007). The positive and negative implications of anonymity in internet social interactions: "On the internet, nobody knows you're a dog". *Computers in Human Behavior, 23*, 3038–3056.

Citron, D. K. (2009). Law's expressive value in combating cyber gender harassment. *Michigan Law Review, 108*(3), 373–416.

Citron, D. K. (2014). *Hate crimes in cyberspace*. Harvard University Press.

Citron, D. K. (2020). Cyber mobs, disinformation, and death videos: The internet as it is (and as it should be). *Michigan Law Review, 118*(6), 1073–1094.

Citron, D. K., & Norton, H. (2011). Intermediaries and hate speech: Fostering digital citizenship for our information age. *Scholarly Commons at Boston University School of Law, 91*, 1435–1484.

Coffé, H. R. (2020). The impact of candidates vocal expression on policy agreement and candidate support: differences between populist radical right and other voters. *Journal of Elections, Public Opinion and Parties, 30*(4), 422–445.

Coleman, E. (2012). Phreaks, hackers, and trolls: The politics of transgression and spectacle. In M. Mandiberg (Ed.). *The social media reader*. NYU Press.

Coleman, S. (2005). New mediation and direct representation: Reconceptualizing representation in the digital age. *New Media and Society, 7*(2), 177–198.

Colliver, B. (2021). Claiming victimhood: Victims of the "transgender agenda". In J. Bailey, A. Flynn, & N. Henry (Eds.), *The Emerald international handbook of technology facilitated violence and abuse (Emerald studies in digital crime, technology and social harms)*. Emerald Publishing Ltd.

Commonwealth Secretariat. (2016). *Women in public sector senior management roles across the Commonwealth*. Retrieved July 21, 2020, from https://thecommonwealth.org/sites/default/files/inline/P14766_SGO_Public_Sector_Mgment_11WAMM-E-copy.pdf

Connolly, I. (2016). Self and identity in cyberspace. In I. Connolly, M. Palmer, H. Barton, & G. Kirwan (Eds.). *An introduction to cyberpsychology*. Routledge.

Cooper, E. (2019, September 26). As the daughter of an MP, I know why Boris Johnson's language is so dangerous. *New Statesman*. Retrieved June 11, 2020, from https://www.newstatesman.com/politics/uk/2019/09/daughter-mp-i-know-why-boris-johnson-s-language-so-dangerous

Corlett, E. (2023, October 14). New Zealand abandons Labour and shifts to the right as country votes for wholesale change. *The Guardian*. Retrieved July 19, 2024, from https://www.theguardian.com/world/2023/oct/14/new-zealand-election-2023-results-national-party-labour-

Cover, R. (2023). Digital hostility, subjectivity and ethics: Theorising the disruption of identity in instances of mass online abuse and hate speech. *Convergence, 29*(2), 308–321.

Cowper-Coles, M. (2020). *Women political leaders: The impact of gender on democracy*. Global Institute for Women's Leadership and the Westminster Foundation for Democracy.

Cracknell, R., & Baker, C. (2024). *General election 2024 results*. House of Commons Library.

Cranston, H. (2015). This is what it's like to have a vagina on the internet. *The Huffington Post*. Retrieved July 29, 2020, from https://www.huffpost.com/entry/this-is-what-its-like-to-have-a-vagina-on-the-internet_b_8808742

Crawford, K. (2009). Following you: Disciplines of listening in social media. *Continuum, 23*(4), 525–535.

Crenshaw, K. (1989). Demarginalizing the intersection of race and sex: A Black feminist critique of antidiscrimination doctrine, feminist theory, and antiracist politics. In K. T. Bartlett & Kennedy (Eds.), *Feminist legal theory* (pp. 57–80). Routledge.

Crewe, E., & Walker, A. (2019). *An extraordinary scandal: The Westminster expenses crisis and why it still matters*. Haus Publishing.

Criado-Perez, C. (2013, August 12). Diary: Internet trolls, Twitter rape threats and putting Jane Austen on our banknotes. *The New Statesman.* 5.

Croall, H. (1995). Target women: Women's victimisation and white-collar crime. In R. E. Dobash, R. P. Dobash, & L. Noaks (Eds.), *Gender and crime.* University of Wales Press.

Crockett, E. (2016). *Nine prominent feminists on what Hillary Clinton's historic candidacy really means.* Retrieved August 13, 2020, from https://www.vox.com/2016/7/28/12300078/hillary-clinton-woman-president-democratic-nomination-feminists

Crown Prosecution Service. (2016). *Guidelines on prosecuting cases involving communications sent via social media.* Retrieved June 17, 2020, from https://www.cps.gov.uk/legal-guidance/social-media-guidelines-prosecuting-cases-involving-communications-sent-social-media

Crown Prosecution Service. (2018). *Social media offences.* Retrieved June 18, 2020, from https://www.cps.gov.uk/cyber-online-crime

Crown Prosecution Service. (2023). *Controlling or coercive behaviour in an intimate or family relationship.* Retrieved July 17, 2024, from https://www.cps.gov.uk/legal-guidance/controlling-or-coercive-behaviour-intimate-or-family-relationship

Cruse, S. (2022). Musk's latest plan to save Twitter: $8 Blue check marks? *The Daily Navigator.* Retrieved June 28, 2024, from https://thedailynavigator.com/news/musks-latest-plan-to-save-twitter-8-blue-check-marks/

Cumming-Potvin, W. (2023). The politics of school dress codes and uniform policies: Towards gender diversity and gender equity in schools. *International Journal of Educational Research, 122,* 102239.

Dahlberg, L. (2007). 'Do-it yourself' digital citizenship: A preliminary interrogation. *New Zealand Sociology, 22*(1), 294–301.

Daly, E. (2021). Making new meanings: The entextualisation of digital communications evidence in English sexual offences trials. *Crime, Media, Culture, 18*(4), 578–596.

David, M. E. (2016). *Reclaiming feminism: Challenging everyday misogyny.* Policy Press.

Davidson, J., Grove-Hills, J., Bifulco, A., Gottschalk, P., Caretti, V., Pham, T., & Webster, S. (2011). Online abuse: Literature review and policy context. *Project Report, European Online Grooming Project, 9,* 1–52.

Davies, P. (2007). Women, victims and crime. In P. Davies, P. Francis, & C. Greer (Eds.), *Victims, crime and society.* Sage.

D'Cruze, S. (2011). Sexual violence in history: A contemporary heritage? In J. M. Brown & S. L. Walklate (Eds.), *Handbook on sexual violence.* Taylor & Francis Group.

DeCook, J. R., & Kelly, M. (2023). Interrogating the "incel menace": Assessing the threat of male supremacy in terrorism studies. In *Gender and the governance of terrorism and violent extremism* (pp. 206–226). Routledge.

De Kimpe, L., Ponnet, K., Walrave, M., Snaphaan, T., Pauwels, L., & Hardyns, W. (2020). Help, I need somebody: Examining the antecedents of social support seeking among cybercrime victims. *Computers in Human Behavior, 108,* 1–11.

DeNardis, L., & Hackl, A. M. (2015). Internet governance by social media platforms. *Telecommunications Policy, 39*(9), 761–770.

Department of Culture, Media and Sport (DCMS). (2017, October 10). *Making Britain the safest place in the world to be online.* Retrieved June 12, 2023, from https://www.gov.uk/government/news/making-britain-the-safest-place-in-the-world-to-be-online

Dewey, C. (2014, October 14). The only guide to Gamergate you will ever need to read. *The Washington Post.* Retrieved July 28, 2020, from https://www.washingtonpost.com/news/the-intersect/wp/2014/10/14/the-only-guide-to-gamergate-you-will-ever-need-to-read/

Dey, S. (2019). Let there be clamor: Exploring the emergence of a new public sphere in India and use of social media as an instrument of activism. *Journal of Communication Inquiry*, 1–21.

Diers-Lawson, A. (2022). "She's Played a Blinder": Nicola Sturgeon as a crisis leader and change agent in Scotland. *Towards a new understanding of masculine habitus and women and leadership in public relations* (pp. 228–246). Routledge.

Dobash, R. E., & Dobash, R. (1998). *Rethinking violence against women*. Sage.

Dobash, R. E., & Dobash, R. (1980). *Violence against wives: A case against the patriarchy*. Open Books.

Dodd, V. (2022, February 1). Met police misogyny: The rot runs even deeper than thought. *The Guardian*. Retrieved April 1. 2022, from https://www.theguardian.com/society/2022/feb/01/revealing-the-rot-police-misogyny-runs-deeper-still

Domestic Abuse Intervention Programs (DAIP). (2022). *Wheels information center*. Retrieved September 6, 2022, from https://www.theduluthmodel.org/wheels/

Donnell, H., & Peacock, C. (2024, May 19). Media oversight one-stop-shop stopped. *RNZ*. Retrieved July 17, 2024, from https://www.rnz.co.nz/national/programmes/mediawatch/audio/2018938976/media-oversight-one-stop-shop-stopped

Dowell, C. (2013, January 21). Mary Beard suffers 'truly vile' online abuse after Question Time. *The Guardian*. Retrieved July 28, 2020, from https://www.theguardian.com/media/2013/jan/21/mary-beard-suffers-twitter-abuse

Doyle, S. (2011, November 10). But how do you know it's sexist? The #mencallmethings round-up. *Tiger Beatdown*. Retrieved August 13, 2020, from http://tigerbeatdown.com/2011/11/10/but-how-do-you-know-its-sexist-the-mencallmethings-round-up/

Doyle, S. (2020, February 20). Elizabeth Warren is marginalized Americans' best hope. *Medium*. Retrieved August 13, 2020, from https://gen.medium.com/elizabeth-warren-is-marginalized-americans-best-hope-d2e1baadfcaf

Dragiewicz, M., & Burgess, J. (2016). Domestic violence on #qanda: The "Man" question in live Twitter discussion on the Australian Broadcasting Corporation's Q&A. *Canadian Journal of Women and the Law = Revue Juridique la Femme et le Droit*, *28*(1), 211–229.

Dragiewicz, M., Burgess, J., Matamoros-Fernández, A., Salter, M., Suzor, N. P., Woodlock, D., & Harris, B. (2018). Technology facilitated coercive control: Domestic violence and the competing roles of digital media platforms. *Feminist Media Studies*, *18*(4), 609–625.

Dragotto, F., Giomi, E., & Melchiorre, S. M. (2020). Putting women back in their place. Reflections on slut-shaming, the case of Asia Argento and Twitter in Italy. *International Review of Sociology*, *30*(1), 46–70.

Drysdale, N. (2023). It's time for women of all parties to stand up to "vile" social media abuse. *Press and Journal*. Retrieved July 26, 2024, from https://www.pressandjournal.co.uk/fp/lifestyle/5940934/saturday-essay-its-time-for-women-of-all-parties-to-stand-up-to-vile-social-media-abuse/

Dubois, E., Minaeian, S., Paquet-Labelle, A., & Beaudry, S. (2020). Who to trust on social media: How opinion leaders and seekers avoid disinformation and echo chambers. *Social Media and Society*, *6*(2), 1–13.

Dubrovsky, V., Kiesler, S., Sproull, L., & Zubrow, D. (1986). Socialization to computing in college: A look beyond the classroom. In R. S. Feldman (Ed.), *The social psychology of education: Current research and theory* (pp. 313–340). Cambridge University Press.

Dubrovsky, V. J., Kiesler, S., & Sethna, B. N. (1991). The equalization phenomenon: Status effects in computer-mediated and face-to-face decision-making groups. *Human-Computer Interaction*, *6*(2), 119–146.

Duffy, B. E., & Chan, N. K. (2019). "You never really know who's looking": Imagined surveillance across social media platforms. *New Media and Society, 21*(1), 119–138.

Dungay, K. (2021). *Violence against women – What can be done?* University Hospital Plymouth Blog. Retrieved December 21, 2021, from https://plymouthhospitalsblog. org/2021/04/10/violence-against-women-what-can-be-done/

Durie, M. (2021). The theological drivers of jihad. *Quadrant, 65*(12), 47–49.

Dutton, D. G., & Corvo, K. (2006). Transforming a flawed policy: A call to revive psychology and science in domestic violence research and practice. *Aggression and Violent Behavior, 11*(5), 457–483.

Dwyer, D. C. (1995). Response to the victims of domestic violence: Analysis and implications of the British experience. *Crime and Delinquency, 41*(4), 527–540.

Ebert, T. L. (1991). The "difference" of postmodern feminism. *College English, 53*(8), 886–904.

Eckert, S. (2018). Fighting for recognition: Online abuse of women bloggers in Germany, Switzerland, the United Kingdom, and the United States. *New Media and Society, 20*(4), 1282–1302.

Edosomwan, S., Prakasan, S. K., Kouame, D., Watson, J., & Seymour, T. (2011). The history of social media and its impact on business. *The Journal of Applied Management and Entrepreneurship, 16*(3), 1–13.

Edström, M. (2016). The trolls disappear in the light: Swedish experiences of mediated sexualised hate speech in the aftermath of Behring Breivik. *International Journal for Crime, Justice and Social Democracy, 5*(2), 96–106.

Edwards, A. (2013). (How) do participants in online discussion forums create "echo chambers"? The inclusion and exclusion of dissenting voices in an online forum about climate change. *Journal of Argumentation in Context, 2*(1), 127–150.

Edwards, C. (2017). The valley vision. *Engineering and Technology, 12*(7), 26–29.

Edwards, R. (1990). Connecting method and epistemology. *Women's Studies International Forum, 13*(5), 477–490.

Elbaum, R. (2019, March 29). Protesters – For and against Brexit – Set up outside Parliament. *NBC News*. Retrieved June 24, 2021, from https://www.nbcnews.com/ storyline/brexit-referendum/protesters-against-brexit-set-outside-parliament-n986961

Elgot, J. (2022, November 29). UK Minister defends U-turn over removing harmful online content. *The Guardian*. Retrieved July 1, 2023, from https://www.theguardian.com/ technology/2022/nov/29/minister-defends-u-turn-over-removing-harmful-online-content-online-safety-bill

Emmerson, C., Farquharson, C., Johnson, P., & Zaranko, B. (2024). *Constraints and trade-offs for the next government.* The IFS. Retrieved January 15, from, https:// doi.org/10.1920/re.ifs.2024.0295

Errity, A. (2016). Human-computer interaction. In I. Connolly, M. Palmer, H. Barton, & G. Kirwan (Eds.), *An introduction to cyberpsychology*. Routledge.

Evans, K. (2013). Rethinking community in the digital age? In K. Orton-Johnson and N. Prior (Eds.). *Digital sociology: Critical perspectives*. Palgrave.

Evolvi, G. (2019). #Islamexit: Inter-group antagonism on Twitter. *Information, Communication and Society, 22*(3), 386–401.

Farrell, T., Fernandez, M., Novotny, J., & Alani, H. (2019, June 26). Exploring misogyny across the manosphere in Reddit. In *Proceedings of the 10th ACM Conference on Web Science. WebSci '19* (pp. 87–96). Association for Computing Machinery.

Femicide Index. (2023). *Women killed by men in 2023*. Retrieved July 18, 2024, from https://kareningalasmith.com/2023/10/02/2023/

Fendt, L. S., Wilson, E., Jenkins, J., Dimmock, K., & Weeks, P. (2014). Presenting phenomenology: Faithfully recreating the lived experiences of Surfer Girls. *Annals of Leisure Research, 17*(4), 398–416.

Fernet, M., Lapierreb, A., Héberta, A., & Cousineau, M. (2019). A systematic review of literature on cyber intimate partner victimization in adolescent girls and women. *Computers in Human Behavior, 100*, 11–25.

Ferraro, K. (1996). Women's fear of victimization: Shadow of sexual assault? *Social Forces, 75*(2), 667–690.

Fessler, L. (2018, May 24). *Thank you very much. An extremely clear definition of emotional labor for anyone who still doesn't get it.* Quartz at Work. Retrieved May 14, 2019, from https://qz.com/work/1286996/an-extremely-clear-definition-of-emotional-labor-from-adam-grants-podcast/

Finegold, A. R. D., & Cooke, L. (2006). Exploring the attitudes, experiences and dynamics of interaction in online groups. *Internet and Higher Education, 9*(3), 201–215.

Fontaine, L. (2017). The early semantics of the neologism BREXIT: A lexicogrammatical approach. *Functional Linguistics, 4*(1), 1–15.

Founta, A. M., Chatzakou, D., Kourtellis, N., Blackburn, J., Vakali, A., & Leontiadis, I. (2019, June 30–July 3). *A unified deep learning architecture for abuse detection.* Proceedings of the 10th Association of Computer Machinery (ACM) Conference on Web Science. Boston, Massachusetts, USA.

Friedan, B. (1963). *The feminine mystique.* Penguin.

Fuchs, C. (2020). The utopian internet, computing, communication, and concrete utopias: Reading William Morris, Peter Kropotkin, Ursula K. Le Guin, and P.M. in the light of digital socialism. Triple C: Communication, capitalism and critique. *Open Access Journal for a Global Sustainable Information Society, 18*(1), 146–186.

Gallacher, J. D., Heerdink, M. W., & Hewstone, M. (2021). Online engagement between opposing political protest groups via social media is linked to physical violence of offline encounters. *Social Media and Society, 7*(1), 1–16.

Galpin, C. (2022). At the digital margins? A theoretical examination of social media engagement using intersectional feminism. *Politics and Governance, 10*(1), 161–171.

Galtung, J. (1969). Violence, peace, and peace research. *Journal of Peace Research, 6*(3), 167–191.

Galtung, J. (1990). Cultural violence. *Journal of Peace Research, 27*(3), 291–305.

Gámez Fuentes, M. J., Gómez Nicolau, E., & Maseda García, R. (2016). Celebrities, gender-based violence and women's rights: Towards the transformation of the framework of recognition? *Revista Latina de Comunicación Social, 71*, 833–852.

Gane, N., & Beer, D. (2008). *New media.* Berg.

Garcia-Moreno, C., & Stöckl, H. (2017). Violence against women. In S. R. Quah (Ed.), *International encyclopaedia of public health* (2nd edn.). Academic Press.

Gardiner, B. (2018). 'It's a terrible way to go to work': What 70 million readers' comments on The Guardian revealed about hostility to women and minorities online. *Feminist Media Studies, 18*(4), 592–608.

Gardiner, B., Mansfield, M., Anderson, I., Holder, J., Louter, D., & Ulmanu, M. (2016, April 12). The dark side of Guardian comments. *The Guardian Newspaper.* Retrieved June 21, 2021, from https://www.theguardian.com/technology/2016/apr/12/the-dark-side-of-guardian-comments

Gardsbane, D., Bukuluki, P., & Musuya, T. (2022). Help-seeking within the context of patriarchy for domestic violence in urban Uganda. *Violence Against Women, 28*(1), 232–254.

Garimella, K., De Francisci Morales, G., Gionis, A., & Mathioudakis, M. (2018). Political discourse on social media: Echo chambers, gatekeepers, and the price of bipartisanship. *Proceedings of the 2018 World Wide Web Conference*, 913–922. https://doi.org/10.1145/3178876.3186139

Gecsoyler, S., & Carrell, S. (2023). Why was Nicola Sturgeon arrested and what does it mean for Scottish independence? *The Guardian.* Retrieved July 16, 2024, from https://www.

theguardian.com/politics/2023/jun/12/why-was-nicola-sturgeon-arrested-and-what-does-it-mean-for-scottish-independence

Gerbaudo, P. (2018). Social media and populism: An elective affinity? *Media Culture & Society*, *40*(5), 745–753.

Gilmore, D. D. (2009). *Misogyny: The male malady*. University of Pennsylvania Press.

Ging, D. (2019). Alphas, betas, and Incels: Theorizing the masculinities of the manosphere. *Men and Masculinities*, *22*(4), 638–657.

Ging, D. (2023). Tactics of hate: Toxic "creativity" in anti-feminist men's rights politics. In K. Boyle & S. Berridge (Eds.), *The routledge companion to gender, media and violence* (1st edn.). Routledge.

Ging, D., Lynn, T., & Rosati, P. (2020). Neologising misogyny: Urban Dictionary's folk-sonomies of sexual abuse. *New Media and Society*, *22*(5), 838–856.

Ging, D., & Siapera, E. (2018). Introduction to special issue on online misogyny. *Feminist Media Studies*, *18*(4), 515–524.

Ginsberg, J. (2019). Trying to shut down women: Women are being forced out of politics as a result of abuse. We need to rally behind them, for all our sakes. *Index on Censorship*, *48*(4), 50–51.

Gizzo, C., Weinstein, L., Bolderas, K., & Rooney, S. (2022). *Australia takes the international lead in social media regulation, social media law bulletin*. Retrieved June 21, 2023, from https://www.socialmedialawbulletin.com/2022/02/australia-takes-the-international-lead-in-social-media-regulation/

Glitch. (2021, April 29). *Glitch working with BT on major new campaign to tackle online abuse*. Retrieved June 28, 2021, from https://glitchcharity.co.uk/drawtheline/

Glitch. (2023). *UK online safety bill*. Retrieved July 28, 2023, from https://glitchcharity.co.uk/uk-online-safety-bill/

Gondolf, E. W. (2011). The weak evidence for batterer program alternatives. *Aggression and Violent Behavior*, *16*(4), 347–353.

Gorrell, G., Bakir, M. E., Roberts, I., Greenwood, M., & Bontcheva, K. (2020). Which politicians receive abuse? Four factors illuminated in the UK general election 2019. *EPJ Data Science*, *9*(1), 9–18.

Graham Hall, J. (1978). Any hope for family courts? *Poly Law Review*, *4*(2), 77–79.

Grant, J. (2021). Indecent exposure: A serious "nuisance" offence. *Women's History Review*, *30*(7), 1219–1224.

Gray, G., & Jones, M. D. (2016). A qualitative narrative policy framework? Examining the policy narratives of US campaign finance regulatory reform. *Public Policy and Administration*, *31*(3), 193–220.

Grebelsky-Lichtman, T., & Katz, R. (2019). When a man debates a woman: Trump vs. Clinton in the first mixed gender presidential debates. *Indian Journal of Gender Studies*, *28*(6), 699–719.

Guo, L. A., Rohde, J., & Wu, H. D. (2020). Who is responsible for Twitter's echo chamber problem? Evidence from 2016 U.S. election networks. *Information, Communication and Society*, *23*(2), 234–251.

Gurak, L. J. (1995). Rhetorical dynamics of corporate communication in cyberspace: The protest over Lotus Market Place. *IEEE Transactions on Professional Communication*, *38*(1), 2–10.

Habermas, J. (2004). *The divided west*. Polity Press.

Habermas, J., Lennox, S., & Lennox, F. (1964). The public sphere: An encyclopaedia article. *New German Critique*, *3*, 49–55.

Hansard. (2017). *UK elections: Abuse and intimidation – Westminster Hall debate*. Retrieved March 24, 2021, from https://hansard.parliament.uk/Commons/2017-07-12/debates/577970DD-1AEF-4071-8AE0-3E3FC6753C6A/UKElectionsAbuseAndIntimidation#contribution-DD641FE6-C9D7-4D0D-8201-C4D9632AA450

Hansard. (2021, July 14). *Questions to the Prime Minister*. Retrieved July 16, 2021, from https://hansard.parliament.uk/Commons/2021-07-14/debates/1e572d49-8faf-4273-a224-36d4ae6f42f7/CommonsChamber

Hardaker, C., & McGlashan, M. (2016). "Real men don't hate women": Twitter rape threats and group identity. *Journal of Pragmatics, 91*, 80–89.

Harel, T. O., Jameson, J. K., & Maoz, I. (2020). The normalization of hatred: Identity, affective polarization, and dehumanization on Facebook in the context of intractable political conflict. *Social Media and Society, 6*(2), 1–10.

Harlow, S., Rowlett, J. T., & Huse, L. K. (2020). "Kim Davis be like ...": A feminist critique of gender humor in online political memes. *Information, Communication and Society, 23*(7), 1057–1073.

Harmer, E. (2017). 'Pink Buses, Leaders' wives and "The Most Dangerous Woman in Britain": Women, the press and politics in the 2015 election. In D. Wring, R. Mortimore, & S. Atkinson (Eds.), *Political communication in Britain: Polling, campaigning and media in the 2015 general election* (pp. 259–272). Springer International Publishing.

Harp, D., Grimm, J., & Loke, J. (2018). Rape, storytelling and social media: How Twitter interrupted the news media's ability to construct collective memory. *Feminist Media Studies, 18*(6), 979–995.

Harris, B., & Vitis, L. (2020). Digital intrusions: Technology, spatiality and violence against women. *Journal of Gender-based Violence, 4*(3), 325–341.

Harrison, G., & Huslage, M. (2023). The curious case of Karen Carney: The argument for equity over equality in curbing the online abuse of women in sports media. In K. Boyle & S. Berridge (Eds.), *The Routledge companion to gender, media and violence* (1st ed.). Routledge.

Hayes, D., Lawless, J. L., & Baitinger, G. (2014). Who cares what they wear? Media, gender, and the influence of candidate appearance. *Social Science Quarterly, 95*(5), 1194–1212.

Haynes, J. (2024, July 5). *Jess Phillips heckled during election result as she says "you can't bear seeing a strong woman up here"*. Birmingham Live. Retrieved July 28, 2024, from https://www.birminghammail.co.uk/news/midlands-news/jess-phillips-heckled-during-election-29480160

Heise, L., Ellsberg, M., & Gottemoeller, M. (1999). Ending violence against women. *Population Reports, 27*(4), 1.

Heiss, R., Schmuck, D., & Matthes, J. (2019). What drives interaction in political actors' Facebook posts? Profile and content predictors of user engagement and political actors' reactions. *Information, Communication and Society, 22*(10), 1497–1513.

Helm, T. (2024, July 7). Where will they all sit? Commons welcomes 334 rookie MPs in most diverse parliament. *The Guardian*. Retrieved July 26, 2024, from https://www.theguardian.com/politics/article/2024/jul/07/commons-334-rookie-mps-diverse-parliament-women-ethnic-minority

Hendricks, J. A., & Schill, D. (2024). The 2020 US Presidential election and social media and Trump. *Social Media Politics*, 1–18.

Henry, N., & Powell, A. (2015). Beyond the 'sext': Technology-facilitated sexual violence and harassment against adult women. *The Australian & New Zealand Journal of Criminology, 48*(1), 104–118.

Hernandez, S. (2020, April 1). Zoom bombing incidents overwhelm online classes and meeting with racist slurs. *Buzzfeed News*. Retrieved December 16, 2020, from https://www.buzzfeednews.com/article/salvadorhernandez/zoom-coronavirus-racist-zoom-bombing

Herrera, G. L. (2016). Cyberspace and sovereignty: Thoughts on physical space and digital space. In M. D. Cavelty & V. Mauer (Eds.), *Power and security in the information age: Investigating the role of the state in cyberspace*. Routledge.

Herring, S., Job-Sluder, Scheckler, R., & Barab, S. (2002). Searching for safety online: Managing 'trolling' in a feminist forum. *The Information Society, 18*(5), 371–384.

Herring, S. C. (1996). Gender differences in CMC: Bringing familiar baggage to the new frontier. In V. Vitanza (Ed.), *CyberReader*. Allyn & Bacon.

Herring, S. C. (2013). Discourse in Web 2.0: Familiar, reconfigured, and emergent. In D. Tannen & A. M. Trester (Eds.), *Discourse 2.0: Language and new media*. Georgetown University Press.

Hester, M. (2006). Making it through the criminal justice system: Attrition and domestic violence. *Social Policy and Society, 5*(1), 79–90.

HM Government. (2024). *The King's Speech background briefing note*. Retrieved July 17, 2024, from https://assets.publishing.service.gov.uk/media/6697f5c10808eaf43b50d18e/The_King_s_Speech_2024_background_briefing_notes.pdf

Hochschild, A. R. (2012). *The managed heart: Commercialization of human feeling* (updated edition). University of California Press.

Hodson, J., Gosse, C., Veletsianos, G., & Houlden, S. (2018). I get by with a little help from my friends: The ecological model and support for women scholars experiencing online harassment. *First Monday, 23*(8).

Holt, A., & Lewis, S. (2021). Constituting child-to-parent violence: Lessons from England and Wales. *The British Journal of Criminology, 61*(3), 792–811.

Holt, S., Øverlien, C., & Devaney, J. (2018). (Eds.). *Responding to domestic violence: Emerging challenges for policy, practice and research in Europe*. Jessica Kingsley Publishers.

Home Affairs Select Committee. (2017). *Hate crime: Abuse, hate and extremism online*. Fourteenth Report of Session 2016–17. HC 609. House of Commons.

Home Office. (2021, April 29). *Landmark domestic abuse bill receives royal assent*. GOV.UK. Retrieve December 21, 2021, from https://www.gov.uk/government/news/landmark-domestic-abuse-bill-receives-royalassent

Houghton, I. (2023). *Social media platforms will lose for disregarding code of practice, Amnesty Kenya*. Retrieved June 21, 2023, from https://www.amnestykenya.org/social-media-platforms-will-lose-for-disregarding-code-of-practice/

House of Commons. (2019a). *Online harms white paper*. HMSO.

House of Commons. (2019b). *Joint committee on human rights: Democracy, freedom of expression and freedom of association: Threats to MPs*. Retrieved June 19, 2021, from https://publications.parliament.uk/pa/jt201919/jtselect/jtrights/37/37.pdf

House of Lords. (2020). *Digital technology and the resurrection of trust*. Select Committee on Democracy and Digital Technologies. HMSO.

Hulley, S. (2021). Defending "co-offending" women: Recognising domestic abuse and coercive control in 'joint enterprise' cases involving women and their intimate partners. *The Howard Journal of Crime and Justice, 60*(4), 580–603.

Humprecht, E., Hellmueller, L., & Lischka, J. A. (2020). Hostile emotions in news comments: A cross-national analysis of Facebook discussions. *Social Media and Society, 6*(1), 1–12.

Hundleby, C. (2011). *Feminist empiricism*. Handbook of feminist research: Theory and praxis: 28–45. Retrieved January 4, 2022, from https://scholar.uwindsor.ca/philosophypub/31

Huntemann, N. (2015). No more excuses: Using Twitter to challenge the symbolic annihilation of women in games. *Feminist Media Studies, 15*(1), 164–167.

Husnain, M., Khalid, A., & Shafi, N. (2021). *A novel preprocessing technique for toxic comment classification*. 2021 International Conference on Artificial Intelligence (ICAI), 22–27.

Hymas, C. (2023, January 9). Record 40 per cent of chief constables are now women amid anti-misogyny drive. *The Daily Telegraph*. Retrieved May 3, 2024, from https://www.

telegraph.co.uk/news/2023/01/09/record-40-per-cent-chief-constables-now-women-amid-anti-misogyny/

IOPC. (2022). *Two Met officers and a former officer charged over WhatsApp messages.* Retrieved April 1, 2022, from https://www.policeconduct.gov.uk/news/two-met-officers-and-former-officer-charged-over-whatsapp-messages

Iudici, A., & Girolimetto, D. (2020). The role of public places in disability hate crimes (DHCs). In V. Ceccato & M. K. Nalla (Eds.), *Crime and fear in public places: Towards safe, inclusive and sustainable cities.* Routledge.

Ivers, C. (2023). Out of order order: Politicians are quitting Westminster in droves, many of them under 40. *The Sunday Times.*

Jackson, M. (2021, July 16). Police and CPS in rape case blame game. *BBC News.* Retrieved July 30, 2021, from https://www.bbc.co.uk/news/uk-57856719

Jackson, S. J., & Banaszczyk, S. (2016). Digital standpoints: Debating gendered violence and racial exclusions in the feminist counterpublic. *The Journal of Communication Inquiry, 40*(4), 391–407.

Jane, E. A. (2014a). 'Your a ugly, whorish, slut': Understanding e-bile. *Feminist Media Studies, 14*(4), 531–546.

Jane, E. A. (2014b). 'Back to the kitchen, cunt': Speaking the unspeakable about online misogyny. *Continuum, 28*(4), 558–570.

Jane, E. A. (2015). Flaming? What flaming?: The pitfalls and potentials of researching online hostility. *Ethics and Information Technology, 17*(1), 65–87.

Jane, E. A. (2016). Online misogyny and feminist digilantism. *Continuum, 30*(3), 284–297.

Jane, E. A. (2017a). *Misogyny online: A short (and brutish) history.* Sage.

Jane, E. (2017b). Feminist flight and fight responses. In M. Segrave (Ed.), *Gender, technology and violence.* Routledge.

Jane, E. A. (2018). Gendered cyberhate as workplace harassment and economic vandalism. *Feminist Media Studies, 18*(4), 575–591.

Jennings, F. J., & Coker, C. R. (2019). 'I just don't think she has a presidential look': The influence of sexism on candidate image. *Information Communication and Society,* 1–15.

Jerath, K. S. (2021). Feminism and gender equality: An ongoing debate. In K. S. Jerath (Ed.) *Science, technology and modernity: An interdisciplinary approach* (pp. 161–176). Springer International Publishing.

Jia, Q., & Xu, S. (2022). An overall analysis of Twitter and Elon Musk M&A deal. *Highlights in business, economics and management* (Vol. 2, pp. 436–441). Darcy & Roy Press Company Limited.

Joachim, J. M. (2007). *Agenda setting, the UN, and NGOs: Gender violence and reproductive rights.* Georgetown University Press.

Johnson, P. (2024). (Re)contextualizing the 'anti-woke discourse: Attitudes towards gender-inclusive language in English and French on X (formerly Twitter). *Journal of Language Aggression and Conflict,* 1–23.

Johnston, M., & True, J. (2019). *Misogyny and violent extremism: Implications for preventing violent extremism.* UN Women.

Jones, H. (2019). More in common: The domestication of misogynist white supremacy and the assassination of Jo Cox, *Ethnic and Racial Studies, 42*(14), 2431–2449.

Jones, P. (2023, November 24). *Domestic abuse in England and Wales overview – Office for National Statistics.* Office for National Statistics. Retrieved July 18, 2024, from https://www.ons.gov.uk/peoplepopulationandcommunity/crimeandjustice/bulletins/domesticabuseinenglandandwalesoverview/november2023

Jones, L., & Wilson, M. (2021). 'It's genetic, init'? Racialising the lockdown. In D. Ellis & A. Voela (Eds.), *After lockdown, opening up. Studies in the psychosocial.* Palgrave Macmillan.

Julios, C. (2022). *Sexual harassment in the UK Parliament: Lessons from the #MeToo era.* Palgrave Macmillan.

Kapidzic, S. (2020). The social academic: A social capital approach to academic relationship management on social media. *Information, Communication and Society, 23*(11), 1673–1688.

Karell, D., & Sachs, J. (2023). How symbols influence social media discourse: An embedding regression analysis of Trump's return to Twitter. *Socius: Sociological Research for a Dynamic World, 9,* https://doi.org/10.1177/23780231231212108

Kargar, S., & Rauchfleisch, A. (2019). State-aligned trolling in Iran and the double-edged affordances of Instagram. *New Media and Society, 21*(7), 1506–1527.

Karl, I. (2007). On/offline: Gender, sexuality and the techno-politics of everyday life. In K. O'Riordan & D. J. Phillips (Eds.), *Queer online: Media, technology and sexuality.* Peter Lang Publishing.

Kasana, M. (2014). Feminisms and the social media sphere, *Women's Studies Quarterly, 42*(3), 236–249.

Katwala, S., & Rutter, J. (2024). *Ethnic and gender diversity in the next parliament: Analysis of candidate selections for the 2024 general election and projections for the new parliament.* British Future. Retrieved July 26, 2024, from https://www.britishfuture. org/wp-content/uploads/2024/06/Diversity-of-parliament-briefing.British-Future-June-2024.pdf

Kaur, S. (2020). *Sex and power 2020.* Fawcett Society.

Kavanagh, E., & Brown, L. (2020). Towards a research agenda for examining online gender-based violence against women academics. *Journal of Further and Higher Education, 44*(10), 1379–1387.

Kelly, L. (1988). *Surviving sexual violence.* Polity Press.

Kelly, L. (2011). Standing the test of time? Reflections on the concept of the continuum of sexual violence. In J. M. Brown & S. L. Walklate (Eds.), *Handbook on sexual violence.* Taylor & Francis Group.

Kelly, L. (2013). A conducive context: Trafficking of persons in Central Asia. In M. Lee (Ed.), *Human trafficking.* Willan.

Kerr, E., & Lee, C. A. L. (2021). Trolls maintained: Baiting technological infrastructures of informational justice. *Information, Communication and Society, 24*(1), 1–18.

Khan, G. F., Swar, B., & Lee, S. K. (2014). Social media risks and benefits: A public sector perspective. *Social Science Computer Review, 32*(5), 606–627.

Khosravinik, M. (2017). Social media discourse and echo chambers. *Insight Turkey, 19*(3), 53–68.

Khosravinik, M., & Esposito, E. (2018). Online hate, digital discourse and critique: Exploring digitally-mediated discursive practices of gender-based hostility. *Lodz Papers in Pragmatics, 14*(1), 45–68.

Kirwan, G. (2016). Computer mediated communication and online media. In I. Connolly, M. Palmer, H. Barton, & G. Kirwan (Eds.), *An introduction to cyberpsychology.* Routledge.

Kligler-Vilenchik, N., Baden, C., & Yarchi, M. (2020). Interpretative polarization across platforms: How political disagreement develops over time on Facebook, Twitter, and WhatsApp. *Social Media and Society, 6*(3), 1–13.

Kong, X., Zhang, A., Xiao, X., Subasish, D., & Zhang, Y. (2022). Work from home in the post-COVID world. *Case Studies on Transport Policy, 10*(2), 1118–1131.

Koulouris, T. (2018). Online misogyny and the alternative right: Debating the undebatable. *Feminist Media Studies, 18*(4), 750–761.

Koziarski, J., & Ree, L. J. (2020). Connecting evidence-based policing and cybercrime. *Policing: An International Journal, 43*(1), 198–211.

Kreiss, D., Finn, M., & Turner, F. (2011). The limits of peer production: Some reminders from Max Weber for the network society. *New Media and Society, 13*(2), 243–259.

Krook, M. L. (2017). Violence against women in politics. *Journal of Democracy*, *28*(1), 74–88.

Krook, M. L. (2020). *Violence against women in politics*. Oxford University Press.

Krug, E. G., Mercy, J. A., Dahlberg, L. L., & Zwi, A. B. (2002). The world report on violence and health. *The Lancet*, *360*(9339), 1083–1088.

Kutiš, R. (2014). Bitcoin – Light at the end of the tunnel for cyber-libertarians. *Masaryk University Journal of Law and Technology*, *8*(2), 209–232.

Lance Bennett, W., & Toft, A. (2009). Identity, technology, and narratives: Transnational activism and social networks. In A. Chadwick and P. N. Howard (Eds.). *The Routledge handbook of internet politics*. Routledge.

Law Commission. (2021). *Hate crime laws: Final report*. Law Comm 402. HC 942. HMSO.

Lea, M. (1992). *Contexts of computer-mediated communication*. Harvester Wheatsheaf.

Lee, C. (2020). Doxxing as discursive action in a social movement, *Critical Discourse Studies*, *19*(3), 326–344.

Lee, S. S., Lane, D. S., & Kwak, N. (2020). When social media get political: How perceptions of open-mindedness influence political expression on Facebook. *Social Media and Society*, *6*(2), 1–12.

Lee, W. L. (2001). Feminist theory: Radical lesbian. In N. J. Smelser and P. B. Baltes (Eds.), *International encyclopedia of the social & behavioral sciences*. Pergamon.

Lees Munoz, E. (2016). *Beyond anecdotal reports: Some hard data about the online abuse of women journalists. New challenges to freedom of expression: Countering online abuse of female journalists*. Organization for Security and Co-operation in Europe. Retrieved July 15, 2021, from https://www.osce.org/fom/220411

Lenhart, A., Ybarra, M., Zickuhr, K., & Price-Feeney, M. (2016). *Online harassment, digital abuse, and cyberstalking in America*. Data & Society and Center for Innovative Public Health Research. Retrieved July 18, 2019, from https://www.datasociety.net/pubs/oh/Online_Harassment_2016.pdf

Lewis, H. (2020). *Difficult women: A history of feminism in 11 fights*. Jonathan Cape.

Lewis, R., Rowe, M., & Wiper, C. (2017). Online abuse of feminists as an emerging form of violence against women and girls. *The British Journal of Criminology*, *57*(6), 1462–1481.

Lewis, R., Rowe, M., & Wiper, C. (2018). Misogyny online: Extending the boundaries of hate crime. *Journal of Gender-based Violence*, *2*(3), 519–536.

Lidsky, L. B. (2000). Silencing John Doe: Defamation and discourse in cyberspace. *Duke Law Journal*, *49*(4), 855–946.

Liem, M. C. A., & Geelen, M. E. F. (2019). The interface between homicide and the internet. A classification. *Aggression and Violent Behavior*, *48*, 65–71.

Lingel, J. (2021). A queer and feminist defense of being anonymous online. In T. X. Bui (Eds.), Translated by NSA. 54th Annual Hawaii International Conference on System Sciences, HICSS 2021, IEEE Computer Society.

Llewelyn Smith, J. (2018, April 29). While I dissect modern Britain, trolls threaten to rape my wife. *The Sunday Times*. Retrieved July 28, 2020, from https://www.thetimes.co.uk/article/stig-abell-while-i-dissect-modern-britain-trolls-threaten-to-rape-my-wife-kxzr2v9bz

Lloyd, B. (2024). Westminster update: New prime minister appoints his cabinet. *The Law Society*. Retrieved July 17, 2024, from https://www.lawsociety.org.uk/topics/blogs/westminster-update-new-prime-minister-appoints-his-cabinet

Loader, B. (1997). *The governance of cyberspace: Politics, technology and global restructuring*. Routledge.

Lopata, H. Z. (1993). Career commitments of American women: The issue of side bets. *The Sociological Quarterly*, *34*(2), 257–277.

Lukianoff, G. (2015). Balancing offence and free speech. *Index on Censorship*, *44*(3), 46–49.

Lumsden, K., & Morgan, H. (2017). Media framing of trolling and online abuse: Silencing strategies, symbolic violence, and victim blaming. *Feminist Media Studies, 17*(6), 926–940.

Lumsden, K., & Morgan, H. M. (2018). Cyber-trolling as symbolic violence. *The Routledge Handbook of Gender and Violence* (pp. 121–132). Routledge.

MacKenzie, D., & Wajcman, J. (1999). *The social shaping of technology*. OUP.

Maguire, M., & Ponting, J. (1988). *Victims and crime: A new deal?* Open University Press.

Mainwaring, S. (2020). Always in control? Sovereign states in cyberspace. *European Journal of International Security, 5*(2), 215–232.

Majó-Vázquez, S., Congosto, M., Nicholls, T., & Nielsen, R. K. (2021). The role of suspended accounts in political discussion on social media: Analysis of the 2017 French, UK and German elections. *Social Media and Society, 7*(3), 1–20.

Mandiberg, M. (2012). *The social media reader*. NYU Press.

Manne, K. (2018). *Down girl: The logic of misogyny*. Oxford University Press.

Mantilla, K. (2013). Gendertrolling: Misogyny adapts to new media. *Feminist Studies: FS, 39*(2), 563–570.

Mantilla, K. (2015). *Gendertrolling: How misogyny went viral*. Praeger.

Marshak, E. (2017). Online harassment: A legislative solution. *Harvard Law Journal, 54*, 501–531.

Martin, F. R., & Murrell, C. (2020). You need a thick skin in this game: Journalists' attitudes to resilience training as a strategy for combatting online violence. *Australian Journalism Review, 42*(1), 93–111.

Marwick, A., & Hargittai, E. (2018). Nothing to hide, nothing to lose? Incentives and disincentives to sharing information with institutions online. *Information, Communication and Society, 22*(12), 1697–1713.

Marwick, A. E., & Miller, R. W. (2014). Online harassment, defamation, and hateful speech: A primer of the legal landscape. *Fordham Center on Law and Information Policy Report*. Fordham University School of Law.

Mason, R. (2019, September 26). PM's divisive "surrender bill" phrase is neither careless nor casual. *The Guardian*. Retrieved June 24, 2021, from http://www.theguardian.com/politics/2019/sep/26/pms-divisive-surrender-bill-phrase-neither-careless-nor-casual

Massanari, A. L. (2018). Rethinking research ethics, power, and the risk of visibility in the era of the 'alt-right' gaze. *Social Media and Society, 4*(2), 1–9.

Matczak, A., Hatzidimitriadou, E., & Lindsay, J. (2011). *Review of domestic violence policies in England and Wales*. Kingston University and St George's, University of London.

Matheson, K. (1992). Women and computer technology: Communicating for herself. In M. Lea (Ed.). *Contexts of computer-mediated communication*. Harvester Wheatsheaf.

Matti, J., & Zhou, Y. (2017). The political economy of Brexit: Explaining the vote. *Applied Economics Letters, 24*(16), 1131–1134.

Mavragani, A., & Tsagarakis, K. P. (2019). Predicting referendum results in the big data era. *Journal of Big Data, 6*(1), 1–20.

Mazúr, J., & Grambličková, B. (2023). New regulatory force of cyberspace: The case of meta's oversight board. *Masaryk University Journal of Law and Technology, 17*(1), 3–32.

McCarthy, B. (2022). "Who unlocked the kitchen?": Online misogyny, YouTube comments and women's professional street skateboarding. *International Review for the Sociology of Sport, 57*(3), 362–380.

McCauley, H. L., Bonomi, A. E., Maas, M. K., Bogen, K. W., & O'Malley, T. L. (2018). #MaybeHeDoesntHitYou: Social media underscore the realities of intimate partner violence. *Journal of Women's Health, 27*(7), 885–891.

McGlynn, C., Rackley, E., & Houghton, R. (2017). Beyond 'revenge porn': The continuum of image-based sexual abuse. *Feminist Legal Studies, 25*, 25–46.

Mckay, F. (2020). A stairheid rammy: Female politicians and gendered discourses in the Scottish press. *Journal of Language and Politics*, *19*(1), 30–47.

McKiernan, J. (2024, June 18). Support for plan to make misogyny a hate crime. *BBC News*. Retrieved July 18, 2024, from https://www.bbc.co.uk/news/articles/c899nxwz3y3o

McLachlan, F., & Harris, B. (2022). Intimate risks: Examining online and offline abuse, homicide flags, and femicide. *Victims and Offenders*, *17*(5), 623–646.

McLaughlin, L. (2004). Feminism and the political economy of the transnational public space. In N. Crossley & J. M. Roberts (Eds.). *After Habermas: New perspectives on the public sphere*. Blackwell.

Mead, R. (2014, September 1). The troll slayer. *New Yorker Magazine*. Retrieved July 28, 2020, from https://www.newyorker.com/magazine/2014/09/01/troll-slayer

Mellado, C., & Hermida, A. (2021). The promoter, celebrity, and joker roles in journalists' social media performance. *Social Media + Society*, *7*(1), 2056305121990643.

Mendes, K., Ringrose, J., & Keller, J. (2018). #MeToo and the promise and pitfalls of challenging rape culture through digital feminist activism. *European Journal of Women's Studies*, *25*(2), 236–246.

Meserve, J. (2014). Recounting virtual brutality. *Democracy Journal*. *32*(Spring), 1–7.

Micalizzi, A. (2021). Exploring gender and sexuality through a Twitter lens: The digital framing effect of the #fertilityday campaign by female users. *Information, Communication and Society*, *24*(8), 1157–1174.

Mill, J. S. (1992). The subjugation of women. In S. Collini (Ed.), *J.S. Mill on liberty and other writings*. Cambridge University Press.

Miller, K. (2009). Public policy dilemma – Gender equality mainstreaming in UK policy formulation. *Public Money and Management*, *29*(1), 43–50.

Ministry of Justice. (2022). *New non-fatal strangulation offence comes into force*. Retrieved September 7, 2022, from https://www.gov.uk/government/news/new-non-fatal-strangulation-offence-comes-into-force

Mooney, J. (2000). *Gender, violence and the social order*. Macmillan.

Moore, M. J., Nakano, T., Enomoto, A., & Suda, T. (2012). Anonymity and roles associated with aggressive posts in an online forum. *Computers in Human Behavior*, *28*, 861–867.

Morales-Campos, D. Y., Casillas, M., & McCurdy, S. A. (2009). From isolation to connection: Understanding a support group for Hispanic women living with gender-based violence in Houston, Texas. *Journal of Immigrant and Minority Health/Center for Minority Public Health*, *11*(1), 57–65.

Morello, B. Y. L. (2015). We can # it. *Nature*, *527*, 148–151.

Mullany, L., & Trickett, L. (2018). *Misogyny hate crime evaluation*. University of Nottingham. Retrieved July 29, 2019, from https://www.nottingham.ac.uk/lipp/documents/press-copy-misogyny-hate-crime-evaluation-exec-summary-june-2018.pdf

Mullen, T. (2014). The Scottish independence referendum 2014. *Journal of Law and Society*, *41*(4), 627–640.

Murray, D. E. (2000). Protean communication: The language of computer-mediated communication. *TESOL Quarterly*, *34*(3), 397–421.

Musk, E. (2022). *Tweet introducing 'Twitter Blue'*. Retrieved July 16, 2024, from https://x.com/elonmusk/status/1587498907336118274?lang=en

Muzaffar, M. (2023, January 19). *Jacinda Ardern resigns: What led the New Zealand prime minister to quit*. The Independent. Retrieved July 16, 2024.

Nagle, A. (2017). *Kill all normies: The online culture wars from Tumblr and 4chan to the alt-right and Trump*. Zero Books.

National Democratic Institute. (2018). *NDI Launches #think10 – A ground-breaking safety planning tool designed to safeguard women in politics*. Retrieved July 15, 2021, from https://www.ndi.org/publications/ndi-launches-think10-groundbreaking-safety-planning-tool-designed-safeguard-women

National Police Chief's Council. (2024). *Call to action as VAWG epidemic deepens.* Retrieved July 28, 2024, from https://news.npcc.police.uk/releases/call-to-action-as-violence-against-women-and-girls-epidemic-deepens-1

Naughton, J. (1999). *A brief history of the future: The origins of the internet.* Weidenfeld & Nicolson

Newman, N. (2018). *Digital news report 2018.* Reuters Institute for the Study of Journalism. Retrieved January 9, 2022, from https://reutersinstitute.politics.ox.ac.uk/sites/default/files/digital-news-report-2018.pdf

New Zealand Department of Internal Affairs. (2023). *Media and online content regulation.* New Zealand Department of Internal Affairs. Retrieved June 21, 2023, from https://www.dia.govt.nz/media-and-online-content-regulation

New Zealand Department of Internal Affairs. (2024). *Safer online services and media platforms.* Department of Internal Affairs, New Zealand Government. Retrieved July 19, 2024, from https://www.dia.govt.nz/diawebsite.nsf/Files/online-content-regulation/$file/Safer-Online-Services-and-Media-Platforms-Summary-of-Submissions-V2.pdf

Nicolson, M., & Korkut, U. (2022). The making and the portrayal of Scottish distinctiveness: How does the narrative create its audience? *International Migration, 60*(5), 151–164.

Norris, P., & Inglehart, R. F. (2018) Understanding Brexit: Cultural resentment versus economic grievances. *SSRN Electronic Journal.* https://doi.org/10.2139/ssrn.3231896

Nugent, C. (2019, June 21). Abuse is a pattern: Why these nations took the lead in criminalizing controlling behavior in relationships. *Time Magazine.* Retrieved August 19, 2021, https://time.com/5610016/coercive-control-domestic-violence/

O'Connor, C. D. (2017). The police on Twitter: Image management, community building, and implications for policing in Canada. *Policing and Society, 27*(8), 899–912.

OECD. (2015). *Women in public sector employment. Government at a glance.* OECD Publishing.

Ofcom. (2016). *Attitudes to potentially offensive language and gestures on TV and radio.* Retrieved December 15, 2021, from https://www.ofcom.org.uk/__data/assets/pdf_file/0022/91624/OfcomOffensiveLanguage.pdf

O'Neill, B. (2011, November 7). The campaign to stamp out misogyny online echoes Victorian efforts to protect women from coarse language. *The Telegraph.* Retrieved December 19, 2018, from http://blogs.telegraph.co.uk/news/brendano neill2/100115868/the-campaign-to-stamp-out-misogyny-onlineechoes-victorian-efforts-to-protect-women-from-coarse-language/

O'Neil, M. (2014). Hacking Weber: Legitimacy, critique, and trust in peer production. *Information, Communication and Society, 17*(7), 872–888.

Ooi, K., Lee, V., Hew, J., & Lin, B. (2021). Mobile social cyberbullying: Why are keyboard warriors raging? *Journal of Computer Information Systems, 61*(4), 371–382.

O'Sullivan, P. B., & Flanagin, A. (2003). Reconceptualizing 'flaming' and other problematic messages. *New Media and Society, 5*, 69–94.

Ouaguira, S. (2024). Electoral Commission chief warns of 'tremendous amount of online abuse' during election campaign. *The Independent.*

Ozalp, S., Williams, M. L., Burnap, P., Liu, H., & Mostafa, M. (2020). Antisemitism on Twitter: Collective efficacy and the role of community organisations in challenging online hate speech. *Social Media and Society, 6*(2), 1–20.

PA Media. (2020, February 13). Tracy Brabin's off-the-shoulder dress raises £20,000 for Girlguiding. *The Guardian.* Retrieved August 13, 2020, from http://www.theguardian.com/politics/2020/feb/13/tracy-brabin-off-the-shoulder-dress-raises-20000-girlguiding

Palmer, B., & Simon, D. (2010). *Breaking the political glass ceiling: Women and congressional elections.* Routledge.

Papacharissi, Z. (2002). The virtual sphere: The internet as a public sphere. *New Media and Society*, *4*(1), 9–27.

Papacharissi, Z. (2009). The virtual sphere 2.0. In A. Chadwick & P. N. Howard (Eds.), *The Routledge handbook of internet politics*. Routledge.

Pariser, E. (2012). *The filter bubble: What the internet is hiding from you*. Penguin.

Parmar, S. (2016). *Protecting female journalists online: An international human rights perspective, new challenges to freedom of expression: Countering online abuse of female journalists*. Vienna: Organization for Security and Co-operation in Europe. Retrieved July 15, 2021, from https://www.osce.org/fom/220411

Patel, N. (2014, February 25). *The internet is fucked (but we can fix it)*. The Verge. Retrieved February 11, 2019, from https://www.theverge.com/2014/2/25/5431382/the-internet-is-fucked

Paul, I., Khattar, A., Kumaraguru, P., Gupta, M., & Chopra, S. (2018). *Elites tweet? Characterizing the Twitter verified user network*. IEEE 35th International Conference on Data Engineering Workshops (ICDEW), Macao, Macao. 278–285.

Pedersen, S., Baxter, G., Burnett, S., Goker, A., Corney, D., & Martin, C. (2014). Backchannel chat: Peaks and troughs in a Twitter response to three televised debates during the Scottish independence referendum campaign 2014. *Aberdeen Business School Working Paper Series*, *7*(2).

Peele, G. (2022). Women and civility in British politics: Reflections on a changing environment. *The Political Quarterly*, *93*(1), 54–63.

Pence, E., & Paymar, M. (1993). *Education groups for men who batter: The Duluth model*. Springer Publishing Company.

Pender, R. L. (2012). ASGW best practice guidelines: An evaluation of the Duluth model. *Journal for Specialists in Group Work*, *37*(3), 218–231.

Pengelly, E. (2019, October 29). Heartbroken MP Heidi Allen won't stand again in General Election. *Cambridge News*. Retrieved June 22, 2021, from https://www.cambridge-news.co.uk/news/cambridge-news/heidi-allen-stands-down-cambs-17165253

Penney, J. W. (2020). Online abuse, chilling effects, and human rights. In E. Dubois & F. Martin-Bariteau (Eds.), *Citizenship in a connected Canada: A research and policy agenda* (pp. 207–220). University of Ottawa Press.

PenzeyMoog, E., & Slakoff, D. C. (2021). As technology evolves, so does domestic violence: Modern-day tech abuse and possible solutions. In B. Jane, F. Asher, & H. Nicola (Eds.), *The Emerald international handbook of technology-facilitated violence and abuse* (pp. 643–662). Emerald Publishing Limited.

Pfeffer, J., Zorbach, T., & Carley, K. M. (2014). Understanding online firestorms: Negative word-of-mouth dynamics in social media networks. *Journal of Marketing Communications*, *20*(1–2), 117–128.

Phillips, D. J. (2009). Location surveillance: Embracing the patterns of our lives. In A. Chadwick and P. N. Howard (Eds.). *The Routledge handbook of internet politics*. Routledge.

Phillips, J. (2017). *Everywoman: One woman's truth about speaking the truth*. Hutchinson.

Phillips, J. (2019). *Truth to power: Seven ways to call time on B.S.* Monoray.

Phillips, W. (2012, October 15). What an academic who wrote her dissertation on trolls thinks of Violentacrez. *The Atlantic*. Retrieved April 5, 2021, from https://www.theatlantic.com/technology/archive/2012/10/what-an-academic-who-wrote-her-dissertation-on-trolls-thinks-of-violentacrez/263631/

Phipps, A. (2014, December 4). The dark side of the impact agenda. *Times Higher Education Supplement*. Retrieved June 19, 2021, from https://www.timeshighereducation.com/comment/opinion/the-dark-side-of-the-impact-agenda/2017299.article

Pickard, S. (2020). On becoming a hag: Gender, ageing and abjection. *Feminist Theory*, *21*(2), 157–173.

Pohle, J., & Voelsen, D. (2022). Centrality and power. The struggle over the techno-political configuration of the Internet and the global digital order. *Policy & Internet, 14*(1), 13–27.

Poland, B. (2016). *Haters: Harassment, abuse, and violence online*. Potomac Books.

Postmes, T., Spears, R., & Lea, M. (2002). Intergroup differentiation in computer- mediated communication: Effects of depersonalization. *Group Dynamics, 6*, 3–16.

Powell, A., & Henry, N. (2018). Policing technology-facilitated sexual violence against adult victims: Police and service sector perspectives. *Policing and Society, 28*(3), 291–307.

Power, G. (2019, October 18). A history of MPs murdered in office. *The Week*. Retrieved June 19, 2021, from https://www.theweek.co.uk/103522/a-history-of-mps-murdered-in-office

Power, S. (2006). Markets and misogyny: Educational research on educational choice. *British Journal of Educational Studies, 54*(2), 175–188.

Pretorius, E. (2018). Men's role in the quest for gender justice: A historical overview of antifeminism and pro-feminism [Mans se rol in die stryd om gendergeregtigheid: 'N Historiese oorsig van antifeminisme en profeminisme]. *Tydskrif vir Geesteswetenskappe, 58*(4), 887–904.

Priddy, S. (2024). *MPs not standing in the 2024 general election*. House of Commons Library.

Prosser, C. (2021). The end of the EU affair: The UK general election of 2019. *West European Politics, 44*(2), 450–461.

Puschmann, C. (2019). An end to the wild west of social media research: A response to Axel Bruns. *Information, Communication and Society, 22*(11), 1582–1589.

Quinlan, S., Shephard, M., & Paterson, L. (2015). Online discussion and the 2014 Scottish independence referendum: Flaming keyboards or forums for deliberation? *Electoral Studies, 38*, 192–205.

Radford, J., & Harne, L. (2008). *Tackling domestic violence: Theories, policies and practice*. McGraw-Hill Education.

Radford, J., & Stanko, B. (1991). Violence against women and children: The contradictions of crime control under patriarchy. In K. M. Stenson & D. Cowell (Eds.), *The politics of crime control*. Sage.

Radu, R. (2019) *Negotiating internet governance*. Oxford University Press.

Rawlinson, K. (2020, February 4). 'I am not a slapper': Labour MP hits back at criticism of attire. *The Guardian*. Retrieved August 13, 2020, from http://www.theguardian.com/politics/2020/feb/04/i-am-not-a-slapper-labour-mp-tracy-brabin-defends-her-commons-attire

Regehr, K., & Ringrose, J. (2018). Celebrity victims and wimpy snowflakes: Using personal narratives to challenge digitally mediated rape culture. In J. R. Vickery & T. Everbach (Eds.), *Mediating misogyny: Gender, technology, and harassment* (pp. 353–369). Springer International Publishing.

Rehman, Y., Kelly, L., & Siddiqui, H. (2013). *Moving in the shadows: Violence in the lives of minority women and children*. Ashgate.

Reisach, U. (2021). The responsibility of social media in times of societal and political manipulation. *European Journal of Operational Research, 291*(3), 906–917.

Renzetti, C. M. (2013). *Feminist criminology*. Routledge.

Rheingold, H. (2000a). *The virtual community: Homesteading on the electronic frontier*. The MIT Press.

Rheingold, H. (2000b). *Tools for thought: The history and future of mind-expanding technology* (2nd edn.). The MIT Press.

Roberts, M. (2024). Five ways attorneys can help gender-based violence survivors vote. *Bifocal: Journal of the ABA Commission on Law and Aging, 46*(1), 19–21.

Rochford, H. I., Brooks, K., Berg, M., & Peek-Asa, C. (2021). COVID-19-related violence trend data challenges and a resource for injury researchers. *Injury Epidemiology, 8*(1), 45–48.

Rodrigues, J. (2012, November 15). 30 years ago: El Vino's treatment of women drinkers ruled unlawful. *The Guardian*. Retrieved November 13, 2021, from https://www.theguardian.com/theguardian/from-the-archive-blog/2012/nov/15/el-vino-women-ban-fleet-street-1982

Rogers, A. (2021). *'Naming "Femicide"', Leading Works in Law and Social Justice* (pp. 85–98) Routledge.

Rogers, M. M., Fisher, C., Ali, P., Allmark, P., & Fontes, L. (2022). Technology-facilitated abuse in intimate relationships: A scoping review. *Trauma, Violence and Abuse*, 15248380221090218.

Rohlinger, D. A., Rose, K., Warren, S., & Shulman, S. (2023). Does the musk Twitter takeover matter? Political influencers, their arguments, and the quality of information they share. *Socius, 9*, 23780231231152193.

Rohlinger, D., & Vaccaro, C. (2021). From "please sir, stay out of it" to "you are an abomination": (in)civility and emotional expression in emails sent to politicians, Information. *Communication and Society, 24*(5), 667–683.

Romano, A. (2020). *What we still haven't learned from Gamergate*. Retrieved April 5, 2024, from https://www.vox.com/culture/2020/1/20/20808875/gamergate-lessons-cultural-impact-changes-harassment-laws

Rosenthal, L. J. (2007). Entertaining women: The actress in eighteenth-century theatre and culture. In *The Cambridge companion to British theatre, 1730–1830* (pp. 159–174). Cambridge University Press.

Rossini, P. (2021). More than just shouting? Distinguishing interpersonal-directed and elite-directed incivility in online political talk. *Social Media and Society, 7*(2), 1–14.

Rutter, D. R. (1987). *Communicating by telephone*. Pergamon Press.

Salin, D., & Hoel, H. (2013). Workplace bullying as a gendered phenomenon. *Journal of Managerial Psychology, 28*(3), 235–251.

Salter, M. (2013). Justice and revenge in online counter-publics: Emerging responses to sexual violence in the age of social media. *Crime, Media, Culture, 9*(3), 225–242.

Salter, M. (2017). *Crime, justice and social media*. Routledge.

Salter, M. (2018). From geek masculinity to Gamergate: The technological rationality of online abuse. *Crime, Media, Culture, 14*(2), 247–264.

Sasidharan, S., & Dhillon, H. S. (2021). The dark shadow pandemic – Assault and sexual violence during COVID-19. *Journal of Medical Science, 41*, 256–260.

Scott, G. G., Brodie, Z. P., Wilson, M. J., Ivory, L., Hand, C. J., & Sereno, S. C. (2020). Celebrity abuse on Twitter: The impact of tweet valence, volume of abuse, and dark triad personality factors on victim blaming and perceptions of severity. *Computers in Human Behavior, 103*, 109–119.

Scott, G. G., Wiencierz, S., & Hand, C. J. (2019). The volume and source of cyberabuse influences victim blame and perceptions of attractiveness. *Computers in Human Behavior, 92*, 119–127.

Searles, K., Spencer, S., & Duru, A. (2020). Don't read the comments: The effects of abusive comments on perceptions of women authors' credibility. *Information, Communication and Society, 23*(7), 947–962.

Segalo, P., & Fine, M. (2020). Underlying conditions of gender-based violence—decolonial feminism meets epistemic ignorance: Critical transnational conversations. *Social and Personality Psychology Compass, 14*(10), 1–10.

Shaw, C. (2018). The lady's not for returning: Memory, mediation and Margaret Thatcher in three contemporary biopics. *Journal of British Cinema and Television, 15*(2), 157–178.

Shirky, C. (2011). The political power of social media: Technology, the public sphere, and political change. *Foreign Affairs, 90*(1), 28–41.

Shreffler, M. B., Murfree, J. R., Huecker, M. R., & Shreffler, J. R. (2023). The impostor phenomenon and work–family conflict: An assessment of higher education. *Management in Education, 37*(1), 5–12.

Siddiqui, H. (2013). True honour: Domestic violence, forced marriage and honour crimes in the UK. In Y. Rehman, L. Kelly, & H. Siddiqui. *Moving in the shadows: Violence in the lives of minority women and children.* Ashgate.

Silvestri, M., & Tong, S. (2020). Women police leaders in Europe: A tale of prejudice and patronage. *European Journal of Criminology,* 1477370820931867.

Sinclair, G. (2024). Euro 2024: Football is a magnet for online abuse – But it is also the ideal platform to challenge it. *The Conversation.* Retrieved July 29, 2024, from http://the-conversation.com/euro-2024-football-is-a-magnet-for-online-abuse-but-it-is-also-the-ideal-platform-to-challenge-it-231836

Smales, L. A. (2017). "Brexit": A case study in the relationship between political and financial market uncertainty. *International Review of Finance, 17*(3), 451–459.

Smith, J. (2019). *Home grown: How domestic violence turns men into terrorists.* Riverrun.

Smith Maguire, J. (2008). The personal is professional: Personal trainers as a case study of cultural intermediaries. *International Journal of Cultural Studies, 11*(2), 211–229.

Snyder, P., Doerfler, P., Kanich, C., & McCoy, D. (2017). *Fifteen minutes of unwanted fame: Detecting and characterizing doxing* (pp. 432–444). Proceedings of the 2017 Internet Measurement Conference. Association for Computing Machinery.

Sobande, F. (2020). *The digital lives of Black women in Britain.* Palgrave Macmillan.

Sohn, S., Chung, H. C., & Park, N. (2019). Private self-awareness and aggression in computer-mediated communication: Abusive user comments on online news articles. *International Journal of Human-Computer Interaction, 35*(13), 1160–1169.

Solace Women's Aid and the Justice Studio. (2021). *When I needed you to protect me, you gave him more power instead. Covid-19 lockdown and domestic abuse.* Retrieved December 21, 2021, from https://gala.gre.ac.uk/id/eprint/34353/7/34353_STENGEL_js_and_solace_when_i_needed_you.pdf

Soontjens, K. (2021). The awareness paradox: (why) politicians overestimate citizens' awareness of parliamentary questions and party initiatives, *Representations, 57*(1), 75–94.

Southworth, C., Finn, J., Dawson, S., Fraser, C., & Tucker, S. (2007). Intimate partner violence, technology, and stalking. *Violence Against Women, 13*(8), 842–856.

Spears, R., & Lea, M. (1992). Social influence and the influence of the 'social' in computer mediated communication. In M. Lea. (Ed). *Contexts of computer mediated communication.* Harvester Wheatsheaf.

Spender, D. (1982). *Women of ideas (and what men have done to them).* Ark.

Stanko, E. A. (1988). Hidden violence against women. In M. Maguire, & J. Ponting (Eds.), *Victims and crime: A new deal?* Open University Press.

Stanko, E. A. (1990). *Everyday violence: How women and men experience sexual and physical danger.* Pandora.

Stark, E. (2009). *Coercive control: How men entrap women in personal life.* Oxford University Press.

Stark, E., & Hester, M. (2019). Coercive control: Update and review. *Violence Against Women, 25*(1), 81–104.

Steinem, G. (2015). *My life on the road.* Oneworld.

Steinþórsdóttir, F. S., & Pétursdóttir, G. M. (2022). To protect and serve while protecting privileges and serving male interests: Hegemonic masculinity and the sense of entitlement within the Icelandic police force. *Policing and Society, 32*(4), 489–503.

Stephens, C., Mays, N., Issa, R., Perkins, L., & Scott, R. (2021). Elder abuse in the UK: Out of the shadows and on to the agenda. *BMJ, 375,* 2828–2829.

Sterner, G., & Felmlee, D. (2017). The social networks of cyberbullying on Twitter. *International Journal of Technoethics, 8*(2), 1–15.

Stöckl, H., & Quigg, Z. (2021). Violence against women and girls. *BMJ, 374*, 1926.

Suler, J. R., & Phillips, W. L. (1998). The bad boys of cyberspace: Deviant behavior in a multimedia chat community. *Cyberpsychology and Behavior, 1*(3), 275–294.

Sunstein, C. R. (2009a). *Going to extremes: How like minds unite and divide*. Oxford University Press.

Sunstein, C. R. (2009b). *Republic.com 2.0*. Princeton University Press.

Suzor, N., Dragiewicz, M., Harris, B., Gillett, R., Burgess, J., & Van Geelen, T. (2019). Human rights by design: The responsibilities of social media platforms to address gender-based violence online. *Policy and Internet, 11*(1), 84–103.

Taddeo, M., & Floridi, L. (2016). The debate on the moral responsibilities of online service providers, *Science and Engineering Ethics, 22*(6), 1575–1603.

Tagg, C. (2015). *Exploring digital communication: Language in action*. Routledge.

Tariq, M., & Syed, J. (2018). An intersectional perspective on Muslim women's issues and experiences in employment. *Gender, Work, and Organization, 25*(5), 495–513.

Taylor-Smith, E., & Smith, C. F. (2019). Investigating the online and offline contexts of day-to-day democracy as participation spaces. *Information, Communication and Society, 22*(13), 1853–1870.

Technopedia. (2013). *Definition of a Twitterstorm*. Retrieved August 13, 2020, from https://www.techopedia.com/definition/29624/twitterstorm

Teotonio, I. (2014, November 5). *Women find power in #BeenRapedNeverReported hashtag*. The Toronto Star. Retrieved January 9, 2022, from https://www.thestar.com/life/2014/11/05/women_find_power_in_beenrapedneverreported_hashtag.html

Terren, L., & Borge-Bravo, R. (2021). Echo chambers on social media: A systematic review of the literature. *Review of Communication Research, 9*, 99–118.

The Barry Amiel and Norman Melburn Trust. (2021). *Red Rag*. Retrieved November 13, 2021, from http://banmarchive.org.uk/collections/redrag/index_frame.htm

The Labour Party. (2024). *Labour Party Manifesto 2024*. Retrieved July 18, 2024, from https://labour.org.uk/wp-content/uploads/2024/06/Labour-Party-manifesto-2024.pdf

The Well. (2019). *Our Story*. The Well website. Retrieved May 9, 2024, from https://www.well.com/about-2/

Thielman, S. (2020, January 31). The harassment of Felicia Sonmez, and the 'fake news' chorus. *Columbia Journalism Review*. Retrieved July 13, 2021, from https://www.cjr.org/cjr_outbox/the-harassment-of-felicia-sonmez-and-the-fake-news-chorus.php

Thomas, K., Akhawe, D., Bailey, M., Boneh, D., Bursztein, E., Consolvo, S., & Dell, N. (2021). SoK: Hate, harassment, and the changing landscape of online abuse. *IEEE Symposium on Security and Privacy (SP)* (Vol. 2021, pp. 247–267). Institute of Electrical and Electronics Engineers Inc.

Thompson, J. D., & Cover, R. (2021). Digital hostility, internet pile-ons and shaming: A case study. *Convergence*, 1–13.

Tierney, W. G., & Lechuga, V. M. (2010). The social significance of academic freedom. *Cultural Studies ↔ Critical Methodologies, 10*(2), 118–133.

Todd, M. (2017). Virtual violence: Cyberspace, misogyny and online abuse. In T. Owen, W. Noble, & F. C. Speed (Eds.), *New perspectives on cybercrime*. Springer International Publishing.

Tomkinson, S., Harper, T., & Attwell, K. (2020). Confronting Incel: Exploring possible policy responses to misogynistic violent extremism. *Australian Journal of Political Science, 55*(2), 152–169.

Tomyn, A. J., Powell, M. B., Cassematis, P., Smallbone, S., & Wortley, R. (2015). Examination of the subjective well-being of Australian internet child exploitation investigators. *Australian Psychologist, 50*(3), 203–211.

Townsend, M. (2021, August 14). Plymouth gunman ranted online that "women are arrogant" days before rampage. *The Guardian*. Retrieved August 16, 2021, from http://

www.theguardian.com/world/2021/aug/14/plymouth-gunman-ranted-online-that-women-are-arrogant-days-before-rampage

Tromble, R., & Koole, K. (2020). She belongs in the kitchen, not in Congress. Political engagement and sexism on Twitter. *Journal of Applied Journalism and Media Studies*, *9*(2), 191–214.

Trottier, D. (2015). Vigilantism and power users. Police and user led investigations on social media. In D. Trottier & C. Fuchs (Eds.), *Social media, politics and the state*. Routledge.

Trottier, D., & Fuchs, C. (2015). (Eds.). *Social media, politics and the state*. Routledge.

Turillazzi, A., Taddeo, M., Floridi, L., & Casolari, F. (2023). The digital services act: An analysis of its ethical, legal, and social implications. *Law, Innovation and Technology*, *15*(1), 83–106.

Turner, A. (2024). Sexism and misogyny as traits of police culture: Problems, red flags and solutions. *International Journal of Police Science & Management*, *26*(2), 279–291.

Turner, F. (2006). How digital technology found utopian ideology: Lessons from the first hackers' conference. In D. Silver & A. Massanari (Eds.), *Critical cyberculture studies: Current terrains, future directions* (pp. 1–22).

Twitter Help Centre. (2021). *Twitter verification requirements – How to get the blue check*. Retrieved May 26, 2021, from https://help.twitter.com/en/managing-your-account/about-twitter-verified-accounts

United Nations Office on Drugs and Crime (UNODC). (2023). *Global study on homicide*. United Nations. Retrieved July 17, 2024, from https://www.unodc.org/unodc/en/data-and-analysis/global-study-on-homicide.html

UN Broadband Commission for Digital Development Working Group on Broadband and Gender. (2015). *Cyber violence against women and girls: A worldwide wake-up call*. United Nations.

United Nations. (1993). *Declaration on the elimination on all forms of violence against women*. United Nations.

Urwin, R. (2013, July 31). *If someone walked up and said, "I'm going to rape you", you'd ring 999: Stella Creasy fights the Twitter trolls*. London Evening Standard. Retrieved July 28, 2020, from https://www.standard.co.uk/lifestyle/london-life/if-someone-walked-up-and-said-i-m-going-to-rape-you-you-d-ring-999-stella-creasy-fights-the-twitter-trolls-8737796.html

Urwin, R. (2021, October 17). Trolls deluge MPs with rape and murder threats. *The Sunday Times*. Retrieved January 9, 2022, from https://www.thetimes.co.uk/article/trolls-deluge-mps-with-rape-and-murder-threats-fcztxltll

Valentine, G. (1989). The geography of women's fear. *Area*, *21*(4), 385–390.

van Dijk, J. A. G. M. (2013). Inequalities in the network society. In K. Orton-Johnson & N. Prior (Eds.). *Digital sociology: Critical perspectives*. Palgrave.

Vasterman, P. (2018). (Ed.) *From media hype to Twitter storm: News explosions and their impact on issues, crises, and public opinion*. Amsterdam University Press.

Veletsianos, G. (2016). *Social media in academia: Networked scholars*. Routledge.

Veletsianos, G., Houlden, S., Hodson, J., & Gosse, C. (2018). Women scholars' experiences with online harassment and abuse: Self-protection, resistance, acceptance, and self-blame. *New Media and Society*, *20*(12), 4689–4708.

Venturini, T., & Rogers, R. (2019). "API-based research" or how can digital sociology and journalism studies learn from the Facebook and Cambridge Analytica data breach. *Digital Journalism*, *7*(4), 532–540.

Vera-Gray, F. (2017). "Talk about a cunt with too much idle time": Trolling feminist research. *Feminist Review*, *115*(1), 61–78.

Vera-Gray, F. (2018). *How women trade freedom for safety*. Bristol University Press.

Vera-Gray, F., & Kelly, L. (2020). Contested gendered space: Public sexual harassment and women's safety work. In *Crime and fear in public places* (pp. 217–231). Routledge.

Vyas, L. (2022). "New normal" at work in a post-COVID world: Work–life balance and labor markets. *Policy and Society*, *41*(1), 155–167.

Wagner, A. (2019). E-victimization and e-predation theory as the dominant aggressive communication: The case of cyber bullying. *Social Semiotics*, *29*(3), 303–318.

Waisbord, S. (2024). Trolling journalists and the risks of digital publicity. In *Journalism and safety* (pp. 61–77). Routledge.

Wajcman, J., Bittman, M., & Brown, J. E. (2008). Families without borders: Mobile phones, connectedness and work-home divisions. *Sociology*, *42*(4), 635–652.

Walby, K., & Joshua, C. (2021). Framing fantasies: Public police recruiting videos and representations of women. *Current Issues in Criminal Justice*, *33*(2), 151–169.

Walby, S., Towers, J., & Francis, B. (2014). Mainstreaming domestic and gender-based violence into sociology and the criminology of violence. *The Sociological Review*, *62*(Suppl 2), 187–214.

Walker, N. (2021). *Brexit timeline: Events leading to the UK's exit from the European Union. House of Commons Briefing Paper* 7960. House of Commons Library.

Walklate, S. (1995). *Gender and crime: An introduction*. Prentice Hall/Harvester Wheatsheaf.

Walklate, S., & Fitz-Gibbon, K. (2021). Why criminalise coercive control? The complicity of the criminal law in punishing women through furthering the power of the state. *International Journal for Crime Justice and Social Democracy*, *10*(4), 1–12. https://doi.org/10.5204/ijcjsd.1829

Wall, D. S. (2007). *Cybercrime: The transformation of crime in the information age*. Polity Press.

Wall, D. S. (2008). Cybercrime, media and insecurity: The shaping of public perceptions of cybercrime. *International Review of Law, Computers and Technology*, *22*(1–2), 45–63.

Ward, S., & McLoughlin, L. (2020). Turds, traitors and tossers: The abuse of UK MPs via Twitter. *The Journal of Legislative Studies*, *26*(1), 47–73.

Waterson, J. (2018, September 17). Ofcom to push for regulation of social networks. *The Guardian*. Retrieved September 18, 2018, from https://www.theguardian.com/media/2018/sep/17/ofcom-to-push-for-regulation-of-social-media-platforms

Watson, S. (2019, November 6). Analysis shows horrifying extent of abuse sent to women MPs via Twitter. *The Conversation*. Retrieved November 25, 2019, from https://theconversation.com/analysis-shows-horrifying-extent-of-abuse-sent-to-women-mps-via-twitter-126166

Watson, S. (2022, November 8). Elon Musk's "Twitter Blue" gives verification for a fee – this could make Twitter even less safe for women. *The Conversation*. Retrieved July 16, 2024, from https://theconversation.com/elon-musks-twitter-blue-gives-verification-for-a-fee-this-could-make-twitter-even-less-safe-for-women-193967

Watson, S. (2025, January 10). Attacks on Jess Phillips show how online abuse of women is intended to keep them out of the public square. *The Conversation*. Retrieved January 15, 2025, from https://theconversation.com/attacks-on-jess-phillips-show-how-online-abuse-of-women-is-intended-to-keep-them-out-of-the-public-square-243631

Watts, L. K., Wagner, J., Velasquez, B., & Behrens, P. I. (2017). Cyberbullying in higher education: A literature review. *Computers in Human Behavior*, *69*, 268–274.

Weathers, M. R., Sanderson, J., Neal, A., & Gramlich, K. (2016). From silence to #WhyIStayed: Locating our stories and finding our voices. *Qualitative Research Reports in Communication*, *17*(1), 60–67.

Wendling, M. (2018). *Alt-right: From 4chan to the White House*. Pluto Press.

Wessels, B. (2010). *Understanding the internet: A socio-cultural perspective*. Palgrave.

West, C. M. (2004). Black women and intimate partner violence: New directions for research. *Journal of Interpersonal Violence*, *19*(12), 1487–1493.

Wiener, C. (2017). Seeing what is 'invisible in plain sight': Policing coercive control. *The Howard Journal of Crime and Justice, 56*(4), 500–515.

Williams, A. A., Bryant, Z., & Carvell, C. (2019). Uncompensated emotional labor, racial battle fatigue, and (in)civility in digital spaces. *Sociology Compass, 13*(2), 1–12.

Williams, L., & Walklate, S. (2020). Policy responses to domestic violence, the criminalisation thesis and "learning from history". *The Howard Journal of Crime and Justice, 59*(3), 305–316.

Williamson, S., Pearce, A., Connor, J., Weeratunga, V., & Dickinson, H. (2022). The future of working from home in the public sector: What does the evidence tell us? *Australian Journal of Public Administration, 81*(4), 640–648.

Wilson, J., & Irwin, A. (2015). Why can't a woman be more like a man? Margaret Thatcher and the discourse of leadership. In J. Wilson and D. Boxer (Eds.), *Discourse, politics and women as global leaders*. John Benjamins Publishing Company.

Winston, J. (2016). *How the trump campaign built an identity database and used Facebook Ads to win the election, startup grind*. Retrieved May 9, 2024, from https://medium.com/startup-grind/how-the-trump-campaign-built-an-identity-database-and-used-facebook-ads-to-win-the-election-4ff7d24269ac

Wise, S., & Stanley, L. (1987). *Georgie Porgie: Sexual harassment in everyday life*. Pandora Press.

Wistrich, H. (2022). Misogyny in the criminal justice system. *The Political Quarterly, 93*(1), 64–68.

Witalisz, W. (2023). "He who destroys a good Booke, kills reason itself": John Milton, Elon Musk and the question of freedom of expression (by way of introduction). In W. Witalisz (Ed.), *Freedom of expression across borders* (pp. 1–14). Jagiellonian University.

Wittes, B., Poplin, C., Quinta, J., & Spera, C. (2016). *Closing the sextortion sentencing gap: A legislative proposal*. Retrieved August 26, 2022, from https://www.brookings.edu/wp-content/uploads/2016/05/sextortion2.pdf

Wolfson, T. (2014). *The birth of the cyber left*. University of Illinois Press.

Wong, R. Y. M., Cheung, C. M. K., Xiao, B., & Thatcher, J. B. (2021). Standing up or standing by: Understanding bystanders' proactive reporting responses to social media harassment. *Information Systems Research, 32*(2), 561–581.

Woodlock, D. (2017). The abuse of technology in domestic violence and stalking. *Violence Against Women, 23*(5), 584–602.

Women's Aid. (2023). *Influencers and attitudes: How will the next generation understand domestic abuse?* Women's Aid.

Worth, A., Augoustinos, M., & Hastie, B. (2016). 'Playing the gender card': Media representations of Julia Gillard's sexism and misogyny speech. *Feminism and Psychology, 26*(1), 52–72.

Wright, S., Trott, V., & Jones, C. (2020). "The pussy ain't worth it, bro": Assessing the discourse and structure of MGTOW. *Information, Communication and Society, 23*(6), 908–925.

Wu, B. (2015). Doxxed: Impact of online threats on women including private details being exposed and 'swatting'. *Index on Censorship, 44*(3), 46–49.

Yar, M., & Drew, J. (2019). Image-based abuse, non-consensual pornography, revenge porn: A study of criminalization and crime prevention in Australia and England & Wales. *International Journal of Cyber Criminology, 13*(2), 578–594.

Yar, M., & Steinmetz, K. F. (2019). *Cybercrime and society* (3rd edn.). Sage.

Yardley, E. (2021a). Technology-facilitated domestic abuse in political economy: A new theoretical framework. *Violence Against Women, 27*(10), 1479–1498.

Yardley, E. (2021b). The killing of women in "sex games gone wrong": An analysis of femicides in Great Britain 2000-2018. *Violence Against Women, 27*(11), 1840–1861.

Yelin, H., & Clancy, L. (2021). Doing impact work while female: Hate tweets, "hot potatoes" and having "enough of experts". *European Journal of Women's Studies*, *28*(2), 175–193.

Zakrzewski, C. (2020, June 10). The technology 202: President Trump's conspiracy theories are putting pressure on Twitter to change its policies. *The Washington Post*. Retrieved June 15, 2020, from https://www.washingtonpost.com/news/powerpost/paloma/the-technology-202/2020/06/10/the-technology-202-president-trump-s-conspiracy-theories-are-putting-pressure-on-twitter-to-change-its-policies/5edfe562602ff12947e888d1/

Zammuner, V. L., & Galli, C. (2005). The relationship with patients: "emotional labor" and its correlates in hospital employees. In C. E. J. Hartel, N. M. Ashkanasy, & W. Zerbe (Eds.), *Emotions in organizational behaviour*, Psychology Press.

Zempi, I., & Smith, J. (2021). *Misogyny as hate crime*. Taylor and Francis.

Zuboff, S. (2015). Big other: Surveillance capitalism and the prospects of an information civilization. *Journal of Information Technology Impact*, *30*(1), 75–89.

Index

www.ingramcontent.com/pod-product-compliance
Lightning Source LLC
Chambersburg PA
CBHW050352270326
41926CB00016B/3702